THE RED COAST

The Red Coast

RADICALISM AND ANTI-RADICALISM IN SOUTHWEST WASHINGTON

Aaron Goings, Brian Barnes, and Roger Snider

Oregon State University Press   Corvallis

Cataloging-in-publication data available from the Library of Congress.

∞ This paper meets the requirements of ANSI/NISO Z39.48-1992
(Permanence of Paper).

First published in 2019 by Oregon State University Press
Printed in the United States of America

Oregon State University
OSU Press

Oregon State University Press
121 The Valley Library
Corvallis OR 97331-4501
541-737-3166 • fax 541-737-3170
www.osupress.oregonstate.edu

Contents

Acknowledgments

First, we are fortunate to have so many supportive coworkers at Saint Martin's University. Thanks especially to those who served on our Organizing Committee as we unionized as part of SEIU Local 925, and voted to strike in the spring of 2017. That so many of our friends and fellow workers risked so much in the face of militant employer resistance continues to inspire us. It's an honor to call this group of academics, who care so deeply for workers' rights and academic freedom, our coworkers and friends.

We thank, applaud, and encourage support for the following institutions: The University of Washington's Labor Archives, the Walter Reuther Library at Wayne State University, the Southwest Washington State Archives and State Archives in Olympia, Washington; the Polson Museum in Hoquiam, Washington; the Pacific County Historical Museum in South Bend, Washington; the Cowlitz County Historical Museum in Kelso, Washington; and the Washington State Library. These institutions hold tremendous collections of materials, and the staffs at all of them are first-rate.

A special thank you to the Saint Martin's University Faculty Development Committee, which awarded us travel funds to support some of the research that went into this book.

We also thank Oregon State University Press, especially Mary Elizabeth Braun, who did so much to encourage this project in all its stages. Thanks as well to the manuscript's peer reviewers who gave us great ideas that helped shape the final product.

This book emerged in part from a course Roger Snider taught that was titled "The Soviet of Washington." Roger sends a big thank you to the many students who made the Soviet of Washington courses at Saint Martin's University such a fruitful experience. Their hard work, enthusiasm, and comments helped inspire *The Red Coast*. Roger would like to dedicate the book to his spouse and friend, Deanna Tabor.

Brian Barnes wishes to dedicate the book to JoAnna Barnes.

Aaron Goings extends his gratitude to everyone who helped make this book possible. I've been fortunate to get to know so many historians and other progressive scholars who have generously contributed their time and ideas to this project. Thanks especially to Matti Roitto, Helena Hirvonen, Keri Graham, Pertti Ahonen, Rex Casillas, David H. Price, Peter Cole, Jeremy Milloy, Gary Kaunonen, Brooke Boulton, Jeremy Hedlund, Brandon Anderson, Laurie Mercier, Chris Henry, Shanna Stevenson, and John Hughes. I owe a special debt of gratitude to my graduate advisers Mark Leier, Betsy Jameson, and Karen Blair for their years of generosity, kindness, and intellectual guidance. And a hearty thank you to my long-time friend and Wobbly enthusiast, Heather Mayer. Her brilliant book, *Beyond the Rebel Girl*, will motivate scholars and activists for years to come.

Funding for *The Red Coast* came from many sources. I owe a tremendous debt to the Finland Fulbright Commission and the History and Ethnology Department (HELA) at the University of Jyväskylä, which granted me a Fulbright Scholars' Fellowship for the 2014–2015 academic year. The Institute of Advanced Social Research at the University of Tampere, which awarded me a two-year research fellowship, has proven to be a researcher's paradise, providing the type of real academic freedom necessary to undertake book-length research and writing projects. And to my fellow fellows at the Institute: your insights and support have been much appreciated. It is no stretch to say that this book would have never been completed without the generous intellectual guidance and financial assistance provided by these fine Finnish academic institutions.

I am indebted to the many archivists and librarians who helped along the way. Thank you to Roy Vataja, John Larson, Tracey Rebstock, Karen Jaskar, Amber Raney, and Lanny Weaver.

My greatest debts are owed to my family—workers all—who taught me the importance of collective struggle. To my lovely aunts and uncles, brothers and cousins, in-laws and nephews—thank you for your sweetness, generosity, and good humor. I dedicate this book to my wonderful parents, Chris and Mike, and my equally wonderful partner, Jess. This book would have been impossible were it not for your love and support.

THE RED COAST

Washington and Oregon from the coast to Interstate 5. Map by Jessica Sheinbaum.

Introduction

During the month of April 1912, headlines of several Pacific Northwest and national publications told of the horrors being committed by "gunmen" and "imported bullies" who physically assaulted female picketers during an Industrial Workers of the World (IWW or Wobbly) lumber strike in the towns of Aberdeen and Hoquiam, Washington.[1] One story in the *Seattle Star* portrayed Finnish American women Anna Kaakinen, Fannie Kaarinen, and Sophy Sipela as brave victims who stood their ground as police sprayed them with a high-powered fire hose. The *Star* reported,

> A fire hose was run out and the water turned on. The stream struck the ground with terrific force at the women's feet, dashing mud and water on their bodies and in their faces.
>
> The imported bullies roared with laughter at the excellent joke.
>
> And the line wavered.
>
> Back and back they fell, half drowned and strangling. Many were knocked down by the force of the stream. The men at the nozzle played it up and down the line.
>
> The line broke.
>
> But one woman—Mrs. Kaakinen—did not retreat. Instead, she advanced upon the men at the nozzle—advanced until the inch stream was hitting her full in the breast. She staggered under the force of it.
>
> And she laughed in the faces of the bullies—laughed sturdily, good-naturedly and called upon the quaking "scabs" to quit work and call the strike.
>
> Then came Miss Kaarinen and Mrs. Sipela and stood by her side; and they, too, laughed.[2]

ke   Here are Mrs. Kaakinen, Miss Kaarinen and Mrs. Sipela, neigh-
ral bors, the plucky women who foiled the gun-men and held the picket line.
the The Star man found them discussing the situation in the yard of the
     first named, 116 Cushing st., Aberdeen.

Finnish American women picketed mills and paraded through Aberdeen and Hoquiam during the
1912 lumber strike. On several occasions, police and vigilantes physically assaulted the women
picketers, including these three "plucky women who foiled the gun-men and held the picket line."
Their photograph appeared on the front page of the *Seattle Star*, April 13, 1912.

Confrontations such as this one between women picketers and groups of
strikebreakers, police, and vigilantes continued throughout much of April as
Grays Harbor women—the wives, daughters, and female friends of lumber
mill strikers—took center stage in what was the Pacific Northwest's largest
lumber strike up to that point.

Women remained on the front lines of the conflict throughout April
1912. Female IWWs and IWW supporters led long lines of marchers through
downtown Aberdeen and Hoquiam, which led the *Seattle Star* to comment:
"There are no men on the picket lines in Aberdeen, but only women and most
of them are Finns. And such women! Tow-headed, solid, they are as strong as
oxen and brave as lions."[3] Agnes C. Laut, a Canadian journalist who observed
the strike, remarked, "Women took an important part in the disturbances at
Aberdeen."[4] The Wobblies' own press celebrated that "women are picketing

every day," and "There will be more women helping on the pickets. Get them all out."[5]

There were several remarkable features of these picket line confrontations. First, they occurred during a strike of several thousand workers in an industry almost entirely ignored by the American Federation of Labor and its affiliate unions. Second, women, who only rarely earned wages in the early twentieth-century Grays Harbor lumber industry, led the pickets against a well-organized and violent body of strikebreakers.[6] Third, less than two years after women won the right to vote in Washington State and eight years before most American women achieved that right, dozens of Grays Harbor women took overtly political stands on the streets and picket lines of Aberdeen and Hoquiam, defying the very real threats of violence at the hands of police, imported strikebreakers, and a "citizens' committee" composed of local employers. The strike also occurred at the same time as a municipal election in which hundreds of working people, including many female Finnish American radicals, elected two socialist city council members. By picketing and voting socialist, the Harbor's working women found two ways to challenge the region's lumber barons who were entrenched in the Republican Party and committed to a program of violent strikebreaking.[7]

The conflict between Grays Harbor employers and the IWW was but one of many flash points in the "labor wars" that raged across the Red Coast during the first four decades of the twentieth century. Like so many of the conflicts that preceded and followed it, the 1912 strike represented a clearly defined class struggle between organized capital and a heterogeneous labor force that, by the early 1910s, began to act in unity to promote class-based goals. These goals included higher wages, improved working conditions, and unionization of all working people, ranging from longshoremen and mill laborers—those routinely identified with the labor movement—to restaurant workers and domestic servants, the women and men whose efforts to unionize met with less success.

What follows is a popular history of those labor, left-wing, and progressive activists who lived, worked, and organized in southwest Washington State from the late nineteenth century to 1940. *The Red Coast* also shines a bright light on the history of the region's employers and their allies who organized to protect the dominant class's interests by forming business clubs and vigilante organizations to fight unions and radicals; on more than one occasion they employed murder and mass deportation to defend against the "threat" of working-class activism.

The Red Coast covers the people, places, and events that made this history, ranging from such well-known events as the 1919 Armistice Day Tragedy in Centralia and the murders of labor activists William McKay and Laura Law in Aberdeen, to the little-known radicals and events that have been lost to posterity. It is our hope that the book reminds readers of the rich history of radicalism and progressive activism in this region—southwest Washington—that is so frequently identified with conservatism. The Red Coast is thus a "hidden history," rescuing the region's activists from obscurity and placing them at the center of its history.

The Red Coast sits along Washington's Pacific Coast, ranging from the Columbia River in the south to the Olympic Peninsula in the north. Coastal settlements developed in tandem with resource extracting industries. Fishing and canning drew residents to both sides of the Columbia River, Astoria to the south, Ilwaco and other small towns to the north. These settlements were filled by white American, European, and Asian settlers who came to the region by the thousands in the decades after 1880.

The Red Coast's massive evergreen forests and the industries that utilized them deeply influenced the region's economic development, as well as its politics, culture, and geography. The Coast's lumber towns—Aberdeen, Hoquiam, Raymond, South Bend, Centralia, and Chehalis—served to connect the region's forests and lumber and shingle mills to the lumber schooners and rails that transported the region's billions of board feet of lumber to California, Hawaii, Mexico, China, and elsewhere. Thousands of men and women labored in the Red Coast's lumber industry during the early twentieth century, performing the work necessary to cut the trees, produce the lumber and shingles, and ship these products to market. In fact, the region included the top lumber-shipping port in the world throughout much of the first four decades of the twentieth century. In 1924, Grays Harbor became the first port in the world to ship over a billion board feet of lumber in a single year, an achievement that led one local newspaper to boast, "Grays Harbor would be the only lumber port in the world able to talk in billions while others were talking millions, in the lumber game."[8]

In the late nineteenth and early twentieth centuries, men held most jobs in southwest Washington's fishing boats, logging camps, and lumber mills. But there were a number of exceptions. In Camas, which sits just east of Vancouver on the Columbia River, forty women held positions in a bag factory owned by the Crown Columbia Paper Company. In 1913, they struck for two weeks, eventually gaining a pay raise and improved working conditions.[9] In Grays Harbor, women made up a sizable percentage of the Cooks and Waiters' Union and the Laundry Workers' Union. Lena Turk was both a union leader and co-owner of the Gloss Steam Laundry, a worker-owned cooperative in Aberdeen during the 1910s.[10] By the First World War, women had gained access to some jobs in the region's logging camps, especially as cooks and servers. At least some of these women formed and led the Domestic Workers' Industrial Union and Foodstuff Workers' Industrial Union, two IWW locals led by women.

To some, southwest Washington no doubt seems an odd starting point for a history of radicalism in the Pacific Northwest, an area with such prominent "red" outposts as Seattle and Portland. Still, even a cursory glance at the region's history shows its numerous, often bloody, labor struggles, and radical working-class organizations. Thousands of workers joined militant trade unions, revolutionary organizations such as the Industrial Workers of the World, and radical political parties during the first four decades of the twentieth century. With some notable exceptions, the Red Coast's radicals hailed primarily from the lumber industry, working in this dirty, dangerous industry as loggers, lumber and shingle mill laborers, longshoremen, sailors, and logging camp waitresses. These men and women formed a diverse array of working-class organizations and political parties to fight their bosses, improve wages and working conditions, push government toward more worker-friendly positions, and in some cases to attempt to overthrow the capitalist system itself.

Men who labored on the Coast's numerous waterways formed the region's first militant trade unions, including the Sailors' Union of the Pacific (SUP), International Longshoremen's Association (ILA), and International Shingle Weavers' Union of America (ISWUA). By 1903, the Aberdeen and Hoquiam waterfront unions were firmly established, representing hundreds of the region's male laborers. Labor activists such as SUP agent Billy Gohl and shingle weaver Jay G. Brown led the labor movement during its early heyday, when it expanded to include thousands of male and female laborers organized into dozens of trade unions that represented workers in jobs ranging from logging to laundry work. By 1910, several of the Coast towns were thoroughly organized.

The Red Coast was not only one of the Northwest's densest areas of labor organization but also one of the most militant. Thousands of Red Coast workers found the mainstream labor movement to be too exclusive and too conservative, and many thought even radical political parties were too tied to what the Industrial Workers of the World labeled parliamentary "slow-cialism."[11] To these men and women, the revolutionary industrial unionism of the IWW held a great and lasting appeal, and it was the union and radical organization of choice for thousands of Red Coast workers between the 1910s and 1930s.

At the heart of this book is a series of vignettes covering the history of class struggle in southwest Washington State. Several of the chapters revolve around struggles waged by the Industrial Workers of the World during its hey-day in the Pacific Northwest. In 1905, a diverse group of socialists, anarchists, and militant trade unionists formed the IWW as an industrial union and revo-lutionary organization for the express purpose of overthrowing the capitalist system. The Industrial Workers saw the world and their place in it through the lens of class: the fundamental division in industrial capitalist America was between those who owned the means of production and those who worked for them. The IWW defined the class system as an antagonistic and exploi-tive relationship between the employing class (capitalist) and the working class (proletariat), with no common interests. As the Preamble of the IWW Constitution proclaims, "The employing class and the working class have nothing in common."[12]

The Wobblies, as members of the IWW were (and are) nicknamed, were keenly aware of their class interests and the legitimacy of those interests. Conversely, they denounced the tyranny and parasitism of the employing class, and were eager "to organize, educate and emancipate" themselves and their fellow workers. This class-based activism—or "class war" as the Wobblies often termed it—was part and parcel of being a Wobbly. According to the Wobblies, not only do the two principal classes have nothing in common, but there can be no peace as long as the employers enjoy the rewards of the workers' toil while workers remain hungry and deprived. "Between these two classes a struggle must go on until the workers of the world organize as a class, take possession of the earth and the machinery of production, and abolish the wage system," they declared.[13]

But as the class-conscious workers who stand at the center of this book were aware, class consciousness is not limited to working people. Red Coast employers were characterized by high levels of class consciousness, and knowing and acting upon their own interest is a virtual hallmark of capitalist profit-centered thought and behavior. Although conflicts among capitalist groups may arise over a variety of issues, capitalists exhibit a remarkable solidarity when challenged *as a class*. Class-conscious capitalists are therefore quick to recognize when workers begin acting in their own interests, and they are more than capable of organizing effectively to exert control over both the workforce and the worker. This response may take the form of propaganda, violence, or repressive laws, but capitalists may also respond more creatively, for example with piecemeal reforms in the workplace—such as shorter hours or better safety conditions—that aim to eliminate or at least minimize working-class consciousness. Given the capitalists' monopoly of resources and their strategic position in the society, these measures are frequently successful. But they do not always succeed. When attempts to subvert working-class militancy fail, the struggle may rise to the level of an overt class war. Confronted by militant and class-conscious workers, the employing class generally calls upon its allies in political circles to wield the authority of the state to deal with the enemy, an enemy that by this time has been defined as a public enemy.

In the past, as in the present, class determined much about individuals' lives. Although one's relationship to the means of production did not dictate that he or she would join a radical political group or the chamber of commerce, it influenced where people lived, how they vacationed, if they vacationed at all, what they ate, what schooling they received, and how they died. Class was also a key ingredient in the formation of people's politics, as they mobilized alongside their fellow workers or fellow employers to court sympathetic politicians, lobby for friendly legislation, and assert themselves as key players in their communities. However, a century ago, several revolutionary possibilities were not only on the table but were the primary animating forces behind the actions of thousands of workers who took to the streets annually. Openly revolutionary workers stood atop soapboxes and on picket lines, offering different, collectivist solutions to the varied oppressions and injuries of class. Thousands of working-class militants and radicals understood full well that theirs was neither a cooperative nor an equal relationship with their boss, a fact underscored in their rhetoric and actions alike. Though a life of brutal conditions, long hours of labor, bouts of poverty, and an early death were the fruits of capitalism, theirs was a world not just of despair, but also of possibilities.

Employers of course had little stomach for the possibilities offered up by the IWW and other labor militants. Some of the earliest anti-labor activism centered on groups calling themselves citizens' committees. During the late nineteenth and early twentieth centuries, these vigilante-style employers' organizations were formed in cities and towns throughout North America to break strikes and suppress worker organizing. For example, employers formed such committees in more than thirty communities in Colorado to combat the Western Federation of Miners in that state.[14]

On the Red Coast, employers formed citizens' committees in Aberdeen in late 1911, and in Aberdeen, Hoquiam, and Raymond in March 1912. The term "citizens' committee" suggests that a unified group of citizens came together to roust the Wobblies from these towns. By using this name, employers sought to position themselves as representatives of their local towns, as "citizens" of the community and country mobilized to do battle with "outsiders," "outside agitators," and "foreigners," just to mention a few of the names used by the mainstream press for the IWW. But citizens' committees were "unions against unions," to use the term coined by historian William Millikan, and little more than front groups for local chambers of commerce.[15] Composed exclusively of employers—lumbermen, small business owners, managers of various types, and conservative newspaper editors—citizens' committees were class-based organizations formed to suppress the Red Coast's radical labor movement using whatever means necessary.

Although the Red Coast's business owners sought legitimacy by calling themselves a committee of citizens, the Wobblies—the men and women on the receiving end of their attacks—went to great lengths to expose and publicize the class-based nature of the citizens' committees. To the Wobblies, the citizens' committee was a "slugging committee of the business men," a group of "piratical masters," "'law and order' thugs" a "gang of scab policemen," and a "bunch of middle-class scissor-bills who are but acting in the interests of the lumber trust." As IWW "Stumpy" Payne wrote, "Their particular names in this instance," included "Banker Patterson, who has 80 per cent of the business houses of Aberdeen and Hoquiam under his thumb," and Robert Lytle, "one of the most vigorous and slimy foes of the Shingle Weavers' Union."[16] For its employers' actions against the IWW, the city of Aberdeen received the nickname "axe-handleville," a moniker that stuck, at least in the radical press, for several years.[17]

When called upon, an impressive lineup of anti-labor militants mobilized alongside citizens' committees to fight working-class and leftwing organizations. The Pinkerton and Thiel detective agencies could be relied on to provide

As seen in this gathering of lumber employers on the Skookum, Red Coast employers depicted themselves as patriotic Americans. Photo courtesy of Jones Photo, Aberdeen, Washington.

labor spies and provocateurs. Scabs and strikebreakers were recruited from the Puget Sound area, Portland, and farther afield. And when they weren't enough to do the job, the employers called on their allies in state and federal government to spy on, infiltrate, and bust the unions. Thus, an extensive espionage network existed in the lumber industry, whose timber and lumber barons felt threatened by militant labor unionists and other radicals.

Several Red Coast towns had large immigrant populations that brought their ethnic traditions and political radicalism to the region's class struggles. The IWW and Socialist Party of America (SPA) found particular strength among immigrant workers who struggled to survive in the lumber industry where low wages, long hours, and dangerous working conditions were the rule. Thousands of immigrants joined thousands more native-born workers to perform the paid and unpaid labor that enabled southwest Washington to produce so much of the world's wood products. Several coastal towns had their own ethnic communities, complete with a diverse array of immigrants and immigrant families, immigrant-owned institutions such as restaurants and newspapers, and rich sets of social and cultural activities based, as often as not, in the groups' meeting halls.

Along much of the Red Coast, Finns constituted the largest immigrant group. Renowned for their political radicalism and labor militancy, working-class Finns led labor movements in many parts of the Upper Midwest and Pacific Northwest. After 1900, the Finnish American community grew to become the region's largest, as thousands of Finns settled in coastal towns that included Ilwaco, Raymond, Aberdeen, and Hoquiam, Washington, as well as Astoria, Oregon. More than 2,000 first- and second-generation Finns settled in Aberdeen and Hoquiam by 1920. Approximately one-half of the residents of Ilwaco, a fishing town on the Columbia, were Finns in 1910. The same was true of Grayland, a beach community numbering approximately 200 residents—more than half of whom were Finns—during the 1920s and 1930s.[18]

As the pages ahead will attest, the Red Coast's immigrants, particularly its radical working-class immigrants, were frequent targets of violence. Employers and their allies raided workers' halls, destroyed their literature and records, and made IWW members "run the gauntlet." Other radicals were tarred and feathered by businessmen and members of the Loyal Legion of Loggers and Lumbermen (4Ls), a military-company union labeled the "Four Hells" by the IWW.[19]

Thus, it was not class alone that drove Red Coast employers to violently and collectively confront Wobblies and other groups of organized laborers. Instead, the intersections of class, gender, ethnicity, and race were visible as the region's bosses—exclusively white men—came together to assert their place as the Red Coast's rightful leadership. Citizens' committee and American Legion members routinely employed gendered language in their attacks on labor radicals. All-male fraternal organizations such as the Elks were equally important as the all-male chambers of commerce in coordinating anti-union drives and anti-radical purges. These "committees" resembled Wild West lynch mobs, when employers joined law enforcement and imported thugs to violently remove problematic individuals and groups from the local area. Moreover, as the case of the 1890 employer-led eviction of Aberdeen's Chinese American residents and the eviction of Raymond's Greeks and Finns twenty-two years later, demonstrated, employers sometimes focused their energies on cleansing communities of "problematic" immigrant groups.

Anti-labor attacks reached a fever pitch during and shortly after World War I as employers joined strikebreakers, patriotic vigilante groups, and state officials in a wide-ranging assault on the IWW and Socialist Party. During World War I, the Wobblies struck, seeking to force employers to grant the eight-hour day and improve working conditions. IWWs and other unionists paralyzed the Pacific Northwest lumber industry. During the struggle, employers orchestrated attacks by police, newspapermen, and vigilantes on unionists and radicals. Picketers were arrested and beaten for the threat they posed to wartime profits and the war effort itself. Striking loggers were forced to seek safety in large groups or pursue more creative means to avoid being assaulted. Bill Amey, an IWW camp delegate, gained notoriety for riding his motorcycle from camp to camp to avoid confrontations with police and vigilantes.[20]

The most infamous incident in the region's labor and left history was the American Legion raid on the Wobbly hall in Centralia on November 11, 1919, the country's first Armistice Day. A mob of Legionnaires suddenly broke from their parade to rush the Wobbly hall, but were met with a hail of bullets from inside the hall and other locations around Centralia. Four Legionnaires died during the raid and its aftermath. That evening, local elites lynched Wobbly Wesley Everest, a logger and veteran of the Great War. The incident turned into a more than decades-long struggle, first by employers, to have Wobblies executed or sentenced to long prison sentences; second, by business and patriotic groups to intimidate witnesses and jurors and later to ensure that the 25- to 40-year sentences remained in place; and third, by labor activists and their supporters to free the IWWs from their long sentences in the Walla Walla Penitentiary. Those efforts finally succeeded in 1933, when, after more than a decade, most of the Centralia prisoners had their sentences commuted by Washington State Governor Clarence Martin.

Joining Wesley Everest as IWW martyrs was Wobbly activist and logger William McKay. In 1923, a gunman shot McKay in the back of the head, killing him, while he picketed at the Bay City Mill in Aberdeen. A year after McKay's murder, Grays Harbor businessmen ran IWW James Rowan's car off the road. He only narrowly escaped lynching by the timely interference of a farm family and a deputy sheriff.[21]

The most notorious anti-labor organization in southwest Washington was the Ku Klux Klan, which surged into prominence in Red Coast towns during the 1920s, much as it did in other parts of the country. On August 1, 1924, the

Chehalis Bee Nugget reported that 15,000 to 20,000 attended a KKK meeting at the Lewis County fairgrounds.[22] Well into the 1930s, long after the Klan resurgence of the twenties had waned, the KKK retained its prominence in the Red Coast towns of Aberdeen and Hoquiam. The hooded knights made headlines during the 1930s by burning crosses in the hills outside Aberdeen and threatening violence against union activists.

The region also produced more than its fair share of reactionaries who tried, sometimes with a great deal of success, to peddle their anti-immigrant and anti-radical views in exchange for votes to elective office. Congressman Albert Johnson rose to prominence on a wave of anti-immigrant and anti-radical hysteria in the early 1910s as editor for the *Daily Washingtonian* of Hoquiam. From DC, the congressman, a darling of the Ku Klux Klan, made an enduring mark on the nation's history. During the early 1920s, he sponsored a series of immigration exclusion bills, culminating in the 1924 Johnson-Reed Immigration Act. The act imposed tight, race-based quotas on immigrant groups that favored those hailing from northern and western European countries. It targeted for exclusion immigrants hailing from Africa and Asia, and it severely restricted the further immigration of Johnson's most-hated Europeans: Greeks, Finns, Italians, and other southern and eastern Europeans drawn to class-conscious politics.

During the 1930s, Red Coast workers joined millions of other Americans in organizing unions and strikes amid the dire conditions of the Depression. With support and leadership from Communists, Red Coast workers expressed a militant class consciousness as they confronted employers in massive and widespread strikes. Owing to the size of their strikes, longshoremen and lumber workers caught the most headlines, but they were not alone in the union drives of the 1930s. By 1938, much of southwest Washington's workforce had organized, as everyone from loggers to clam diggers, shingle weavers to beauticians, belonged to unions. By the end of the decade, southwest Washington was home to approximately 200 unions.[23]

The Red Coast is organized into a series of thematic chapters arranged in rough chronological order. It uncovers a history of working-class radicalism and employer reaction in a region that has long been identified with the Right. It tells the history of working-class resistance that, we contend, offers the potential to show that at one time southwest Washingtonians organized by the thousands to protest injustices great and small, ranging from the horrors of laboring in a deadly workplace to the insult of a short paycheck.

1

The Gillnet Wars

In the darkness of night, May 23, 1887, some three hundred gillnet fishermen and their boats gathered in Baker Bay, near the mouth of the Columbia
River in southwest Washington Territory, to destroy the fish traps that caused
them so much hardship. They began with the trap of Fred Colbert, a well-to-
do resident of Ilwaco. In the previous week the fishermen had regularly cut
adrift the pile driver that Colbert used to build fish traps. Colbert, expecting
trouble, stationed three employees named Miller, Murray, and Russ on a large
scow near his trap with orders to protect his property. But confronted with
an overwhelming force of armed men, Colbert's employees were unable to
do their boss's bidding. Instead, the gillnetters took them from the scow and
put them to work destroying traps. Russ was taken to Daniel Markham's traps
"and forced at the point of the pistol to cut that trap away." Miller was forced
"to destroy and mutilate as much as possible Colbert's pile driver; in other
words, abuse the property of his employer." The gillnetters set fire to Colbert's
scow and trap equipment, then continued up the river "to destroy everything
in the shape of a fish trap" before disappearing into the darkness. Miller and
Russ were left on a scow off Sand Island. Murray was taken away in a small skiff
without oars and left anchored in the bay. The residents of Ilwaco, where most
of the trap-men lived, awoke to the sound of ringing school bells and the sight
of Colbert's scow aflame. They "rushed out armed but it was too late; the ruin
was accomplished and the miscreants had sailed away."[1]

The next night, three Ilwaco trap-owners, A. E. King, Archie Ross, and Al
Green, went out to check on some newly tarred trap net that had been left out
to dry. They saw a Native man, Tom Dalzan, near the net. Believing he was a
gillnetter bent on sabotage, they pursued and fired at him. He returned fire and
both King and Ross were shot, with Ross dying of his wounds. This shooting
turned out to be an accident, since Dalzan had been hired by trap-man Fred

Colbert to guard his equipment.[2] But the May raid on the fish traps of Baker Bay was just one of the first skirmishes in a long series of conflicts between union gillnet fishermen, non-union fishermen, trap-men, and cannery operators on the Columbia River. This conflict took form in the 1880s and did not end completely until fixed fishing gear, such as fish wheels and fish traps, were outlawed by a series of Oregon and Washington popular initiatives between 1926 and 1948.[3] The first blood spilled in this conflict may have been the result of an accident, but later bloodshed was very intentional. During the 1896 Gillnet Strike the violence seemed serious enough that both the Oregon and Washington National Guard were called to the river, and even the US Army was involved before all was said and done. Taken together, the conflicts might well be called the Gillnet Wars.[4]

The root cause of the Gillnet Wars was class conflict on the lower Columbia River where, by the end of the 1880s, some 2,600 fishermen and 3,000 cannery workers made their living from the enormous but already declining runs of salmon.[5] The conflict pitted working-class gillnetters of the Columbia River Fishermen's Protective Union (CRFPU) against property-owning fish-trap operators, against the cannery operators with whom the trap-men were sometimes allied, and against scabbing fishermen, often farmers who worked seasonally at fishing to supplement their income, and who were less likely to observe strikes. These conflicts were critical in forging a largely pan-ethnic and working-class movement among the diverse communities of the lower Columbia River.[6]

The gillnetters' profession was an extremely dangerous one, even by the standards of nineteenth-century industrial capitalism. Gillnetters set out on the Columbia River in a centerboard boat of about twenty-six feet in length and eight feet in beam, and set a net of 1,800 feet in length and twenty-five to thirty feet in depth that drifted with the ebb down the river. Each boat was operated by two men, a fisherman and a boat puller. They generally owned their net, but rented the boat from the cannery for the season, which ran from April until August of each year. Fishing was often done at night, and the fishermen sometimes slept while the net drifted. They ran a risk of being overturned and drowned if bad weather arose suddenly, if their net was snagged, and most fatally, if they could not gather in their net in time before being swept over the deadly bar at the river's mouth. Between twenty and sixty gillnetters died each year, and it is not without reason that a government report on the Columbia River fisheries stated that gillnetting "develops a hardy and brave set of men."[7]

Gillnet fishing on
the Columbia River.
Photo courtesy
of the Freshwater
and Marine Image
Bank, University of
Washington Libraries.

GILL-NET FISHING ON THE COLUMBIA RIVER.

These men who ventured out in their small boats onto the dangerous waters of the Columbia were, as one would expect, working-class fishermen. In the early years of the industry they were often migrant workers, moving seasonally between the Sacramento River Delta and the Columbia. Many of them were also immigrants. In 1890, the CRFPU reported that 40 percent of its members were born in another country, with Scandinavians leading the way, followed by Finns and Austrians.[8] Gillnetters lived on both the Oregon and Washington sides of the Columbia, but most lived on the Oregon side, and the largest concentration was in Astoria, where they developed numerous social clubs and ethnic enclaves. In 1888, according to the calculations of the CRFPU, each fisherman grossed an average of $312, and netted $187.50 for the 120-day season, for an average daily earnings of $1.57. They were "lamentable small wages, these, for risking life and property and for laying out on the stormy waters night and day and suffering the many hardships incidental to a fisherman's avocation."[9]

Unfortunately for the gillnetters, their profession was made both more dangerous and less remunerative by the use of fish traps on the most productive fishing grounds, and especially at Baker Bay, across from Astoria. Fish traps were large fixed-gear devices that consisted of a net or lattice structure attached to a row of piles driven into the river bed. This barrier might extend up to 800 feet into the river, and when fish heading upstream to the spawning grounds encountered it, they swam along this lead until entering a circular pound, from which they could not escape, since their instinct compelled them to swim only upstream.[10] For this reason, the devices were also called pound nets. The first was installed on the Columbia in 1879. By 1900, there were 500 of the devices on the lower river, with around 400 in Baker Bay.[11] An 1897 article in *Frank Leslie's Popular Monthly* described the scene: "Here is a perfect labyrinth of nets filling the water for miles and miles, and one wonders how it is possible for fish entering this bay to get past the leaders and pounds which, like gigantic spider webs, invite to destruction all fish unwary enough to come within their folds."[12]

The owners of these traps had little in common with the gillnetters. Whereas gillnetters were working-class fishermen who risked their lives for a modest subsistence, the trap-men were property-owning capitalists who either owned or leased the land on which they trapped. Moreover, constructing fish traps was a capital intensive project. The trap was based on indigenous fishing technologies, but they soon evolved into massive structures built by work crews operating steam-powered pile drivers. Some owners possessed multiple traps, and the traps might be just one of a capitalist's many business ventures. Some traps were also owned directly by the canneries, which threatened to cut the gillnetters out of the industry altogether.[13] Another difference between the gillnetters and the trap-men was that whereas most of the gillnetters lived on the Oregon side of the river, most traps were on the Washington side. This meant that the gillnetters could not appeal successfully to their own state government to regulate the trap-men, even if the state had been inclined to do so. Trap-owners, meanwhile, could inflame public sentiment against the gillnetters by presenting any actions they took against fish traps as an attack by outsiders—and foreign outsiders at that—on Washingtonians.

The gillnetters resented the traps and the trap-men for multiple practical reasons. One was that as more and more traps were constructed, their very presence excluded gillnetters from the places where they were built, since they could not set their nets where fish traps obstructed their drift.[14] Since the traps were naturally built where the fishing was best, the gillnetters found themselves elbowed out of the prime fishing grounds. Another reason was a concern for safety. The traps were an obstacle not only to fishing but to navigation, and fishermen fishing close to the traps sometimes themselves became entangled in them and drowned.[15] In addition to this, the monopolization of prime fishing grounds by the traps encouraged some fishermen to fish other productive, but more dangerous drifts, such as the approach to the Columbia River Bar.[16] Finally, although gillnetters took a majority of the harvest, the additional supply produced by the trap-men certainly limited the prices gillnetters could get for their catch, and trap-men's willingness to provide fish to canneries during strikes was particularly offensive.

On April 11, 1886, the gillnetters came together to form the CRFPU in order to improve their condition.[17] This workers' organization had many functions. It was a mutual aid society for gillnetters; a trade group that pulled snags and other impediments to fishing from the river; a pressure group that lobbied for the elimination of fish traps and other practices that gillnetters regarded as destructive, such as fish wheels. Of course, the CRFPU was primarily a union that sought to force canneries to pay fair prices for the fruits of fishermen's labor.[18]

It is clear that the fishermen who formed and joined the union understood their struggle to be a class struggle. The preamble to the union's constitution and bylaws declared:

> A combination exists among the capitalists of this river, whose avowed object is to so control the labor market as to deprive us of our share in the general prosperity, and to obtain the product of our labor, without rendering therefor a fair equivalent. Knowing as we do that if this condition of things is allowed to go unchecked and the few be allowed to control the many, it is only a question of a very short time when we as well as other laborers must be dependent upon the will and caprices of a few unscrupulous men. Knowing as we do that any individual effort to maintain our rights and uphold the dignity of labor is sure to meet with failure, we but feebly imitate the example which capital has set up; to organize and protect ourselves against the unjust efforts of the capitalists to reduce us to a state of absolute dependence.[19]

The CRPFU proclaimed that "labor alone gives life and value to capital," asserted "the right of every member to receive fair and just remuneration for his labor," and maintained that "an injury to one is the concern of us all." It seems initially to have admitted only gillnet fishermen, but it eventually welcomed "Any Gillnetters, Gillnetter employees, Seine employees, Canneries employees and Fish Buyers employees." However, the union would admit "no liquor dealer, gambler, politician, capitalist, lawyer, agent of or for capitalists, nor persons holding office, whether under the National, State or Municipal government." [20] In an unfortunate sign of the racism common to Pacific Coast whites, the union was also strongly opposed to Chinese labor, and the advent of the union drove the small number of Chinese fishermen from the river and restricted their participation in net-weaving.[21]

The CRFPU had real and immediate success raising wages for its members. Before the opening of each season, union members gathered and set a price at which they would provide salmon to the canneries. In 1886, the first year of the union, canneries offered $0.45 for fish caught on gear provided by the canneries, and $0.55 for fish caught on gear owned by the fishermen. This the fishermen "quietly but firmly refused," offering to provide fish at $0.55 and $0.65 instead. After a costly strike, the canneries met the union demands. As a result of the strike, the canneries "learned to fear and respect the power of the laboring men when they stand united, and the fishermen learned that their only hope to better their condition, lay in banding together and enforcing their rights through organized effort." Over the next three years, the union obtained further increases, so that by 1889, fishermen received $1.00 and $1.25. According to the union's calculations, over the first four years of the union, this amounted to an increase in pay of "$1,500,000 in clear cash over and above what they would have received had they remained unorganized." These increases appear to have increased workers' security to such a degree that many abandoned the migrant lifestyle and established more settled lives.[22]

However, in the 1890 season the position of the gillnetters began to erode. The union sought the same price for fish as fishermen had received in 1889, but the canneries refused, and a strike ensued. One pressing problem for the union was that the number of fishermen on the river had increased, and many of them did not join the union or observe its work stoppages. Many of these non-union workers were "cowboy fishermen" who had recently emigrated from the Midwest and settled upriver of Astoria. Many were not professional fishermen, but fished for subsistence and to raise funds to improve their land claims. The union had no objection to subsistence fishing during a strike, but cowboy fishermen often accepted the canneries' offer of gear to fish during the strike and sold fish to the canneries at the canneries' price. [23] This the union sought to discourage for obvious reasons. During the 1890 strike, depending on whose account you choose to believe, union fishermen cruised up and down the river, either ordering or entreating non-union fishermen to combine with them and demand $1.25 per fish.[24] Probably both persuasion and compulsion, especially in the form of cutting nets, were widely employed by the striking workers. Whatever the case, tensions ran high, and violence broke out.

On the morning of April 29, 1890, three boats filled with union men went upriver to discourage fishing during the strike. Among them was CRFPU fisherman Nicholas John, who described what followed. Near Rainier, Oregon, the union fishermen encountered a body of non-union men, and held a conference with them. The non-union men appeared "reluctant" to cooperate with the union, and pointed the union men toward another boat and said, "Go to those men in that scow, and see if they will agree to this." As the union boats approached the scow, they were fired upon from both the non-union boats and the shore. Several were wounded, including Nicholas John, who was hit with buckshot in the wrist, arm, and head. Three union men, including Jack Hayman and Nicholas Andrew, died of their wounds. A third man, named as "Olsen" in the *Morning Astorian*, likewise perished from his wounds. In Astoria, on May 2, "over 500 men and 100 women," formed a funeral procession headed by the "brass band of the Scandinavian Temperance society" to carry Hayman's and Andrew's bodies through streets crowded with union families.[25]

On April 30, August Linstrom, one of the non-union men who did the killing, testified at the inquest that followed the violence. He regarded his action as self-defense, and boasted how he had "fixed 'em, and if any more had come we'd have made it hot for 'em." Asked how many he had killed, he replied, "Oh, I don't know; three or four."[26] Of course, it is impossible to tell who started the violence on April 29, but it does appear that the fact that many of the union gillnetters were immigrants and members of despised ethnicities made them less sympathetic in the eyes of many. The same day Linstrom testified, many non-union fishermen visited Portland to stock up on rifles and ammunition so that they could fish when they pleased. "As to whether there will be more bloodshed," they said, "depends entirely on the piratical dagos of the fishermen's union, and if they dare again to come up from their haunts at Astoria to browbeat and terrorize peaceable American citizens and destroy their nets and drive them off the river, there will be plenty of bloodshed." "These union fishermen," the *Seattle Post-Intelligencer* explained, "are mostly Greeks, Austrians, and Russian Finns who came to Astoria for the fishing season and who literally run that town while there." The non-union, "up-river fishermen, are mostly American citizens, Scandinavians and others."[27] In the end, the union men had to accept $1.00 per fish for that season, which was subsequently reduced to $0.75 by the canneries, with full price paid only for fish above fifteen pounds.[28]

The most tumultuous strike on the river, and perhaps the most significant, was the 1896 strike. During the 1893 season, the price paid for salmon was changed from a per fish price to a per pound price. In that season, the price paid for salmon was five cents per pound, and the same price was paid the next two seasons. In 1896, however, the cannery men, operating in solidarity with their fellow capitalists, formed an association and pledged to offer only four cents per pound. As a way of holding the line, the cannery owners even posted a bond that would be paid to other owners should they pay more to the fishermen. At least that's what the CRFPU believed.[29] Two thousand fishermen attended a mass meeting in Astoria on April 8 and determined to strike on opening day, April 10, rather than accept less than five cents.[30]

The disputes of that season actually commenced before the season opened with a series of raids reminiscent of the 1887 raid on the Baker Bay fish traps. It is uncertain whether the motive for the early raids had more to do with the price the canneries offered or with the fishermen's continuing anger that traps presented a hazard to fishing and navigation, as the union's secretary claimed. In any event, gillnetters were as mad as ever at the trap-men. The largest of these raids occurred at Baker Bay on April 3. According to Sheriff Thomas Roney of Pacific County, Washington, a flotilla of "between two hundred and three hundred men[,] most of whom [were] residents of Astoria, Oregon, [and were] armed with knives, hatchets, and other deadly weapons," descended on Baker Bay. There they encountered Washingtonians driving piles for fish traps and, threatening to hang them, the unionists compelled the Washingtonians to pull up their piles before cutting their pile drivers adrift to float over the Columbia River Bar. According to Roney, the gillnetters bragged that they were supported by the CRFPU and stated bluntly that they would continue to destroy traps and prevent trap-fishing in the bay that season.[31]

The union, through its secretary, Sofus Jensen, officially disavowed violence and coercion, claiming that the pulling of piles was carried out only for the sake of safety. But it seems probable that the fishermen were determined to prevent the fish traps, whether owned privately or by the canneries, from supplying fish to the canneries at cannery prices. As Jensen himself pointed out the following week, "The trappers of Ilwaco have always, in former strikes, in a more or less degree, carried on fishing."[32] So the union men had good reason to believe that the trap-men would undermine their strike, and on April 11, the *Daily Morning Astorian* reported that the Ilwaco trap-men would provide salmon to Seaborg's cannery at four cents per pound. On that same day, the

Baker Bay trap-men met at the Ilwaco Opera House and issued a series of resolutions denouncing the gillnetters' destruction of property and proclaiming
the "inalienable right of each and every citizen to prosecute and carry on the
means of earning an honest livelihood for the support of ourselves and families at a price for our labor which we as individuals may deem just and right."[33]

The trap-men were no doubt emboldened to disregard the work stoppage
by the actions of Washington State Governor John McGraw. After the raid
on Baker's Bay, McGraw sent forty soldiers from the state National Guard
to protect the traps. Sheriff Roney, meanwhile, headed a volunteer army of
forty-five men and patrolled the river with a 63-foot steamer equipped with
a six-inch cannon.[34] The *South Bend Journal*, published in the Pacific County
town of South Bend, expressed confidence that these forces would "intimidate the Dago-Oregon fishermen," and the trap-men commenced the fishing
season.[35] The gillnetters found no opportunity to strike again at Baker Bay,
but did continue to discourage fishing upriver and cut nets of those found to
be scabbing.[36] On the night of June 8, a cannery of the North Shore Packing
Company, on the Washington side of the river, went up in flames.[37] On June
15, Oregon Governor William Lord ordered the First regiment of the Oregon
National Guard to Astoria to "preserve the peace among striking fishermen."
The "radical element" saw matters a bit differently. The CRFPU called it the
"4 ½-cent" militia, assuming that it was there to end the strike and help the
cannery operators win their struggle to cut the workers' wages.[38] In fact, by the
end of the month the strike was settled at four and a half cents, and an Astoria
businessman was celebrating that "the union has lost its fight, and its influence,
at least for the present, is gone. If matters are handled from this time on in a
business manner it will be a difficult matter for the organization to recoup."[39]

The 1896 strike was lost by the union, but it was not a complete failure.
During the 1896 season, the canneries had formed an association—essentially
a trust—in order to increase their leverage in the struggle with the CRFPU
over prices. Once formed into this combination, they reduced the price they
offered to the fishermen and, even as the strike wore on, none of the canneries
gave in and began paying the rate demanded by the union. This placed the can-
nerymen in an extremely strong position, since they were united along class
lines while the suppliers of fish—which included both union and non-union
gillnetters, and trap-men—were divided. Confronted with such a power, and
undermined by trap-men, scabs, and their own state governments, the union
gillnetters couldn't get fair pay for a fair day's work. Many union fishermen

realized they would need to control production themselves, and a group of "about 200 mostly Finnish fisherman pooled their resources" to establish the Union Fishermen's Cooperative Packing Company, a cannery of their own, which operated until 1975.[40] In 1926, Oregon gillnetters joined with the Oregon State Grange and the Oregon Federation of Labor to support an initiative banning fixed fishing gear on portions of the river. All of the Astoria canneries opposed the successful measure, except the Union Cooperative.[41]

2
The Aberdeen Outrage

On November 8, 1890, a mob of Aberdeen citizens, following up on ulti-matums made by the anti-Chinese league they had formed that September, rioted against the Chinese residents of that city. Most of them wore masks when, in the dead of the night, they rounded up the last of Aberdeen's Chinese residents, forced them onto the steamer *Wishkah Chief*—robbing and beat-ing those who resisted—and transported them twelve miles up the Chehalis River to Montesano, leaving them with the instruction to "keep going." By the standards of late-nineteenth-century attacks on Chinese immigrants in the western United States, this riot was neither particularly large nor particularly bloody; wholesale massacres of Chinese immigrants had occurred in Rock Springs, Wyoming (1885), and on the Snake River, in Oregon (1887). Nor was the mass deportation—expulsion from town—of a town's entire Chinese American population unusual; this had occurred on a much larger scale sev-eral years earlier in Tacoma (1885) and Seattle (1886), and was repeated in countless towns and cities in the western United States.[1] What is surprising about the expulsion of Aberdeen's Chinese residents is the degree to which the historical record of it is filled not with white workers who resented competi-tion with Chinese labor, but with Aberdeen's merchant elite.

The Aberdeen expulsion came toward the end of more than a decade of anti-Chinese agitation, legislation, and violence that swept the western United States in the late nineteenth century. The anti-Chinese outcry was first raised in California by Denis Kearney's Workingmen's Party. In an 1878 address, Kearney argued that capitalists imported Chinese as "cheap working slave[s]" in order to "further . . . degrade white Labor."[2] His Workingmen's Party lob-bied for restrictive policies at both the state and national level. Going further, Kearney declared, "The Chinese Must Go!"—a cry that soon echoed up and down the coast. In Washington, matters came to a head in Puget Sound in 1885, where a coalition of city leaders and white workers, often part of the Knights of Labor, pioneered the "Tacoma Method" to deport Chinese residents from that city: they formed an anti-Chinese league, declared that all Chinese residents must leave the city by a certain date, and then proceeded, with the complicity of the city's law enforcement and political leaders, to round up and forcibly deport all those who remained. The 1886 Seattle sequel to the Tacoma expulsion was more controversial. It played out as a "brutal charade" in which those who wanted the immediate expulsion of the Chinese by force, which included a strong labor element, were opposed unsuccessfully by the "Opera House" faction, led by city leaders. The latter acquiesced to the anti-Chinese movement, but sought to drive the Chinese out without violence or lawlessness.[3]

These anti-Chinese campaigns coincided with a period of increased joblessness and worker anxiety. In the 1880s, as the transcontinental railroads were completed and workers were laid off, white workers increasingly took up Kearney's cry and turned against Chinese workers, with whom they refused to identify. At least in its rhetoric, if not in its methods, the anti-Chinese movement of the era closely resembles the anti-immigrant movement of our own time. Chinese workers, their opponents argued, entered the United States illegally, refused to assimilate, sent their earnings home, and undercut white wages. In a time of economic dislocation, the Chinese immigrant minority proved an attractive scapegoat for workers' economic problems, and organizations like the Workingmen's Party and the Knights of Labor clearly exploited this in their drive to increase membership. Yet the Aberdeen expulsion suggests that elites could also harness or even instigate these movements to serve their own class interests.

The expulsion movement appears to have taken shape in mid-September 1890 under the leadership of Aberdeen's elites. The spark for the anti-Chinese movement was "occasioned by one of the citizens renting a building on F Street, which is one of the principal thoroughfares, to some Chinamen." Neighboring "property owners," perhaps fearing a decline in their rents or property values, sought the support of the Board of Trade, a forerunner to Aberdeen's Chamber of Commerce. At a special session of this body "a mass meeting was called for . . . having for its object the removal of all Chinese from the city limits."[4] In a letter from Tsui Kwo Yin, of the Chinese Legation in Washington, DC, to James Blaine, Secretary of State, and dated September 14, Tsui reported that the Chinese residents of Aberdeen had been writing to the Imperial Consul

General at San Francisco, stating that they had been told to leave Aberdeen "at once" and that "their lives and property were in great peril."[5]

A more formal demand that the Chinese leave Aberdeen was the result of the September 15 gathering that had been recommended by the Board of Trade. This meeting was held at Aberdeen's Opera House and presided over by Aberdeen's mayor, J. B. Maling, who later reported that "the celestials were coming in such large numbers that the citizens said it must be stopped."[6] This characterization, if accurate, shows a very high degree of intolerance indeed, since Aberdeen's 40 Chinese represented just 2.4 percent of Aberdeen's population of 1,638. After "many speeches," the meeting passed a resolution requiring all of the forty or so Chinese residents of Aberdeen to leave within one week, by noon on September 23, and appointed a "committee of forty" to ensure the resolution was carried out.[7] About this time, if not at this very meeting, the leaders of the anti-Chinese movement also hatched a plan to take up a subscription to buy out at least the property owned by launderer John Wing, who was seemingly the most prosperous Chinese resident of Aberdeen.[8]

Aberdeen's Chinese had a good reason to be afraid: five men might make a committee, but a "committee of forty" was nothing less than a mob. Understandably, some—perhaps half—appear to have left shortly after the Opera House meeting. They were undoubtedly well aware of the history of anti-Chinese mobs in other cities, and some of them may even have experienced them prior to their residence in Aberdeen. There was also a report that some members of the anti-Chinese movement, worried that their order to leave the city would not be followed, held a second meeting in which they required all Chinese to leave the city within forty-eight hours.[9] But the remaining Chinese residents, though threatened with violence if they remained, instead sought protection through the Chinese embassy. On the day of the Opera House meeting, the following telegram was sent to the Chinese Consul in San Francisco: "The Aberdeen citizens say our Chinese must go on September 23rd. Telegraph the Government to have them protected at once. Signed—Woo Lee and Chinese at Hoquiam, Wash."[10] This plea for protection was forwarded to the Chinese Legation, which in turn forwarded it to the Secretary of State, along with a request for action. After corresponding with the Chinese Legation, Acting US Secretary of State William Wharton asked Washington State Governor Elisha Ferry to preserve the peace and protect the rights of the Chinese in Aberdeen.[11]

But Governor Ferry appeared determined not to act. On September 17, he announced that "the people of Aberdeen, as free citizens, can hold what meetings they choose and pass resolutions that the Chinese or anybody else must go, but I cannot assume that violation of the law is intended in the case that the Chinese do not go." On September 21, the *Seattle Post-Intelligencer* reported that "a riot had broken out [at Aberdeen] to such an extent that the life and property not only of coolies, but of citizens, were at stake, and that an appeal had been sent to the governor to call out the militia to quell the uprising."

Whether a full-blown riot occurred at this point is uncertain. The governor appeared to deny it, but his claims often lack credibility. It is perhaps more significant that a September riot is not reported in other newspapers, or in the most reliable source on these events, the testimony of John Wing. But it is certain at least that a state of lawlessness prevailed, that violence was threatened, and that the threat was taken seriously by both Chinese and non-Chinese residents of Aberdeen. Speaking several days after the report, the governor affirmed that the request for militia came from "some of the best citizens of Aberdeen." However, using some rather bizarre reasoning, the governor claimed that he could not call out the militia to preserve the peace without a request from Aberdeen's city government, since civil authority must remain superior to military authority. Of course, the governor was the state's supreme civil authority, and he himself commanded the militia. Furthermore, the governor claimed—also quite incorrectly—the matter was now resolved peacefully, since the Chinese had left.[12]

In fact, about twenty Chinese residents remained in Aberdeen as of the first week of November. One of these was laundryman John Wing, or John Wing Ham, who "had resided in Aberdeen for many years, was highly respected, unobtrusive, public spirited and wealthy."[13] At the beginning of the expulsion movement, he had been told by the anti-Chinese committee that he must leave town within ten days, an amount of time which seemed to him "rather short notice after being in business six years." The committee told him that his business would be bought out by the subscription fund, that "he would be paid in full," and that he should "take stock." However, when the committee returned, it refused to pay more than $250 for his "stock, building and lease." Since Wing valued his stock alone at $1384, he refused. The committee, apparently deciding that the Chinese could not be bought out at a price they were willing to pay, returned the funds to subscribers, and John Wing considered the matter dropped.[14]

The anti-Chinese league, however, did not consider the matter dropped, and on the night of November 7, the masked mob, this time about fifty strong, and with many of Aberdeen's elite at its forefront, completed its work of expelling Aberdeen's Chinese. At ten o'clock that night John Wing was at home, where he lived with two other Chinese residents, John and Emma Sing, when the mob appeared. When he refused to answer his door, the mob "beat down its doors and windows." Shoemaker John Henson burst in "with a pistol in one hand and a candle in the other. He said: 'Wing[,] You got to go now; pack up.'"[15] Wing, along with John and Emma Sing, were forced down to the river and on board the steamer *Wishkah Chief*, where they joined the rest of Aberdeen's Chinese, some twenty in all, who had been likewise gathered up by the mob. Under the escort of four armed and masked men they were steamed up the river to Montesano. At some time during all this, Wing was robbed of $580 "together with his watch and other valuables," and he was "badly hurt, kicked and bruised" when, at three o'clock in the morning, he was left on the dock in Montesano.[16]

A *Seattle Post-Intelligencer* reporter named Whalley was on hand in Montesano to record Wing's account of the riot while Wing recovered in the home of a Chinese launderer in that city.[17] Thanks to Wing's testimony, and to the apparently earnest though futile efforts of Montesano's prosecuting attorney, George Moody, to bring the perpetrators to justice, we can gain some insight into the composition of the mob that expelled Wing and his fellow Chinese. Given the history of the expulsions of Chinese from other cities, we might expect the list of perpetrators to be filled with wage earners who resented competing with Chinese laborers for jobs. But although we cannot rule out the possibility that some workers participated in the riot, the fact of the matter is that none of the persons named in the case are clearly identifiable as wage workers. In fact, from the time Mayor Maling presided over the Opera House meeting to the release of the perpetrators, John Wing's case reads practically like a who's who of Aberdeen's elite.

Ultimately, six men were indicted for burglary in connection with the robbery of John Wing. In Wing's interview with Whalley of the *Seattle Post-Intelligencer*, Wing stated that most of the mob wore masks, but that he identified three men. Two of these were certainly leading men of Aberdeen. One of them, Francis R. Wall, was a graduate of the US Naval Academy and Tulane University, a lawyer, and the owner and editor of Aberdeen's Democratic newspaper, the *Aberdeen Herald*, which he often used to ridicule the Chinese.[18]

Captain S. C. Mitchell was a merchant shipowner who in 1896 was elected as a "conservative" member of the city council.[19] The third man Wing identified, John Henson, was a shoemaker, and his social status is harder to determine. If he worked for himself, he is probably best classified as a member of the petit bourgeoisie. His position to others involved in the case, though, may be a bit anomalous. The *Seattle Post-Intelligencer* described him as "formerly of Port Angeles and a disciple of George Venable Smith."[20] Smith was a lawyer who agitated in support of the Chinese expulsion from Seattle in 1886, and also a socialist who founded a cooperative community in Port Angeles.[21]

By the time Prosecutor Moody brought charges of burglary against Wall, Mitchell, and Henson, three more perpetrators had been identified, and Moody brought charges against them also for their role in the attack on Wing. Joseph M. Stallings was a hotel operator.[22] Gus Forssell was listed as a laborer in the 1892 county census, but he was one of three brothers involved in construction businesses and who acquired large real estate holdings in Aberdeen.[23] Christopher Natwick was listed as a laborer in 1889,[24] but in 1890 his motive in the expulsion was clear: he was about to become the proprietor of a laundry. He bought advertising space in Wall's *Herald*, and in return Wall endorsed the laundry, writing, "When this institution opens for business, there will be no vestige of an excuse for patronizing the Chinese, and the heathen should not receive one dollar's worth of work."[25]

If the apparent perpetrators of the attack were men of some prominence, this is also true of those who came to their aid. Samuel Benn and John W. Farquhar acted as surety for Hanson, Mitchell, Stallings, and Wall when they were released on bond. Benn was the founding father of Aberdeen, a landowner with large holdings and a former cannery operator, who, in 1891, succeeded Maling as mayor.[26] The city of Aberdeen holds Benn in great reverence. The city's high school gymnasium and most prominent public park bear Benn's name. Farquhar was a "well known merchant," a "timber land dealer," and the present owner of a newly constructed "commodious dwelling" in Aberdeen.[27] E. L. Koehler and R. P. Waldon acted as surety for Natwick's bond. Koehler was also a substantial merchant, who at the time was erecting a new building and running for Chehalis County Treasurer on the Democratic ticket. Acting as surety for Gus Forssell were Thomas C. Moulton and John Steen. Moulton was a furniture dealer, a real estate developer, and a member of Aberdeen's first chamber of commerce. John Steen was "Noble grand" of the local International

Order of Odd-Fellows and future marshall, water superintendent, and street commissioner of Aberdeen.[28]

Those who had led the expulsion, predictably, were never brought to justice. Part of this is because of the pervasive climate of racism against and hostility toward Chinese immigrants, whatever their profession or class, both in Aberdeen and elsewhere. Some Washingtonians did condemn the assault on Aberdeen's Chinese. The *Seattle Post-Intelligencer* published an editorial that strongly condemned "The Aberdeen Outrage" and openly doubted the account of those responsible for it.[29] Yet the same paper, just two weeks later, also editorialized that "there is a definite and profound objection to the Chinese as an element of the population," that this was "not merely sentimental" but "was based upon considerations of the most substantial and important sort." Among these considerations, the editorial argued, were that:

> The Chinese belong to another race and another civilisation and it is impossible that they should ever become assimilated with the American people. They not only cheapen labor but they degrade it. They bring the lowest vices among us. They absorb large sums of money which they send out of this country and which is lost as much as if it were cast into the sea. All these—and others which might be enumerated—are sound and legitimate objections.[30]

On its own, this pervasive climate of racism very likely would have prevented convictions of those involved in the expulsion.

However, the high social status of those most visibly involved additionally insulated them from prosecution, no matter how well-intentioned Prosecutor Moody may have been. Mayor Maling denied that there had been any violence or robbery in the expulsion and claimed that it was "Wing's gang" that was disorderly.[31] F. R. Wall used his paper to both celebrate the expulsion and undermine Wing's credibility. He wrote that "no one seems to know or care how [the Chinese] went," but stated, "It is said Wing tried to set fire to his old shack where he had a laundry . . . and left much dirty linen behind." Many called attention to the social status of the accuser and the accused. Wall was outraged that charges were brought "based simply upon the word of a Chinaman."[32] The *Spokane Globe* argued that "while the method employed at Aberdeen was probably too harsh, the word of a Chinaman . . . should be taken with a great deal of allowance. A Chinaman cares no more than a hyena would for a Christian oath."[33] A report from the *Morning Oregonian* claimed that even if the accused participated in the expulsion, "not one of the accused would commit such a crime."[34] Another report from Aberdeen published in the *Seattle Post-Intelligencer* explained that the "best citizens of the county" did not want any arrests to be made, and claimed that John Wing's injuries were self-inflicted.[35] F. R. Wall, S. C. Mitchell, and John Henson sued Wing for libel. Prosecutor Moody saw this for what it was, an attempt to intimidate witnesses in the case against the perpetrators. Interestingly, one of the most prominent of Aberdeen's citizens, Captain J. M. Weatherwax, acted as surety for Wing's release in the libel case. Perhaps Weatherwax was a man of principle who believed Wing had been wronged. Or perhaps he acted in the interests of his fellow leading-citizens and encouraged Wing to make things easier on himself and disappear. In either event, while the libel suit was dismissed, so were the charges against the rioters.

In the end, the perpetrators of the Aberdeen Outrage may not only have been protected by their status as members of Aberdeen's merchant and employing class, but they may also have had a strong motive for their participation in the Chinese expulsion movement. This is startlingly obvious for Natwick, who found in the expulsion an opportunity to rid himself of his competition in the laundry business. A slightly less direct motive may have existed for Wall. He had just acquired the *Aberdeen Herald* in 1889 and may have seen the anti-Chinese agitation in which he took such evident delight as a boon to circulation. Others, too, may have profited from their participation. Most appear to have been prominent businessmen, and many may have been among the "property owners" who initiated the expulsion by complaining of the Chinese rental of property on F street. A number also had political aspirations, and as any support for the Chinese was seen as an impediment to success in the November 1890 elections, they may have seen leadership in the movement as a way to enhance their prestige.[36] Without exculpating the Workingmen's Party or Knights of Labor for their infamous roles in their campaigns to drive out the Chinese residents of the West Coast, the Aberdeen Outrage does demonstrate the need to reexamine the role of elites, especially employers, in these atrocities. What is certain is that in this particular case the historical record demonstrates that the expulsion effort was led by the city's elites, not by its laborers. The forty Chinese in Aberdeen, most of whom must have worked as launderers, cooks, domestic workers, and in canneries, cannot have materially affected the wages of other workers. And although they were expelled, the Chinese workers did maintain a presence in Grays Harbor. Although they were doubtless the targets of racism, they were never again driven out, and they were welcomed to the class struggle by a later generation of workers carrying the card of the IWW.

"Red" Finn Hall in Aberdeen, the main meeting place for lumber strikers during the first four decades of the twentieth century. Photo courtesy of Aaron Goings collection.

3
Red Finn Halls

In June 1928, students drawn from many parts of the American West traveled to the Red Coast town of Woodland to attend a Communist summer school held at the Woodland Finn Hall. In her memoir, Peggy Dennis, Woodland summer school student and future Communist leader, recounted her early impressions of the school:

> We came by car and bus and the hitchhiker's thumb from cities and towns across California, Oregon, and Washington State. Five miles outside of Woodland, somewhere between Portland and Seattle, the meeting house of the Finnish Cooperative Society was to be home to fifty-four of us.... The barn-like white building stood on a knoll overlooking the icy Lewis river, surrounded by flat fields and dense forests. An idyllic vacation spot; but we had come for a more serious purpose.[1]

Professional Communist organizers joined young activists to "aid in equipping the vanguard of the workers with the essential theoretical and practical training and knowledge to enable them to take active part in the struggle for the freedom of the working class from its bondage, the yoke of capitalist production."[2] Written by an anonymous student, the school's song gave a good idea of its educational goals:

> Hail Pacific Workers' Summer School!
> Students who have come to learn the rule
> Of workers' education
> Building for our organization
> Hail, Pacific Workers' Summer School!

Hail to workers' solidarity.
We aim to gain more clarity
Of struggles present and past
That we may fight to the last
For victory![3]

Students took a rigorous set of classes covering subjects such as Marxian eco-
nomics, American social and labor history, public speaking, and labor journalism. Like others who used the "Red" Finn halls, the young Communists took
part in social activities. One participant recalled "always organizing athletic
events, art festivals, agitprop theater, and the weekend dances to which came
our Finnish hosts, also oldtime socialists from the logging camps and shingle
weavers and fishermen's unions."[4] They also left the relatively safe confines of
the classroom to engage in political activities including touring the non-union
Long-Bell Mill in Longview, Washington, giving speeches at Portland and
Seattle union meetings, and visiting Portland to sing revolutionary songs to
celebrate the opening of Tualatin Park.[5] Peggy Dennis recalled, "Each Sunday
morning we climbed the soapbox in the city park at Woodland to discourse on
current events at home and abroad."[6]

The Woodland Communist summer school's activities were illustrative of
the left-wing activities organized by Finnish Americans in multiple cities and
towns across the Red Coast. Indeed, hall-building and hall events were important aspects of the Finnish American labor and socialist movements, as well
as the wider Finnish American culture. Finns built halls in several Red Coast
towns, much as they did in ethnic enclaves stretching across North America.
While many of these structures were demolished long ago, a few remain,
potent reminders of the impressive Finnish American labor and radical movements that played such notable roles in early twentieth-century US history.[7]

Socialist, union, Communist, and Wobbly Finn halls provided spaces for
meetings, plays, dances, dinners, and reading rooms. In short, they encouraged cultural continuity, served as second homes for immigrants, and provided headquarters for immigrant radicals as they challenged capitalism.
Finnish workers' halls dotted the geography of Washington State, stretching from Spokane to Ilwaco and several points in between. During the first
decades of the twentieth century, Finnish American workers built several
structures devoted to promoting the class struggle along the "Red Coast."
Built in varying shapes and sizes, these halls were constructed in the Grays

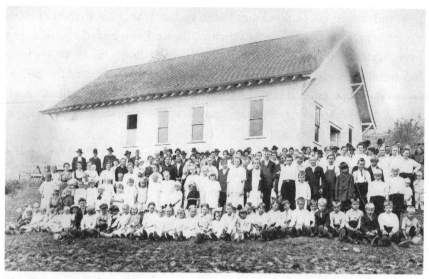

This photograph, taken around 1916, shows approximately two hundred individuals posing in front of the massive Woodland Finnish Workers' Hall. Like most Red Finn Hall events, this gathering featured women, men, and children—Finnish American families—who collectively made up the Finnish Socialist movement in the United States. Photo courtesy of Clark County Historical Society & Museum.

Harbor lumber towns of Aberdeen and Hoquiam, the Columbia River fishing village of Ilwaco, the beach and cranberry-farming community of Grayland, the tiny farming and logging settlements of Woodland and Winlock, and the Pacific County lumber town of Raymond.

"Red" halls were not the only, or even the first, such structures built by Finnish Americans to house their sociocultural activities. The trajectory of hall building followed a predictable pattern. The first Finnish hall builders constructed a temperance hall where members of the immigrant group met away from the temptations of alcohol. Finns from a variety of political persuasions, including conservative Lutherans and small-business people, joined the temperance clubs. In many Finnish communities, including Aberdeen, Raymond, and Ilwaco, a large majority of local Finns hailed from the working class. Quite commonly, local temperance movements divided into "Red" and "White" camps over issues such as dancing and support for the labor movement. During the first decade of the twentieth century, these divisions hardened as Red (socialist) Finnish organizations either took over the local temperance hall or constructed or purchased a preexisting hall of their own.[8]

Just such a process played out in the tiny fishing town of Ilwaco, near the mouth of the Columbia River. By 1910, Ilwaco's 664 residents included 296 first- and second-generation Finns.[9] With such a large concentration of Finns eager to engage in familiar social activities, Ilwaco Finns gained control over a large meeting hall they called Columbia Hall. Built during the 1890s, the large hall stood as one of Ilwaco's main community spaces. Finns used the hall for lectures, dances, musical programs, wedding receptions, and political meetings. A Finnish temperance group, known as the Benevolent Society, organized most of the Finns' activities.[10]

As was true in other Red Coast towns, most of Ilwaco's Finns were working people, many of them fishermen and members of the Columbia River Fishermen's Protective Union. Like their fellow Finns on the south side of the Columbia River, in the early twentieth century, many of these working-class Finns were drawn to socialist politics. Founded in 1911, the Ilwaco local of the Finnish Socialist Federation provided a class-based alternative to the temperance activities of the Benevolent Society. Topping out around 70 members in the 1910s, the socialists tried, and failed, to gain ownership of the hall for themselves. Following a court ruling that granted control of the hall to the conservative group, Ilwaco's Red Finns set out on an independent path. In 1915, they constructed a hall of their own, called the Workers' Hall. In March 1915, Ilwaco's Finnish Socialists held a three-day celebration to mark the hall's opening. The festivities included music and theater performed by Red Coast Finns. Showing the importance of class struggle to Ilwaco's Finnish socialist community, they put on a play depicting a long and bloody strike eventually won by the strikers.[11] Hosting events such as this, the Workers' Hall remained a fixture in the community until the Depression forced the leftists to sell it in the 1930s.[12]

In Ilwaco and beyond, most of the actions planned and carried out by Red Finns were the product of working-class families, as men, women, and children all contributed to the success and persistence of the Finnish left. Part of the reason for women's uncommonly deep involvement in the Finnish locals of the Socialist Party of America was the unique form of socialism developed by Finnish Americans, which was rooted in their "Red" Finn halls. These halls became centers of strike support, where Finnish American women blended public and private spheres through their work in union auxiliaries, soup kitchens, and radical cultural groups. Hundreds of radical Finnish American men and women participated in the Red Coast's vibrant hall culture, where they met, sang, danced, and engaged in political debate.

Although the Red Finn halls hosted a number of activities that were explicitly didactic—ranging from political meetings to fundraisers for class-war prisoners—much of the lively activity that took place within the halls was social in nature, as the halls operated as much like community centers as union halls. The large buildings—some as large as 20,000 square feet—also provided radical Finnish workers with large meeting spaces, libraries, theaters, gymnasiums, and offices to conduct workers' business. Finns in Woodland fondly recalled hosting a great variety of activities at their hall. These included plays, funerals, athletic events, language classes, wedding anniversaries, and wedding dances, which Woodland Finn Helen Basso described as "a combined wedding shower and reception honoring a newly married couple."[13]

The size and amenities of Finn halls made them attractive locations for use by local, regional, or national groups run both by Finns and non-Finns. In the Summer of 1927, the Winlock Finn hall served as the site for a summer school hosted by the Young Workers' League (YWL), a communist organization. The six-week-long course mixed classroom instruction with political speeches, dances, plays, and outdoor gatherings. Students participated in extracurricular activities ranging from swimming parties and wiener roasts to putting on English- and Finnish-language plays, and they published a weekly newspaper called the *Red Star*.[14]

Aberdeen Finns built their own hall in 1903. Located at 717 Randall Street and known as the Kansankoti Hall, it was built and paid for by the Kansankoti Club of Aberdeen. This structure was originally home to both the socialist "Red" and conservative "White" Finns. The name "Kansankoti Hall," meaning people's hall, is significant. It indicates a "people's" rather than an employer's ownership of the space.[15]

Aberdeen's Finnish socialists built their own hall, the famous Red Finn Hall at 718 E. First Street in 1906, leaving the Kansankoti hall for the more conservative Finnish group to maintain. In this radical space, Finnish workers met several times per week, discussed jobs, community events, and politics, and formulated varied responses to a political and socioeconomic system working against their interests. Amenities in the hall included a restaurant, dining hall, gymnasium, theater, apartments, and office space. By 1912, according to one newspaper article, the hall hosted "two Socialist orders, a Finnish Sunday school, the Finnish band, the women's committee of the Socialist party, and diverse other organizations."[16] The Finnish leftists who met at these halls produced an impressive array of arts and crafts, ranging from poetry to textiles. In

1918, Kyllikki Salo, a member of an Aberdeen Finnish Socialist youth organization that met at that city's Red Finn Hall, wrote a poem titled "Punalippu," intended as an ode to the red flag.[17] A decade later, the Finnish American Wobbly Hilja Karvonen penned "The Child Worker." In stanzas such as the following, she expressed her belief in the importance of organizing unions for the good of future generations.

> From early morn till late at night
> I toil as busy as a bee.
> I serve the greedy masters right—
> Oh, workers, join and make me
>   free! [18]

Each time Aberdeen and Hoquiam's Finnish laborers struck, they met at their "Red" halls to discuss tactics, coordinate picket assignments and negotiation teams, and establish soup kitchens and commissaries. Between 1905 and 1939, not only the Finns, but many groups of striking lumber workers— regardless of ethnicity—used the friendly confines of the Finn halls as their primary strike headquarters.[19] This was the case during the 1912 Grays Harbor and Pacific County Lumber Strike, when hundreds of Finnish American mill hands joined in the IWW-led strike. Wobbly halls were too small to accommodate such a large strike force, so they used the Red Finn Hall as their primary meeting place.

Because of their importance to the IWW and to Finnish socialist unionist strikers, Red Finn halls sometimes fell victim to vigilantes, soldiers, and municipal police forces that raided, vandalized, and occasionally even destroyed the buildings. During the 1912 strike, Aberdeen officials closed the Red Finn hall, arguing (correctly) that it served as a major recruiting area and headquarters for the strikers. From employers' and strikebreakers' perspective, closing the Red Finn Hall made perfect sense. In one fell swoop, police shut down the center of the Harbor's radical community and a fruitful training ground for Finnish American activists. After all, Aberdeen Mayor James Parks blamed "agitation carried on at the Red Finnish Hall on First Street" for bringing about the 1912 strike.[20] Harbor socialists requested a court injunction against the city, stating that "great mental, moral, and spiritual 'suffering' has been caused by the act of the city administration in nailing up the doors of the resort."[21]

The strike soon spread south into the mills of Pacific County where hundreds of lumber mill workers organized with the IWW. Strikers held their activities at the Raymond Finn Hall until local employers and their allies raided and shut the place down. The *Industrial Worker* described the raid: "The hall, which belongs to the Finns, was raided by a gang of from 60 to 70 citizens and everything in sight was taken, books, supplies, stamps, etc. The front entrance was nailed up despite the fact that the hall is private property." Authorities posted a sign reading: "Closed by order of the County."[22]

Several years later, in 1919, the Aberdeen Red Finn Hall narrowly averted destruction at the hands of a patriotic mob when Wobbly Ralph Chaplin's visit to the hall provided the town's thugs with an opportunity to terrorize local radicals. Chaplin was among the best-known IWW activists, the man who penned the labor anthem "Solidarity Forever" and an important Wobbly newspaper editor. In 1918, Chaplin was one of dozens of well-known Wobblies convicted and sentenced to lengthy prison terms in the *United States v. Haywood et al.* case. When vigilantes threatened the Aberdeen Wobbly hall, two thousand Wobblies turned out to protect it, many of them "armed with a loaded baseball bat." Recognizing the precariousness of Chaplin's situation, one of the armed Wobblies warned him that "there's going to be hell-popping" and "we don't want you in on it. You're married and have a long sentence hanging over your head already."[23] According to Chaplin, the presence of so many armed guards helped de-escalate the confrontation without violence.

A decade later, radicals from the American Communist youth movements experienced a similar threat from vigilantes while staying at Woodland's Red Finn Hall. During the 1928 Pacific Coast Summer School, dozens of radicals from across the West met at the hall for what was to be six weeks of radical pedagogy (as described at the beginning of the chapter). But nothing in the classroom could match the lessons on class struggle learned on the second night of the school, when "friends from Woodland" informed the students and staff of threats to destroy the school. Peggy Dennis, a student and a future leader of the Communist Party, recalled how students, staff, and working-class allies in the community met the vigilante threat:

On the second night they came, seventy young bully-boys itching
for a fight, motors revving, exhausts backfiring. Under strict orders
to ignore all verbal provocations and fight back only if physically
attacked, we apprehensively waited as [school leader Oliver] Carlson

and his persuasion group urged the ringleaders inside to talk. Pouring coffee and passing cookies, Carlson quietly discoursed upon our constitutional right against theirs. Outside the intruders circled around us, taunting and daring us to fight. With sweaty fists clutching clubs and pepper/salt bags, we were grateful for the presence of the seasoned loggers and shinglers who had arrived earlier to aid us.[24]

Dennis concluded this anecdote by noting that the "persuasion group won no converts that night, but the uncomfortable guests scuffed their way out, and with a gruff 'les go' to their disappointed stalwarts, they piled into their cars and drove off." One suspects that the presence of "seasoned" loggers and shingle weavers had something to do with the thugs' choice to flee rather than fight.[25]

As the Woodland incident suggests, many of the Red Finn halls retained their importance to the Pacific Northwest labor and left movements during the 1920s and 1930s. They housed local unions, served as headquarters for the region's Communist organizations, and hosted a variety of major events during the Depression decade. This was especially true of Aberdeen's towering Red hall, where progressives and leftists met to host a great variety of activities. In October 1929, radical unionists affiliated with Communist organizations held what they termed a unity conference in hopes of "smash[ing]" the "corrupt" AFL unions.[26]

For many Red Finn groups, the Depression decade brought not only joblessness and poverty to their members, but also a decline and sometimes demise of their institutional life. Several Red Coast Finnish radical groups, including the Ilwaco Communists, lost so many members during the 1930s that they were forced to sell their halls.[27] All too frequently, Finnish workers' halls fell victim to accidental fires or arsonist's matches, which sometimes devastated the buildings and the organization's records held within. Built in 1912, Woodland's Finnish Workers Hall was destroyed by a fire in 1915.[28] At least some local socialists blamed arsonists from the more conservative Finnish community for burning down the hall. "The unexplained burning down of the new hall, where excellent plays were produced and popular dances held, didn't warm up friendship between the two groups of Finns," noted one study of Woodland's Finns. Persevering through this hardship, in 1916 Woodland-area socialist Finns built a new, larger hall only a quarter-mile from the burned structure. The new hall remained an active meeting spot—first for socialists, later for Communists—into the early 1950s.[29]

Perhaps the most blatant assault on the Red Coast's Finnish workers' movement came on December 2, 1939, when vigilantes raided and pillaged Aberdeen's mighty Red Finn Hall. To protest the recent Soviet invasion of Finland, many of the Harbor's anti-Communists planned to picket a planned dance at the hall. Although the Red Finns canceled their dance, a "picket line" of 300 to 400 people still formed around the darkened and empty hall. Soon thereafter, some of the mob broke down the front door and began ransacking the premises. Over the course of several hours, the vandals pulled up floor boards; smashed windows, light fixtures, dishes, appliances, and furniture; and ransacked the hall's extensive library, destroying books, periodicals, and other materials. Much of the literature ended up tossed on a bonfire in the street, a painful end to an impressive collection of radical materials accumulated during the local group's thirty-plus years in existence. As tools and symbols of the leftist movement, the Finnish workers' stage, theater scenery, and piano also fell victim to the vandals. Some of the worst damage came when members of the mob shattered a fountain, flooding the hall's bottom floor.[30]

The attack continued for three to four hours as the crowd looked on. Police were reportedly on hand at the initiation of the raid and made several passes in their cruisers as it continued, but they made no move to stop it. They later claimed that they were not aware of the attack, but the fact that the demonstration was well advertised both in print and on the radio, and that the police station was only a few short blocks from the Red Finn Hall casts considerable doubt on these assertions.[31] Even though a photographer for the *Aberdeen Daily World* photographed a number of those engaged in the raid, only two men were eventually arrested after a nationwide public outcry shamed the local authorities into taking action.[32] The suspects, Ward Penning, of the right-wing Order of Better Americans, and Joe LaLande, executive board member of an anti-Communist AFL union, were set free after a twenty-minute jury deliberation.[33]

As we write, only a few of the halls constructed and used by Red Finns to promote their class interests still stand. Those structures that still exist have long since become the property of other groups or businesses, and a carefully planned "whitening" has been somewhat successful in removing many of the "Red" traces of the region's history. Efforts to erase class struggle and impose a conservative consensus on the region's history have been captured by James

Loewen, the sociologist and best-selling author of *Lies Across America*. The "Finn Hall Marker" placed at the site of the Finnish Workers' Hall in Woodland caught Loewen's attention. The marker reads:

> In 1916 Finnish immigrants constructed a hall near the site under the name of a literary association (Kirjallisuus Seura), forming a lending library. Although they brought their diet, language, and saunas with them, some old country beliefs were left behind. These people found it necessary to meet where they could study the social customs of their new country, challenge and question partisan politics, and reflect on new technological insights. At this cultural center were held language classes, meetings, athletic activities, wedding dances, funerals, and programs with oratory, drama, poetry, vocal and instrumental music. Steaming kettles of coffee and the warmth of dignified waltzes, pulsating polkas, and schottisches brought togetherness to these rugged individualists. Life to them was involvement.[34]

Loewen describes this marker as little more than a straightforward cover-up. "Passionate political debates and intellectual controversies raged in this hall, especially in its early years when the Woodrow Wilson administration had declared war on all leftists," notes Loewen. He continues: "'Life to them was involvement'—well, yes. But involvement in *what*? In a communist society in rural southwest Washington? No one would envision *that* without help, and this historical marker hardly provides the necessary assistance."[35]

Loewen's critical comments brought much-needed attention to the widespread practice of rewriting, distorting, and sterilizing history. Unfortunately, the rewriting does not end at the edges of Woodland's Finn Hall marker. In fact, it might be more accurate to say that the history of Red Finn Halls has been erased. Despite the halls' importance in the lives of thousands of Red Coast radicals during the early twentieth century, the "Finn Hall Marker," flawed though it is, remains the sole public display commemorating the history of the region's radical spaces.

4
The Aberdeen Free Speech Fight

On October 11, 1911, the Aberdeen City Council met to reconsider Ordinance 1084, which criminalized street speaking outside of a two-block area in downtown Aberdeen. The goal of the controversial ordinance, which was passed that August, was clear. It would not be used against Salvation Army speakers, who employed street speaking for the purpose of proselytization. Instead, it would be enforced selectively to deter IWW agitation among the working people of that city. The ordinance provoked the ire of both socialists and Wobblies, who regarded it as blatantly unconstitutional. Wobbly organizer William Thorn attended the October 11 council meeting, but was greatly disappointed when it adjourned so that members could attend a performance at the Grand Theatre. Hoping to voice his displeasure with the law, Thorn followed Mayor James Parks and Councilman John Myles, a former police officer, into the lobby, where he harassed the officials. During the argument, Myles knocked out Thorn with a punch to the face. The following day, in a matter befitting the anti-labor stance of Chehalis County's commercial press, the *Aberdeen Herald* ran a headline that read, "IWW Leader Given a Knockout Punch by John Myles," and followed it up with an article that justified the assault.[1]

The appearance of hostilities between Myles and Thorn during this episode signaled the growing conflict between the Wobblies and the Aberdeen city government. These conflicts recurred over the subsequent months of the Aberdeen Free Speech Fight, and marked one of the most violent periods in the Red Coast's history. In one sense, the Aberdeen Free Speech Fight of 1911–1912 represents just one battle in the war that Wobblies waged for free speech across the western United States over the ensuing decade. From San Diego to Vancouver, BC, employers and city officials regularly prohibited street speaking in an attempt to quell the IWW threat, thereby setting off spectacular conflicts with the rebel unionists determined to defend their rights. The Aberdeen

Free Speech Fight, however, is significant in a number of ways. First, the IWW struggle for the right to use city streets for meetings polarized Aberdeen's citizenry, with the working class on one side and those who promoted ruling class interests on the other. Second, during this fight Aberdeen's ruling class of businessmen, city officials, and police used violent and vigilante tactics in an attempt to defeat the Wobblies, tactics that would subsequently be exported to other cities. Finally, in winning the Aberdeen Free Speech Fight, Wobblies demonstrated an ability to improvise, build alliances, and act pragmatically, abilities that helped lay the foundation for future labor activism in the region.

The Wobblies' challenge to the street-speaking ordinance began in earnest on Tuesday, November 21, when William Thorn and James Train, another IWW organizer, took to the corner of H and Heron Streets with the intention of violating the ordinance.[2] Thorn mounted the soapbox first and orated on "changing the shape of the world," before Police Chief Templeman ordered his arrest. Next, Train stepped up and denounced "the national administration, the local administration, the millowners, the business folk, the union officials, and the local police."[3] His arrest followed, and both men spent the night in jail before being bailed out by the Wobblies.[4] The next night three more Wobbly speakers were arrested.

At this point in the conflict, the Aberdeen Free Speech Fight appeared much the same as previous fights, and the Aberdeen local followed the advice of IWW General Secretary Vincent St. John, who stated, "Whenever any local union becomes involved in a free-speech fight, they notify the general office and that information is sent to all the local unions . . . with the request that if they have any members that are footloose to send them along."[5] The Wobbly tactic, as the ruling class well recognized, was one of civil disobedience. Wobblies would publicly defy the law, fill the jails, and "cripple the city financially" so that the government would give in and repeal the ordinance.[6]

Events accelerated quickly over the next two days as both workers and employers assembled in full on the Aberdeen streets to test the others' resolve. On Thursday, November 23, Thorn delivered a speech that drew an estimated crowd of 250 Wobblies and more than 1,500 sympathizers.[7] This massive demonstration showed the wide appeal of the IWW, which only a few months earlier took out a union charter with a mere thirty-one members. The union strengthened its appeal by building partnerships with socialists and trade unionists, and received outpourings of support from those who identified with IWW efforts. At the height of their support from the area's working class, IWW meetings regularly drew crowds of close to 2,000 people, a major accomplishment, especially considering Aberdeen's meager population of 13,660.[8]

Following Thorn's speech, a crowd carrying red banners and singing labor songs marched behind IWW organizers to City Hall to demand the repeal of the ordinance and the release of prisoners.[9] Chief Templeman attempted to break up the crowd, which refused to disperse. Police arrested Thorn a second time, and the fire department sprayed the crowd with a high-power water hose.[10] Weeks later, Wobbly activist "Stumpy" Payne described the melee: "Here the fire hose was brought into play and thousands of men, women, and children were drenched for being 'rioters.' A demonstration of working men in their own interest is a 'riot,' but violence and terrorism on the part of the capitalists and their tools is 'law and order.'"[11]

This incident marked a turning point in the tactics utilized to suppress demonstrations, as the organized working class met an equally organized employer class that was willing to use violence to suppress the IWW efforts. Wobblies looked positively on the incident, noting that the police-inflicted violence raised sympathy for the union, which was able to sell "thousands of red free speech tags" that read "free speech, free press, and free assembladge [sic]," and declared a willingness "to go to jail for our rights."[12] However, Chief Templeman's use of the fire hose was just the beginning of city leaders' escalation of the violence, and the Wobblies were clearly unprepared for what was to follow.

On the afternoon of Friday, November 24, the day after the demonstration, Aberdeen's ruling class—represented by the executive committee of the Chamber of Commerce—held a special meeting at the Hotel Washington to decide upon a course of action. The Chamber claimed that it sought to "preserve order and uphold law." Indeed, Aberdeen's elites certainly intended to uphold the street speaking prohibition. But in general, these men cared little about the laws of the land, and as subsequent events demonstrated, they violated laws far more serious than an ordinance restricting street meetings. The anti-Wobbly *Aberdeen Herald* stated their real design more clearly: rather than allow Wobblies to practice civil disobedience and fill up the jails, city leaders would give the radicals "a dose of their favorite doctrine."[13] In other words, the ruling class would turn to lawlessness to suppress the Wobblies.

Mayor Parks, who participated in the chamber meeting, decided that the help of the entire city would be needed to achieve this aim, so a mass meeting was called for two o'clock that day at the Aberdeen Elks. The second meeting showed the solidarity among the city's ruling elite, as five hundred men, "numbering among them the most prominent business and professional men in the city" attended, and the "little sawdust town was practically closed up when 3:00 o'clock rolled around."[14] Those who attended the Elks meeting adopted a number of resolutions, one of which pledged attendees' "service until such a time as the invading force of Workers shall be quelled or run out of town."[15] The attendees also established a program for dealing with the IWW, including the closure of saloons after 6 p.m., the patrol of all roads leading to and from Aberdeen, the arrest of all "suspicious characters," and the deputization of five hundred businessmen to serve as special police.[16]

The five hundred men of the citizens' committee met at seven in the evening and reported to police headquarters, where they were split into squads to patrol the town. One party of citizens' committee members raided the IWW headquarters at 406 East Heron Street. When they found the hall empty, they proceeded to confiscate and destroy union literature and propaganda.[17] Meanwhile, other committee members patrolled the streets. The Wobblies had scheduled a mass meeting that night at the Empire Theater to discuss the speaking ordinance, and the deputies roped off H Street at Heron so as to not allow entrance into the theater. Outside, they arrested at least thirty IWW members and escorted them to jail. In a move befitting their leadership of Grays Harbor employers, banker W. J. Patterson and Dudley G. Allen, two officers in the Chamber of Commerce, made the first arrests.[18]

Debate over what to do with the prisoners ensued, at which time the citizens' committee decided to ship them out of town by train. However, officials at the Northern Pacific Railway refused to participate, and other courses of action came up for debate. Finally, they all decided to simply escort the men out of town. Later that night, with two citizens' committee members assigned to each Wobbly, the prisoners were marched through a rain storm past East Wishkah to the base of Dabney Hill. As the *Daily Washingtonian* suggested, "Judging from the demand for clubs and wagon spokes, when the procession moved from the city hall at 11:25 o'clock, the treatment [of the captives] was not gentle."[19] Two weeks later, Tracy Newell, one of the deportees, described the night in a sworn oath to a notary public. Newell "was standing in front of the Empire Theater" when "he was attacked by a body of men armed with clubs and guns [,] arrested by the said body of men, and taken to the City Jail at Aberdeen," before being escorted by the mob beyond the city limits.[20]

Newell's description was merely the most formal of the many complaints lodged against the tactics used by the citizens' committee to remove the Wobblies from town. Still, such deportations became commonplace throughout the winter of 1911–1912, and tactics became more violent as committee members became more irritated by IWW persistence in challenging the law.

Before the citizens' committee expelled the Wobblies, they warned, "What we have done we did by taking the law in our own hands. You men go and never return. God bless you if you remain away, but God help you if you ever return."[21] This warning served both to intimidate the Wobblies against returning to Aberdeen, and to show them that the citizens' committee acted outside the constraints of law, and thus could subject the IWW to whatever treatment they pleased without fear of retribution. The Wobblies each received a loaf of bread from the citizens' committee and marched out of town on the Northern Pacific Railroad tracks.

Meanwhile, in Aberdeen, martial law prevailed. The citizens' committee patrolled the streets wearing white tags and arresting anyone they suspected of IWW sympathies. Special police guarded all roads and railroads into town, and questioned each person who tried to enter. Curfew notices were sent out to parents ordering children under the age of eighteen to stay at home after dark, and the citizens' committee rigorously enforced the ban on group meetings.[22] Citizens' committee members' biggest fear was that Wobblies "will keep on coming to the Harbor country, and finding that they can not work their way into the city, will mass at Junction City," until enough of them are present to invade the city. These fears proved justified when, following the deportations, the train patrol captured twenty-eight IWW men attempting to reach Aberdeen. Committee members ordered the men to leave, thus increasing the number of deportees to well over fifty men.[23]

The deportation of rabble-rousing Wobblies represented a marked change in the strategy for dealing with the IWW during free speech fights.[24] The actions taken against the radical unionists served both as a sign of things to come, and as a warning to Wobblies to remain out of town. That most of the Wobblies had broken no law and that their only offense was their affiliation with a revolutionary industrial union did not matter to the citizens' committee. The citizens' committee's new tactics, however, successfully countered the tactics of the IWW. Rather than allow IWW members to break the law, fill the jail, and drain the city treasury, the citizens' committee decided to simply remove the problem from town.

The deported Wobblies secured a temporary residence in Montesano, a small town and county seat located ten miles to the northeast of Aberdeen, and considered their options.[25] They were now faced with the reality that their usual tactics for waging a free speech fight could not work effectively. They had been confronted by a well-organized, relentless group of vigilante businessmen, and many of their members had been driven from town, while those who remained behind were handicapped by prohibitions on speech, press, and assembly. Unable to re-enter the well-guarded town, and denied the use of their headquarters, the Wobblies were forced to reconsider their tactics and develop untested methods for waging free speech fights from the outside. That the Wobblies, in the weeks and months that followed, were successful in this attempt, and were able to launch a major strike in the Grays Harbor lumber industry, cemented the union's role as a major player in the region.

Now working from headquarters in Tacoma, the IWW sought to influence Aberdeen's elites using indirect means of political and economic action. The distance between Tacoma and Aberdeen limited communication between the two, but the IWW sent Clarence E. "Stumpy" Payne, a well-known IWW organizer and writer, to Aberdeen to assist in the fight's organization. Arriving in Aberdeen in early November, Payne immediately took on the union's journalistic responsibilities, wrote stories for the *Industrial Worker*, and issued calls for assistance from Wobbly locals. In keeping with the colorful tradition of IWW members, "Stumpy" worked in a number of occupations during his long life, including laboring as a carpenter, farm hand, and railroad worker. A lifetime member of the IWW, Payne was the only person to attend both the 1905 founding convention, and its fifty-year convention in 1955.[26] Payne was somehow able to avoid detection in Aberdeen, and his efforts kept up IWW spirits and provided the best record of the town's goings-on. He remained in the area throughout the conflict and was not imprisoned until the waning hours of the free speech fight.

Lacking the strength to make an immediate assault, the IWW needed time to gather the men and money necessary to continue the struggle. In the meantime, headquarters printed Payne's reports, solicited donations from around the nation, and forged alliances between friendly organizations whose members could act collectively to check the citizens' committee. The *Industrial Worker* also called upon volunteers to travel into Grays Harbor and await a time when a direct challenge could be made to the law. The paper directed

This cartoon from the IWW's *Industrial Worker* (Spokane, WA), November 30, 1911, issue was one of several front-page Wobbly cartoons based on events from the Aberdeen Free Speech Fight and the 1912 Grays Harbor Lumber strike. Here, an Aberdeen police officer beats a Wobbly at the behest of the Aberdeen lumber barons.

those interested to travel to Tacoma to await further instructions, or secretly drift into Aberdeen, leaving "all buttons, badges, cards and literature with your own local, as the police are making close search of all suspects."[27] The IWW also advised their more impatient members to arrive in Aberdeen and immediately test the law, thereby applying constant pressure on city officials.[28]

Meanwhile, Wobblies began a campaign to apply economic pressure to Aberdeen's ruling elites. According to the *Industrial Worker*, "The worst fear of the 'business' men . . . is that they will lose their trade, and this fear is greater than the fear of hell." Operating on this assumption, the IWW declared boycotts against businesses owned and operated by members of the citizens' committee, as well as anyone who supported the "Aberdeen Thugs."[29] On December 14, the *Industrial Worker* declared "BOYCOTT IS ON IN ABERDEEN," and the next week it published a "Do Not Patronize List." The list named a number of small businessmen, the Hayes and Hayes Bank, the mayor, city councilmen O'Hare and Miles, all of the Aberdeen and Hoquiam newspapers, and W. B. Mack, a mill superintendent whose anti-union stance became prominent a few months later during the IWW lumber strike. Meanwhile, in an attempt to fracture businessmen's class solidarity, the paper promised that workers would purchase from those "business men who were manly enough to refuse to line up with the Lumber Barons in suppressing the I. W. W."[30]

The Wobblies were a minority of the population, but they belonged to the working-class majority. To secure victory in the free speech fight through methods such as boycott, they needed to win support across all segments of that community. Above all, for a boycott to succeed, it required the enthusiastic support of working-class women, whose domestic roles dictated their control over most families' purchasing power.[31] An *Industrial Worker* story described one woman's observations of the boycott:

> The proprietor of a large department store here was asked to carry a
> club on November 24, but he said, "Nothing doing, I make my living
> off the working people, and I won't help drive them out of town." A
> few days before Christmas a lady went into this department store
> for some goods, and found all the clerks jumping sideways to wait
> on customers, while the shelves had been stripped almost bare by
> the holiday shoppers. Presently she crossed the street to the store of
> George J. Wolf, one of the ax handle merchants, but there the clerks
> were standing with folded arms and the shelves were piled with goods
> as if they had hardly been touched.[32]

The article followed up with the humorous, albeit hopeful, quip: "May the U.S. bankruptcy courts soon have a good reason to make Aberdeen their general headquarters."[33]

The boycott's success or failure depended not just on the active support of female consumers, but also on the cross-organizational alliances formed between the IWW and others. Wobblies succeeded in this pursuit by mobilizing assistance from sympathetic groups—such as AFL affiliates and socialists—who opposed the ordinance's infringement on civil liberties, the violence of the citizens' committee, and admired the passive resistance of the IWW.[34] In response to the continued enforcement of the speaking law and citizens' committee violence, Hoquiam socialists advised "the working men of Hoquiam and Grays Harbor to buy nothing from a single Aberdeen merchant engaged in the work of persecution."[35]

According to IWW member A. J. Giblin, by early December, all of Aberdeen's workers had stopped patronizing stores owned by citizens' committee members, while victims of citizens' committee violence filed $100,000 in personal damage lawsuits against the city.[36] These economic actions united Aberdeen's workers along class lines, and coordinated their opposition to citizens' committee methods of waging the free speech fight. Thus, even with much of its membership removed from embattled Aberdeen, the IWW helped "the workers of Aberdeen realize that an injury to one is an injury to all."[37]

However, economic pressure alone could not secure an IWW victory in the Aberdeen Free Speech Fight. Although the rebel unionists showed the ability to harness tactics such as the boycott, they did not abandon their primary tactic, direct action. During the first six weeks after the November 24 deportation, Wobblies and their sympathizers again risked life, liberty, and property to sneak back into Aberdeen. A bold *Industrial Worker* headline read "TO ABERDEEN OR BUST" and claimed that one hundred Spokane Wobblies were on their way to assist in the free speech effort, while the *Spokesman Review* claimed a force three times as large was en route from Vancouver, British Columbia, to directly challenge the law.[38]

For their troubles, the IWW met resistance from the citizens' committee, elected officials, and the commercial press. On December 6, a few members returned to Aberdeen and opened the IWW hall.[39] In response, an angry citizens' committee raided the hall, arrested the men, and drove them from town. Two of the Wobblies, Aloyzy Pierog and Christian E. Pederson, were blindfolded, punched and kicked, and forcibly expelled from town.[40] This treatment, like other similar incidents in December and January, was merely an extension of the tactics used by the citizens' committee throughout the affair. That members used their axe handles and clubs instead of merely threatening to do so, was simply their attempt to make good on their violent promises. On January 6, the city council passed an even more restrictive ordinance, which banned all speaking "upon any street, alley or sidewalk within the territorial limits of the city of Aberdeen."[41] Local newspapers, controlled by the ruling elite, rushed to defend the law.[42]

On January 7, seven hundred Grays Harbor residents attended a meeting at the Aberdeen "Red" Finnish Hall to hear lectures from Socialist Party members and to protest against the strict new speaking ordinance. During his speech, socialist Adam Schubert vowed to fight the law once "the weather gets warmer."[43] In the meantime, the socialists, who were well organized and a major force in Aberdeen politics, began to act as arbiters of the dispute between the Wobblies and Aberdeen's elites. But Wobblies were less patient than their socialist allies; more than 150 free speech fighters were in Chehalis County, waiting for their chance to directly challenge Aberdeen's speaking prohibition.[44]

At six o'clock on January 10, fifteen IWWs hit the streets of Aberdeen to challenge the law. Within a few moments, 3,000 observers gathered around the orators to listen and await the conflict that would surely follow.[45] Members of the citizens' committee arrived quickly and began to break up the meeting with their pick handles, but the Wobblies once again improvised their tactics to deal with the attacks by splitting up into smaller groups and spreading themselves throughout the streets.[46] After considerable confusion, the citizens' committee and police force rounded up and arrested the speakers. Anyone suspected of belonging to the IWW was taken to jail and held all night.[47] "Stumpy" Payne, who took notes and cheered from the crowd, was the last man arrested. In a 1919 article he wrote for the One Big Union Monthly, Payne emphasized the multi-ethnic character of the fighters, noting that among their ranks was a "Down East Yankee," "a short, swarthy German," a "raw-boned Irishman," and an Italian.[48] Regardless of ethnicity, each of these men took to the soapbox, addressed his "Fellow Workers," and was arrested. Payne's description demonstrated that the IWW appeal cut across traditional ethnic boundaries, and as subsequent events suggested, the Wobblies' inter-ethnic appeal was one of the chief reasons for their successful transition from a free speech fight into an industrial union capable of shutting down the region's lumber mills.

Realizing the enormous appeal of their street meetings, and willing to risk the dangers involved, the IWW intended to put ten speakers on the streets every night for the following two weeks.[49] However, Aberdeen's officials, fed up with the struggle, were ready to settle with the IWW.[50] Mayor Parks sent "anxious inquiries" to the Hoquiam headquarters of the IWW, asking to meet with a committee to settle the Free Speech Fight, but union members informed him that only the men in jail had the power to end the conflict. Parks met with the imprisoned Wobblies and arranged the terms under which a truce could be reached. As a token of his good intentions, he released all Wobblies from prison, and both sides declared a temporary truce until January 15.[51]

The following day, delegates from the citizens' committee and the IWW met twice and decided on final terms for the truce. Both sides claimed that the other started the negotiation process out of desperation, crowed over the success of their tactics, and claimed final victory in the Free Speech Fight. Predictably, the Industrial Worker issued the most belligerent version of the fight's waning moments, declaring complete victory in the conflict. The only catch, it claimed, was that the Industrial Worker was advised to "use headlines that are not OVER two feet tall" to brag of their victory. A week later, "Stumpy" declared the IWW received everything it had demanded in negotiations, and that "the Free Speech in Aberdeen passes into history as a clean-cut, unqualified victory for the Industrial Workers of the World."[52]

At first glance, it seems odd that the citizens' committee, which had resorted to brutal techniques of repressing free speech during the previous three months, was so willing to negotiate with the Wobblies. The citizens' boycott, the IWW press's depictions of Aberdeen officials as lawless thugs, and the pressure exerted by union members and socialists must have all factored into the decision. Aberdeen's elites perhaps also sought to avoid a drawn-out conflict that might tarnish the city's image. Throughout the early 1910s, Chehalis County experienced an economic boom: the establishment of the Port of Grays Harbor, the county's connection to the Milwaukee Railroad, and the construction of numerous new lumber mills all led to the rapid expansion of the area's industry.[53] Thus, it is likely that the same businessmen who were so concerned in autumn about silencing IWW organizers and expelling rabble-rousers were also concerned about the prospect of losing face if a massive, Spokane-type conflict occurred in Aberdeen.[54]

Regardless of how one views the specifics of the outcome, the IWW, through both heroic and pragmatic efforts, undoubtedly did achieve its primary goal: the ability to use Aberdeen's streets to hold organizational and educational meetings.[55] Like their predecessors in Missoula, Spokane, Fresno, and other cities across the western United States, Aberdeen IWW members put themselves at risk to regain their freedom of expression and to establish a stable, effective labor organization in Grays Harbor. However, unlike previous free speech fighters, who failed to transition the union from the role of agitator to that of a structured labor union, the actions taken by Aberdeen IWW members led directly to the union's leadership in the Grays Harbor labor movement. The Chehalis County IWW immediately undertook the act of solidifying the gains made during the free speech fight. On January 18, the IWW held a large street meeting to celebrate the free speech fight victory and discuss organizational options. Many police attended, but did not interfere, as the meeting was both legal and orderly.[56] The celebration reached new proportions three days later during a meeting in which those in attendance decided to follow up the organizational gains made during the free speech fight with a mass organizational drive across Chehalis County. Immediately, four organizers went to work among the area's logging camps and lumber mills.[57] The

tactics implemented as a result of this meeting built on the free speech fighters'
successes and laid the foundation for the future conflicts that enveloped the
region in the spring of 1912.

5
The War of Grays Harbor

During the winter of 1912, the workplaces, boardinghouses, and streets of Aberdeen and Hoquiam were filled with discussions of socialism, industrial unionism, and anarchism, carried on in a variety of languages as diverse as the region's working class. Fresh from their victory in the Aberdeen Free Speech Fight, local Wobblies and Socialists delivered soapbox orations on Aberdeen's street corners to hundreds of eager listeners. Workers flooded into locals of the IWW's lumber and maritime workers' unions, and read about their workplace and community struggles in the pages of the *Industrial Worker*. Those who preferred to receive their radicalism in the comfort of indoor heating also had plenty of options. Local Wobblies and Socialists had their own halls, and the Aberdeen Red Finn Hall provided local leftists with an auditorium that could comfortably accommodate several hundred persons for speeches, dances, or theatrical performances. Throughout the winter, Grays Harbor socialists took part in the Socialist Party of America's Lyceum course, which hosted speeches by prominent leftists in the Empire Theater and the Aberdeen Red Finn Hall.[1]

For Red Coast radicals, however, speeches, meetings, and the "right" to assemble on the streets were not enough. They did little to improve the horrid conditions experienced by working men and women in a region dominated by the lumber trust. In the early months of 1912, working people united across differences of skill, occupation, race, ethnicity, and sex to wage the Grays and Pacific County Lumber Strike of 1912, the largest pre–World War I Pacific Northwest lumber strike. To maintain their tight grip over the Red Coast communities, mills, and logging camps, Grays and Willapa harbor employers formed vigilante "citizens' committees" that used violence to break the strike and, on occasion, to break the strikers' skulls. Alongside the bosses marched an impressive array of anti-union municipal officials and newspaper editors, men who had for years collaborated in the Chamber of Commerce, the Elks club, and other employer-class associations. Given the scale and intensity of the struggle, it is not surprising that the strike came to be known as The War of Grays Harbor.

The strike began on March 14, 1912, when two hundred workers walked off the job at the Northwest Lumber Company in Hoquiam.[2] The IWW soon took control of the strike. Even at this early juncture, it became apparent that the Wobblies possessed the ability to lead large numbers of workers. After walking out, IWW organizers and strikers marched to Hoquiam's Finn Hall to hold a meeting, where they determined to march on the Hoquiam Lumber and Shingle Company, owned by Robert F. Lytle. On reaching the mill, the Wobblies found it surrounded by a twelve-foot fence. Undaunted, they climbed the fence and encouraged the mill labourers to join the strike. The IWW press later mocked Lytle's use of the fence to encircle "his slave dump.... If he thinks that a flimsy fence or wire will keep out men who should wish to take a peep into this establishment of slave conditions, he is badly mistaken."[3] Soon after entering this mill, the Wobblies convinced enough men to leave their jobs to shut down production.

Strikers utilized the region's numerous Finn Halls as headquarters during the strike, and recruited many of their most faithful members from within this ethnic group. On the strike's first day, at the Hoquiam Finn Hall, Wobbly organizers, strikers, and sympathizers celebrated the closure of the North Western and Hoquiam Lumber and Shingle mills, discussed future plans, and cemented their organizational gains among the striking mill hands. The meeting proved extremely successful, as the IWW immediately signed up 147 new members. Strikers later named George L. Holmes and Fred Isler officers, and elected a multi-ethnic committee to lead the strike negotiations.[4]

The next day, the strike committee issued a statement demanding immediate pay raises for the "common laborer" of twenty-five cents per day, and a minimum of $2.25 per day.[5] The *Daily Washingtonian* cited even more ambitious demands by the strikers: the "Greeks" demanded $2.50 per day, "and the I.W.W. men declar[ed] they will not work for less than $3."[6] Before the strike, Dr. Herman Titus, a prominent Washington State socialist who visited the strikers, wrote that they "received but $1.75 per day, and that no man with a family could live on such wages."[7] The employers, however, were unmoved. Led by manager Al Kuhn of the Hoquiam Lumber and Shingle Company, they refused the strikers' demands and began soliciting applications for replacement workers.[8]

Meanwhile, the IWW expanded their strike and led out sixty "previously loyal" mill yard employees at the Lytle Mill. This expansion of the strike led to the first substantive victory when the E. K. Wood Company, responding to a strike threat, raised its wages twenty-five cents per day. Hopeful strikers, however, were disappointed when the Lytle and North Western mills refused to conform to the E. K. Wood example.[9]

As the strike expanded throughout March, the strikers continued in solidarity across ethnic, gender, occupation, skill, geographic, and union lines. Two weeks into the strike, production had come to a halt in all of the mills in Grays Harbor, and also in much of the Grays Harbor and Puget Sound logging industry. Workers from all sectors of the lumber industry participated in the work stoppage, including the skilled saw operators, shingle weavers, and unskilled mill hands. Sailors and longshoremen pitched in by refusing to load cargo produced by scab labor. At a March 18 mass meeting, picketers held signs that read "Keep Away From Ships," and declared the support from longshoremen.[10] The *Industrial Worker* described the support of both the shingle weavers and the longshoremen:

> The shingle weavers are pledged to give their support in this strike and the strikers have all agreed not to return to work until their demands are granted and no discrimination shown.
>
> The Longshoremen in Aberdeen, both of the I.W.W. and the I.L.A. [International Longshoremen's Association], are standing with the strikers and in Hoquiam they will do the same.[11]

The most substantial support came from the shingle weavers, who struck against many of the same employers as mill hands affiliated with the Wobblies. The Everett Washington Trades Council, center of the International Shingle Weavers' Union of America (ISWUA) activities, voiced the shared interests of the ISWUA and IWW during the strike, asserting that "skilled workmen, members of the A.F. of L. unions, and common laborers affiliated with the I.W.W. are alike engaged in the strike."[12]

The alliance between the trade union locals and the IWW during the lumber strike drew attention from the AFL's top leadership. Washington State Federation of Labor President C. R. Case visited Grays Harbor to investigate the causes of the tumult. AFL-IWW alliances in the Northwest were rare, but

Case praised the Wobblies' actions, and cited the actions of Grays Harbor lumbermen as the cause of the trouble:

> I called attention to the spirit of discontent that was arousing the
> employes of the "saw dust ring" of southwestern Washington, to
> the suppression of free speech and free press by city officials who
> were owned or controlled by these vast lumber barons and to the
> probabilities of an early outbreak against the damnable un-American
> and unendurable conditions of employment.[13]

During a speech in Everett, Jay G. Brown, president of the ISWUA and a long-time Grays Harbor labor activist, reinforced Case's arguments and called attention to the inter-union solidarity shown by the strikers. According to Brown, "For intensity and solidarity of action, [the 1912 strike] ranks second to no strike of recent years in any part of the country."[14] The shingle weavers, longshoremen, and sailors continued their participation in the strike, and with few exceptions, maintained a united working-class front against Grays Harbor employers until the waning days of the conflict.

As the strike extended into its third week, IWW general strike threats appeared to come true as workers throughout the region declared sympathy strikes with the Grays Harbor lumber workers:

> Practically every saw mill in Aberdeen, Hoquiam, Raymond, and
> South Bend is closed down. The longshoremen of these four cities are
> out in sympathy with the mill workers and have tied up the shipping
> of lumber. Boats arriving in California harbor from the strike district
> here find that union men will not unload the lumber.[15]

Organizing across ethnic lines became vital as the IWW efforts spread into Raymond and South Bend, the two principal lumber towns located on Willapa Harbor, twenty-five miles south of the "twin cities." From their headquarters at the Raymond Finn Hall, the IWW organized primarily among the Finnish and Greek communities, but their ranks also included many native-born Americans and South Asians.[16]

Workers in large cities also displayed their solidarity with the strikers. In Tacoma, a number of mills went out in sympathy with the Harbor strikers:

A big delegation of pickets have gone over to Tacoma to help to keep
the St. Paul mill closed down. . . .

The latest report from Tacoma is that out of 1,150 employees only
293 are working today [the 9th] and they are acting as watch dogs for
the bosses property but are not producing very much lumber.[17]

Later, the Tacoma Central Labor Council voiced its resounding support of
IWW efforts and endorsed the strike. In Seattle, IWW locals actively supported the strike, both by calling sympathy strikes and collecting funds for
the Chehalis County strikers. As a show of support, Seattle Wobblies and
sympathizers held a "monster meeting" at Dreamland Rink in support of the
IWW, and collected $140.92 for the strikers. Fred Allison, a prominent Pacific
Northwest Wobbly, spoke at the meeting and drew enormous applause when
he stated that union organizer William Thorn was "the most hated agitator in
Grays Harbor."[18]

The strongest support, however, came from the Pacific Northwest's loggers. On April 3, nine Chehalis County Wobblies traveled to the logging camp
of George Hulet to meet with sympathetic loggers.[19] Similar efforts throughout the region led loggers at ten camps along the Tacoma Eastern Railway to
walk out in sympathy with the Grays Harbor mill workers. In mid-April, the
ambitious Wobblies called a general strike among lumber workers for April
19. Although it never reached its proposed dimensions, the logging strike did
have an impact. On May 9, the Industrial Worker contended that five thousand
loggers had come out of the camps, with more still to come. "Over forty camps
are affected, either completely closed or so badly crippled that they are unable
to operate," it reported.[20]

Thus, the huge strike showed the potential power of a united body of lumber workers. At one early April strike meeting, eight thousand union members and sympathizers paraded through town toward a ball field that could not
accommodate the size of the crowd. The Industrial Worker described the meeting: "There were speakers in many different languages, in fact more speakers
than time would permit to hear. Among those who spoke were organizers and
representatives of the I.W.W., A.F. of L. and Socialist organizations which are
jointly conducting this strike." Workers were divided by ethnic, organizational,
and occupational lines, but brought together by their support of working-class
interests, had effectively brought the entire Grays Harbor lumber industry
to its knees. The Industrial Worker admitted that the power of working-class

Strikers march through Hoquiam during the 1912 Grays Harbor Lumber Strike. Led by the IWW, the strike spread from Grays Harbor to mills and logging camps in Pacific County and the Puget Sound. Photo courtesy of Polson Museum, Hoquiam, Washington.

radicalism had even gone beyond the union's control, suggesting that "this was not what could be called an I.W.W. strike, but instead it was a revolt and protest alike of those unorganized as well as organized."[21]

Red Coast employers responded to this workers' revolt by forming a united strikebreaking front that waged a multifaceted war against the strikers. They attempted to starve out workers by denying them credit at local businesses; they formed what they called "citizens' committees," but which were, in fact, violent vigilante organizations; they hired strikebreakers and company guards to open the mills; they sponsored a widespread anti-radical propaganda campaign in the mainstream press; and they worked to divide workers along ethnic lines by offering wage increases to native-born "American" workers.

Employers knew that striking workers were unlikely to have much savings and would need to make their purchases on credit when they stopped receiving their paychecks. Within the first week of the strike, employers furnished local grocery stores with lists of strikers and asked merchants to refuse them credit.[22] By employing these "no credit" lists, mill owners sought to eliminate the possibility of a long, drawn-out strike, and starve the strikers back to their jobs. The best opportunity for employers to exploit their power in this way came in the company town of Cosmopolis. Here, Neil Cooney, the manager of the Grays Harbor Commercial Company, had authority over the stores, restaurants, and homes of his workers, a state of affairs that enabled him to threaten striking employees with a loss of store credit and eviction from their homes.[23]

Without credit at local stores, union members sought other ways to feed their families. Each week the *Industrial Worker* asked outsiders to send money and food to aid the strikers. Appealing to supporters' sympathies, these reports often cast the strikers as desperate, hungry, and in need of immediate relief. As IWW member J. S. Biscay wrote, "The many workers who are now struggling for a slight increase in wages have had a hard winter and are mostly in debt. The employers have caused the merchants to refuse credit. That means that many will go hungry unless there is prompt relief from the outside."[24] In addition to the funds solicited from outside Grays Harbor, strikers also received financial support from a number of friendly merchants. With these funds, union members established soup kitchens in Aberdeen and Hoquiam, but operating the kitchens proved to be dangerous. In early April, members of the Aberdeen Citizens' Committee ransacked the soup kitchen and fired shots through its walls to terrorize those who aided the strikers.[25]

Violence was central to the employers' strikebreaking tactics. Shortly after the strike commenced, Grays Harbor police, professional strikebreakers, and a 1,000-member citizens' committee organized a two-week campaign of violent resistance to the workers' revolt. During this time, police, strikebreakers, and vigilantes beat, jailed, kidnapped, and deported the male strikers. The first such violence came on March 18, during a picket at the North Western Mill. Shortly before the plant opened for the day, as Greek strikers urged other workers to join the strike, special police interfered, and a fight broke out. During the ruckus, one Greek striker was hit over the head with a brick. Four strikers were arrested for disorderly conduct, but no charges were brought against the officer who assaulted the striker.[26]

Mass expulsion from town was, in fact, the official policy of Aberdeen officials and employers who acted to curb the Wobbly threat. Banker William J. Patterson, the head of the Aberdeen Citizens' Committee, described the group's actions: "We organized that night a vigilante committee—a Citizens' Committee, I think we called it— to put down the strike by intimidation and force. . . . [W]e got hundreds of heavy clubs of the weight and size of pick-handles, armed our vigilantes with them, and that night raided all the IWW headquarters, rounded up as many of them as we could find, and escorted them out of town."[27]

Although employer violence was almost totally ignored by the local mainstream press, large urban dailies joined union and Wobbly papers in publicizing the violence the citizens' committees directed against the strikers. The *Morning Oregonian* reported, "A citizens' police force of 200 men, . . . armed with shotguns and part mounted and all carrying clubs and some kind of guns," had been dispatched so as to "preserve order."[28] The *Tacoma Times* publicized the efforts of the Aberdeen police chief to tour the state recruiting "experienced policemen to go to Aberdeen to fight the IWW workers."[29] The Wobbly press was even more explicit in its denunciations of boss violence. In one *Industrial Worker* article, a Wobbly reported: "Yesterday four of the pickets arrested at the North Western, and the captain, a Greek, had his head split with a hammer in the hands of a scab. We know them and will do some arresting also." Another article declared the violent actions of the owner of the Anderson and Middleton Mill: "Mill owner Anderson, swinging a heavy club and brandishing a revolver, urged his thugs to shoot down the workers. . . . He had shot a workingman who had come after his pay and who was leaving the vicinity of violence. Shot from behind. He may recover."[30]

In Hoquiam, where Mayor Harry Ferguson initially refused to endorse the creation of a citizens' committee, Police Chief Quinn created a special force of mill police serving on company payrolls to enforce order around the mills.[31] The *Seattle Union Record* added that although Ferguson blocked the creation of a government-endorsed citizens' committee, "mill superintendents, foremen, corporation attorneys, doctors and small businessmen" nevertheless formed a vigilante "mob" to attack and deport strikers.[32]

Aberdeen did form a citizens' committee, and it directed its energies to beating, harassing, and deporting Wobblies and other strikers. Its members earned a reputation as "thugs" from the IWW press.[33] During a March 26 picket at the Anderson and Middleton Mill, the citizens' committee and regular police officers "freely used" clubs and guns to break up the demonstration; one Greek striker was shot, and twenty others were injured. Similar incidents occurred throughout late March, as officers and vigilantes fought to keep picketers away from the mills by force.[34]

One might wonder how employers, who were, after all, greatly outnumbered by their striking employees, could possibly hope to suppress a strike through violence. In fact, one of the purposes of employers' use of violence

Two workers arrested and jailed in Hoquiam during the 1912 Lumber Strike. The men are showing their bare arms to demonstrate the injuries they sustained while in jail. The bottom of the photo reads: "Yager and Anderson who were stungup [sic] to the cages in the City Jail of Hoquiam, Wash., during the Lumber Workers' Strik [sic] of May 1912, by Rube Quinn, who was Chief of Police of Hoquiam in May 1912 and filled the jail with strikers and handled them rough." Photo courtesy of Polson Museum, Hoquiam, Washington.

was to win the support of the "law and order" crowd and bring state intervention. Having first instigated violence, the lumbermen met on March 28 in Aberdeen to write to Governor Marion Hay, requesting that he send in the militia to disperse the picketers.[35] In response to their request, the Washington State attorney general ordered the state cavalry and "a battalion of infantry from Seattle" to be prepared to go to the embattled region and ensure the reopening of the area's mills.[36] Although state troops did not intervene in this conflict, the threat of their involvement was a potent reminder to workers of the long history of government strikebreaking.

Local public officials also used the violence the mill owners created as justification for their anti-worker positions. For example, Mayor Parks of Aberdeen issued an anti-strike proclamation in which he claimed that the closing of striking workers' halls was necessary to preserve law and order. In response to the mayor's proclamation, the IWW pointed out that it was not the workers, but "the city authorities, acting at the behest of the mill owners in this district [who] have brought about a condition of lawlessness." They beseeched the "good citizens to aid us in the restoration of good order and to rid the city of gun men and thugs imported here from the slum districts of other cities and to restore to the working men here their rights peaceably to assemble in the pursuit of their affairs."[37] Despite the Wobbly plea, the citizens' committee members kept their wagon spokes handy during the entirety of the lumber strike.

The mainstream press had no difficulty excusing the violent actions employed by the police and vigilantes. In mid-April, the *Aberdeen Herald* congratulated the officers for their discretion during the conflict:

> Under the trying conditions existing in Aberdeen for the past month,
> too much praise cannot be bestowed on the police department
> and Chief Templeman. It was a time for discretion, and it was used
> admirably. Mistakes may have been made—the wonder would be if
> they were not—but, so far as the Herald can learn, the officers were
> determined upon but one point—to preserve the peace.[38]

In fact, the citizens' committee was responsible for a number of assaults, jailings, and illegal deportations of union members throughout the strike. On March 21, a fire hose was used to disperse a meeting of striking workers at the Cooperage Mill. Although this was clearly an act of violence, the *Aberdeen Daily World* boasted of the perpetrators' actions: "Shortly after 4 o'clock several hundred strikers practically surrounded the mill and the usual tactics which are employed to induce men to abandon their work were used. Three lines of hose were placed in operation and for several minutes the strikers were held back."[39]

Because the lumbermen and other anti-union forces controlled the machinery of state, they were able to present their violence as lawful and the activities of striking workers as a menace to law and order. Aberdeen's Socialist Party, its second-largest political party, therefore opened another front in the class war when they organized for municipal elections in early April 1912. However, lumbermen were not about to let democracy come between them and their profits. In an attempt to intimidate socialists away from the polls, sixty-one strikers and socialists were arrested and jailed when they gathered at a political rally on April 1.[40] Later that day, police raided the strikers' chief meeting points: Aberdeen's Red Finn Hall, the Aberdeen Croatian Hall, and the Greek pool hall.[41] A few days later, the citizens' committee changed their tactics. Instead of simply arresting strikers, they began kidnapping and deporting their targets. In Hoquiam, vigilantes attempted to deport 150 strikers on boxcars, but were stopped by railroad workers.[42]

Despite these continued outrages, Socialist candidates for Aberdeen city council seats captured 34 percent of the total votes, winning two out of six seats and losing a third by only thirty-one votes. Not simply a protest vote, the large Socialist turnout reflected sharp ethnic and class divisions in the city. Wards One, Two, and Six—those where Socialists polled best—housed much of Aberdeen's Finnish working-class population.[43] Socialist and union official E. E. Milette earned a victory in Ward Six.[44]

Despite the tremendous economic and political power that the bosses brought to bear in the War of Grays Harbor, workers might yet have succeeded in their revolt had they been able to maintain solidarity. From the first days of the strike, bosses went to great lengths to divide the workers based on skill, ethnicity, and race, and they ultimately succeeded. Many of the strikers were immigrants, and local newspapers—all edited by local Chamber of Commerce leaders—urged local mill owners to replace these men with "All American Labor." On March 15, just a day after the strike began, Al Kuhn, the manager of the Hoquiam Lumber and Shingle Company, noted the presence of a large group of "blacks" picketing outside his mill, and asked that they be replaced by "white men with families."[45] As the strike progressed, the mills began offering higher wages—without union recognition—to white American-born men who returned to work. Mills also refused to rehire strike leaders and IWW members.[46] In early April, a headline in the *Daily Washingtonian* proclaimed: "Hoquiam Is To Be A White Man's Town."[47]

Employers' efforts to divide and conquer appealed to some Grays Harbor workers, who, having been granted their wage demands, began returning to the mills. Certainly, a number of radicals remained on the picket lines, yet other workers fell into the category described by the *Aberdeen Herald* as, "men [who] had struck for $2.25 a day and got it. . . . They want work and fair wages, not revolution."[48] The increased wages succeeded in drawing enough men back to work that, by the first week in April, the Anderson and Middleton, and the Aberdeen Lumber and Shingle Company had reopened. Acknowledging the Wobblies' partial victory during the strike, IWW Fred Allison stated that because of the strike, laborers earned higher wages, but that "The flag of slaveocracy [still] floats over the bull pens of Grays Harbor."[49] A week later, the

American Mill, the last affected by the strike, resumed operations, and the strike ended.[50]

Many Wobblies left Grays Harbor in early May 1912, but the region's workers retained a close affiliation with the IWW for years thereafter. In an editorial titled "Never Lost A Strike," an anonymous IWW member wrote that the Grays Harbor strike will cause "further organization until the day is reached when the workers manage industry in their own interest."[51] Although this grand prediction proved to be an exaggeration, the 1911–1912 period of IWW activity in the region's lumber industry laid the foundation for future radical working-class movements in Grays Harbor. In fact, the IWW remained a potent force in Grays Harbor. In 1917 and 1923 Wobblies launched major strikes against the region's lumber owners, while in 1919–1922 Grays Harbor radicals were among the most widely targeted victims of Washington State's criminal syndicalism law.[52]

6
Moving Day in Raymond

"March 30—Today was moving day in Raymond," the *Aberdeen Herald* proclaimed during the 1912 Grays Harbor and Pacific County Lumber Strike, "and if the census were taken tomorrow Raymond's population would be shy some 150 names, unless all signs fail. Hereafter Raymond is to be strictly an American city." Earlier that morning, a mob went to Raymond's Greek settlement and told all striking workers that those who did not return to work in the mills by 1:00 would be run out of the city.[1] Striking millworker and socialist candidate for the city council L. A. Jacobson was awakened by banging on his door. "When I opened it [millman] A. C. L[ittl]e, exmayor, and one of his trusted deputies stood there. L[ittl]e shook his fist in my face and told me I would either go to work in the mills or be thrown in jail." But the workers hung together, and the mob set about its work. Raymond's striking Finns were rounded up and deported by boat to Nahcotta, and then on to Astoria. Greek workers were deported by railroad. Deported Greek millworker John Pallas described the scene: "Friday they grab us. Everybody have guns, clubs, break in our houses, say: 'You go to work.' We say, 'No we not want to work.' Then woof! Hit us with gun and throw us in box car like cattle. Ship 120 to Chehalis."[2] The Greek workers, determined to return to their homes, enlisted the aid of the Greek consul and attempted to return to the city. They were again met by a mob, beaten and deported, this time to Menlo, where they were held in a corral, before being carried to Tacoma. The mob that met their train, and which planned also to prevent Raymond's Finns from returning, was said to be determined that "hereafter Raymond will be known as the home of the white laboring man."[3] Decades later, Robert C. Bailey, who grew up in Raymond, observed "There is no doubt that the furor was whipped up by the mill operators."[4]

These deportations, carried out at the urging of the Red Coast's major employers and the newspapers they controlled were not without precedent. The late nineteenth century saw a wave of violence and mass deportations of Chinese American immigrants in the Pacific Northwest. Tragically, organized labor, and especially the Knights of Labor, often took the lead in these nineteenth-century campaigns. The Knights argued that Chinese labor was used by the capitalists to depress white wages and reduce white workers to slavery, and they urged white workers to drive the Chinese out. However, the 1912 deportations out of Raymond were not a spontaneous outbreak of anti-immigrant racism among anxious workers. On the contrary, these deportations were part of employers' carefully orchestrated and increasingly sophisticated attempt to undermine worker solidarity and divide workers by race. An important distinction between the two deportations, indeed, is that while Chinese immigrants were deported *because* they worked, Greek, Finnish, and other laborers were deported because they refused to do so— because they *struck*. These latter deportations were a response to a new generation of workers, often organizing under the anti-racist IWW, who called on all workers to stand together against the employing class. "We take in all nationalities and colors," the IWW, proclaimed, "because the interests of all workers are the same and the only foreigner we know is the boss."[5] In the face of such solidarity, the employing class sought to stigmatize strikers as foreign radicals, co-opt "American" workers with offers of white privilege, and enlist the support of the middle class in their strikebreaking campaigns through appeals to "law and order."

The Raymond deportations were some of the culminating events in the 1912 Grays Harbor and Pacific County Lumber Strike, also known as the War of Grays Harbor, described in the preceding chapter; it was the largest strike in the region up to that time. Grays Harbor employers, with their mills closed by the strike, filled their orders at mills in Raymond, in neighboring Pacific County. On Monday, March 25, workers gathered in Raymond's Finn Hall to discuss the situation. After hearing speeches in several languages, they decided this had to stop. They struck in sympathy.[6]

In Raymond, while "the strike caught the millmen wholly unprepared," they responded quickly. At eight o'clock on the evening of Tuesday, March 26, with Raymond's mills closed indefinitely by the strike, the town's businessmen gathered in Raymond's Commercial Club to decide on a course of action. The meeting was called to order by ex-mayor and millman A. C. Little, and chaired by banker J. J. Haggerty. Little delivered an impassioned speech, asking all those who "believed in the American flag . . . without interference from a foreign element to stand up." All in attendance rose, and shouted, "We are with you." They created a number of committees, including a conference committee, of which Little was a member, directed to "consult with the mill-men and ascertain in what way the businessmen could aid them in adjusting the strike."[7] The Finnish-language socialist newspaper *Toveri*, published in Astoria, Oregon, provided a detailed description of the meeting. One of the speakers was "that notorious Doctor Overmayer," who concluded that "the strike must be ended by the unified activities of the policemen and business-men. He said he, too, would be ready to take on any possible measures for that end."[8]

The method they chose was to create a mob and endow it with police authority to threaten, beat, imprison, and deport the workers who sought higher wages through direct action. A citizens' committee, which included 460 "mill men, business men, and all employees who wished to work," set about suppressing the strike by attacking rank-and-file workers.[9] The deputies were issued badges with instructions to "keep the agitators moving and pre-vent any gathering of the strikers." Those who couldn't explain their business were ushered out of town or imprisoned and charged with inciting to riot.[10] On Wednesday, March 27, Sheriff Stephens and Deputy Sheriff McDonald led a party of the "law and order brigade" against strikers and strike sympa-thizers at Raymond's Finn Hall and a Greek grocery where strikers gathered. The hall was nailed shut, its banners were torn down, and a dozen workers were imprisoned under armed guard at the city jail where, with the con-nivance of Chief of Police Ray Wheaton, they were sometimes taken out at night and beaten. Many of the city's Finns were card-carrying members of the Socialist Party who subscribed to, and occasionally wrote articles for, *Toveri*. One *Toveri* writer provided a powerful description of the attacks made against Raymond's strikers: "Without showing any mercy the police beat everybody they could get their hands on with the butts of their revolvers and batons. They did not even spare the women, at least Mrs. Leena Hagzvist got her hands beaten bloody and bruised."[11] A sign reading "Closed by order of the county" was posted on the Finn hall, while banners reading "I.W.W. Headquarters" and "Apply for Membership Here" were displayed at the city jail.[12]

Meanwhile, the mob of special police, under the command of Chief Wheaton, armed itself and prepared for its final attack on strikers, a "determined

During the 1912 Lumber Strike, Pacific County authorities and employers jailed striking workers. In this image, the Raymond City Jail is labeled "IWW Headquarters." Photo courtesy of Pacific County Historical Society, South Bend, Washington.

effort to drive the strikers and transient agitators bodily out of the city" by force of arms. On Saturday morning, March 30, "it was put up to the strikers to go to work or quit the town." The armed mob went from door to door, and to the Greek and Finnish boarding houses, herding onto boats or packing "into boxcars like sardines" all those who chose not to work on terms dictated by the employers.[13] In an article titled "RUSSIANIZED RAYMOND," the *Industrial Worker* described the continued vigilantism in Raymond and South Bend, as well as the presence of "pinks," by which they meant Pinkertons, the country's most notorious labor spy organization:

> Raymond, Washington, resembles a city besieged. Special officers
> are guarding the various entrances to the city. Watchmen search all
> incoming trains for agitators and I.W.W. men. As soon as a man arrives
> in town, the "pinks" ask him his business.
> The city jail has a large banner with the inscription "I.W.W.
> Headquarters," "Apply for Membership Here," signed by the citizens'
> committee. They have for a slogan, "This is no heathen town."[14]

Demonstrating that antipathy toward labor extended well beyond the ranks of the radical IWW, local authorities assaulted President Holmes of the shingle weavers' union with a rifle.[15] Again showing the unity between vigilante businessmen and the commercial press, the local newspapers praised the citizens' committee's actions. The *Willapa Harbor Pilot* crowed, "Ex Mayor A. C. Little, Mayor E. E. Case and citizens of Raymond nipped the agitation in the bud, but were forced to take heroic measures to rid the city of the I.W.W. crowd."[16]

Yet for all the naked brutality of the employers' strikebreaking techniques, it is clear that the multiethnic nature of the movement was threatening enough to the employing class that employers believed they would be required to use more than force alone to break it. If beatings, arrests, and deportations were the stick in employers' strikebreaking strategy, they also held out a carrot to American-born workers in the form of preferential hiring and promised wage increases. The strategy here was to channel worker frustrations into energies directed at other workers, rather than the boss, thereby weakening class solidarity and preventing truly revolutionary action. As the *Industrial Worker* explained, "The bosses think they can use the scissorbill [an anti-union worker] to scab on the Greeks."[17] A column in the industry mouthpiece *Aberdeen Herald* from March 18 gives a clear indication that this was part of the bosses' strategy from early in the strike, just days after it began: "The strike of the I.W. W. members and of the Greek and other Slavic laborers in the mills of this city is still on. . . . It seems certain that the foreigners will be replaced in the mills by American men of families. . . . That the strike will result in married men securing positions and possibl[y] in an increase in wages, there is little doubt."[18]

Employers, then, sought to divide workers by depicting the strike as a product of radical foreigners, and they were even willing to offer concessions to "American" workers as a reward for scabbing on the strikers. The strike began as a strike for increased wages. Employers, confronted with workers organizing along class lines, were willing to accede to their wage demands, at least in the short term, but that willingness was combined with another offer intended to transform the nature of the strike: they offered to settle the strike on a "white basis." They would raise workers' wages to $2.25, but they would deport striking immigrants and give hiring preference to "American" men with families. The Tacoma Strike Committee of the IWW described the lumbermen's promises: "The men were told at the time of the strike that if they helped drive out the Greeks and other foreigners . . . it would give the American citizens a chance to work and wages would immediately go up to meet the 'high standard of living enjoyed by the American working man."

Of course, the lumbermen defined the strike as the product of immigrant radicals, so "all I.W.W. men are considered foreigners."[19]

This argument, moreover, was not intended only to seduce "American" working men into betraying their fellow workers. It was also part of a strategy to win the middle classes to the side of the timber barons. The barons, after all, needed these good "citizens" to swing the clubs and point the rifles and shotguns used by the citizens' committees against the workers. IWW organizer Bruce Rogers summed up the lumber barons' argument, and the citizens' reaction, thus:

> "The mill barons now turned to the innocent, calf-eyed citizenry
> and said: "Behold! our foreign slaves have revolted against the good
> American working conditions. Let us have the American working
> man with his family. He will scab the undesirable foreigner out of 'our
> fair city.'" The good citizens feebly reply: "Deal with your workers
> alone, but we are with you for law and order."[20]

While employers, supported by these co-opted citizens, continued their attacks on strikers, they also aggressively recruited scab labor. The *Aberdeen Herald* declared that "the authorities will rigidly enforce the vagrancy law" against striking workers, and predicted that "before the end of the week the I. W. W. leaders will either be in jail or on the road to new fields in quest of fresh dupes, while all idle men in the city, without visible means of support will either be deported or prosecuted as vagrants." To fill the shoes of the deported workers, scabs would be recruited from outside the Red Coast. "[A] man will be sent to the [Puget] Sound to secure a sufficient number of home-making American families to take the place of the striking foreigners," the *Herald* stated.[21] This man had apparently arrived in Tacoma by the following day, because on April 2 the *Tacoma Times* reported that "local employment offices got an order today for 4,600 mill workers to go to Hoquiam, while Raymond wants 50. Only 'white men,' the advertisements read, are wanted, Finlanders and 'hunkies' being barred."[22] The *Herald* predicted, "The advantage to Aberdeen," "in exchanging a horde of unassimilating foreign men without families for English speaking men of family ties, who come here to make homes, will cause the strike to assume the form of a blessing before the end of two years."[23]

Employers' two-pronged assault on the workers' movement, which combined ruthless repression of striking workers with promises of increased wages for "American" workers, soon bore fruit. Some laborers returned to work, accepting the bosses' promises of increased wages. Those who refused were beaten, imprisoned, deported, or themselves returned to work later, once it became clear that the strike was broken. Horrified by the violent repression, one Wobbly editorialist wrote, "The lumber strike at Grays Harbor presents a scene that resembles a composite photograph of the atrocities at Lawrence, Mass., and the barbarities at San Diego, Cal."[24] But although employer repression broke the 1912 strike, it did not break the Wobblies. In fact, in some ways the bonds between the Wobblies and their community were solidified by employers' militant anti-unionism.

Of the hundreds—if not thousands—of Grays Harbor workers who joined the IWW in 1912, many retained an informal affiliation with the Wobblies, one that was revived four years later when local workers again organized themselves into IWW branches. Others remained in the IWW during the mid-1910s, refusing to drop their membership in the union.

It is also worth pointing out that the employing class's efforts to depict striking workers as foreign radicals and enemies of the local community of "American" whites was not unique to the 1912 Lumber Strike. Instead, it was part of an increasingly sophisticated technique employers rolled out at times of labor unrest to divide and conquer workers. Depictions of Greek and Finnish workers as unassimilated outsiders without families drew on the anti-Chinese movement of the previous century. This characterization was far from accurate. Immigrant laborers did have families, and they were deeply rooted in the communities in which they worked, as evidenced by their many halls and societies. That the employing class was itself all too willing to undermine community is evident in their frequent resort to such tactics as deportation and the recruitment of scab labor from far afield. However, despite the falsity of employers' claims, they proved useful because they could be combined with state power, which the capitalists controlled, and because they were often accepted by the middle classes, which sympathized instinctively with the capitalists whenever they were persuaded "law and order" was threatened. As a consequence, these techniques were trotted out again and again on the Red Coast during successive Red Scares.

Radical men and women, meanwhile, continued in a class struggle to bring justice for all workers, whether through the IWW, or later, through the

Communist Party or the International Woodworkers of America. In the summer of 1912, the *Industrial Worker* urged laborers to avoid distractions from the main issue:

> There is a decided attempt on the part of the employing class,
> particularly upon the Pacific Coast, to attack the I.W.W. and the
> radical section of the Socialist party on the proposition of reverence
> for the flag. . . . While we must preach and teach and burn into the
> hearts and minds of the workers the fact that there are but two
> nations, the exploited and the exploiters, let us not be drawn into
> a controversy about the merits or demerits of national emblems or
> symbols. Organize at the point of production; that is the main issue.[25]

In a separate post-strike autopsy, the *Industrial Worker* summed up the main takeaway from the strike:

> The working men generally have awakened to the realization that the
> 'flag' and the 'foreigners' were not the issue of the strike, but were
> used by the bosses to mislead and delude the working men from
> taking any class action to benefit their condition. American working
> men now are aware that the boss does not love them any more than he
> does a "foreigner," but uses them to further his own ends.[26]

As for Raymond, Robert C. Bailey recalled, "Later, Raymond became a very unionized and union-supporting town. Most people that are aware of the events and others that followed would like to erase and forget them. Unfortunately, it was not easy to do."[27]

7

"The Home Defender"

ALBERT JOHNSON'S WAR ON RADICALS AND IMMIGRANTS

On November 5, 1912, the voters of the Red Coast congressional district elected Albert Johnson, editor of the popular *Daily Washingtonian*, to serve as their member of Congress by a margin of thirteen hundred votes.[1] Over the next twenty years, Johnson became one of the most powerful congressional leaders in the United States, serving in nine successive congresses until his defeat in the 1932 landslide that swept Franklin D. Roosevelt and the Democrats into power. Without doubt, Johnson's greatest legacy was the 1924 Johnson-Reed Act, which applied a stringent quota system to American immigration policies, and is widely regarded as the most important piece of restrictive immigration legislation in United States history. Johnson's anti-immigrant policies, though inherently racist, were not without a larger motive. An examination of Johnson's career as a newspaper editor suggests that his anti-immigrant policies were, in fact, a product of his wars with and hatred for Grays Harbor radicals.

His election came only a few short months after Johnson played a key role in "The War of Grays Harbor," lending a steady hand to his fellow employers as they combined to battle a strike led by radical members of the IWW. The editor's meteoric rise from battling the radicals of Grays Harbor to becoming a major player in one of the world's great power centers was certainly impressive. Born on March 25, 1869, in Springfield, Illinois, Johnson learned the printers' trade before embarking on his long career in journalism. During his youth, he worked at a variety of newspapers around the United States, including the *St. Louis Globe Democrat*, the *New Haven Register*, and the *Morning Post* in Washington, DC. In 1898, he was lured from a job at the *Washington Post* to Tacoma with the promise of a job as managing editor of the *Tacoma News*. After a stint there and at *The Seattle Times*, Johnson moved to Hoquiam, Washington, in 1909, where he purchased and became editor of the *Daily Washingtonian* and supported the Republican Party and President Taft, in his political feud with Theodore Roosevelt.[2]

But it was the growth of the radical labor movement in Grays Harbor that provided the popular plank on which Johnson built his publishing empire and launched his political career. Both the future congressman's chief interests—opposition to radicalism and support for immigrant restriction—were given full play during his days as a Hoquiam newspaperman. When Billy Gohl, the militant agent for the Aberdeen local of the Sailors' Union of the Pacific, was arrested on murder charges, Johnson urged vigilante action from his "respectable" fellow citizens. He seemed to take sadistic pleasure in imagining Gohl's lynching. His newspaper asked: "Do you imagine that you hear the roar of the mob in pursuit of a human being? A mob swayed by passion! William Gohl, can you hear it? The yelp of the wolf, the horrid laugh of the hyena, the growl of the bear, the howl of the dog, all combining to make the wild cry of the mob, seeking in vengeance the blood of a fellow man?"[3]

During the Aberdeen Free Speech Fight and the War of Grays Harbor, Johnson and his fellow Grays Harbor editors served as loud and enthusiastic mouthpieces for the anti-Wobbly drive. The *Aberdeen Daily World* and Johnson's own *Daily Washingtonian* functioned as Republican organs, whereas the *Aberdeen Herald* strongly supported the Democratic Party, but the newspapermen put aside their party differences to fight the Wobblies. John Carney, Democratic editor of the *Aberdeen Herald*, left little doubt as to this fact: "The issue is not free speech; it is not whether or not street speaking be permitted or denied, but who shall control Aberdeen, its resident citizens or a bunch of irresponsibles gathered under the red banner of anarchy by a small coterie of grafting officials parading under the high sounding name of the Industrial Workers of the World."[4] Not to be outdone by its cross-town "rival" paper, the *Aberdeen Daily World* praised the good work of the citizens' committee: "It was inspiring to see the law-abiding men of this city—hundreds of them—rise in Elks' hall yesterday and pledge their aid to the preservation of order in this community." The *World* continued by describing the IWW as a "red menace," a revolutionary "horde of men" who sought to import chaos into the Harbor towns. The *Aberdeen Daily World* complimented the citizens' committee for its vigilance: "The city will not place them [the IWWs] in jail, nor will meals be furnished them. They will be shipped out by the carload or train load, if necessary, and as soon as enough of them have been collected to make up a shipment."[5] Johnson battled the radicals not just with the pen, but with the sword. He joined a citizens' committee composed of Grays Harbor businessmen that assaulted Wobblies, socialists, and their family members, and drove large numbers of them out of Hoquiam and Aberdeen.

Johnson's war with the Red Coast Wobblies, many of whom were newly arrived immigrants from southern and eastern Europe, shaped his extreme attitudes about radicalism and immigration restriction. In response to his need to more fully express his anti-radical and anti-immigrant attitudes, Johnson established a second newspaper, the *Home Defender*, in May 1912. The opening issue of the monthly newspaper explained that its goal was "to take an active part against the spread of radical, revolutionary socialism."[6] The *Home Defender* also expressed anti-immigrant positions that might have shocked the less-bigoted *Washingtonian* subscribers. "The Growth of Socialism in this country," he wrote:

> may be directly charged to this great incoming heterogeneous mass
> of undesirable wage-cutting inhabitants, many of them admittedly
> temporary inhabitants—who, before they have learned to speak our
> language and before they know of our customs and institutions, are
> taught by foreign-born agitators to hate the United States and to
> contribute their money and their energies to a revolution, bloodless
> or otherwise, which plots the downfall of our present form of
> government.[7]

Johnson was therefore explicit in his desire to use immigration restriction to fight the IWW. He relied on the much-used caricature of the anarchist immigrant to strengthen his argument for restriction. Johnson preferred to let the occasional "blind grandmother" and "crippled child" into the United States than "an immigrant with red in his heart and a bomb in his hand." Johnson assured his supporters that any "discussion of immigration leads at once to a discussion of the I.W.W.," and that the combination of these two issues created the greatest and most immediate threat to the United States.[8]

Johnson also positioned himself as a champion of a specific type of progressive activism during a period of progressive ascendance. He supported, in turn, women's suffrage, trade unions, and prohibition. But throughout his career as editor and politician, Johnson campaigned on a particularly vicious "anti-socialistic" platform that considered immigration restriction to be the best remedy against "the pernicious spread of socialism."[9] A sample of his vituperative editorializing came out during the campaign when he uttered: "The greatest menace to the Republic today is the open door it affords to the ignorant hordes from Eastern and Southern Europe, whose lawlessness flourishes and civilization is ebbing into barbarism."[10] With a reputation for battling Wobblies and socialism, Johnson proved his conservative bona fides and gained the full support of the third district's business community.[11]

Like many white progressives, Johnson's antipathy toward the IWW and revolutionary socialists did not extend to members, and especially leaders, of trade unions affiliated with the American Federation of Labor (AFL). In fact, the editor was a long-time member of the Typographical Union.[12] He also received a good deal of positive press from certain labor unions and their umbrella organizations. His own union journal, the *Typographical Journal*, which sometimes came out in support of radical movements and labor conflicts, heaped praise upon the editor-congressman: "Congressman Albert Johnson, at one time a member of Tacoma Typographical Union No. 170, now a member of the Aberdeen local, recently returned from the front line trenches and has given several interesting talks in Tacoma of what he has seen in war-ridden Europe."[13] The *Bricklayer, Mason, and Plasterer*, another AFL union periodical, praised the election of Johnson, whom it termed another member of the "labor group in Congress."[14] Johnson considered AFL founder and president Samuel Gompers a personal friend and even attended his sixty-fourth birthday party.[15]

It's not surprising, then, that as someone who stood front and center in local employers' assaults on Wobblies and Socialists during the Harbor's labor conflicts of 1911–1912, he received immediate support from Grays Harbor businessmen when he declared himself a candidate for the House of Representatives in early 1912. He received numerous endorsements, including the entire Grays Harbor press corps, the Aberdeen Chamber of Commerce, the Hoquiam Commercial Club, and the dominant regional lumber interests. [16] E. G. Ames of the Puget Mill Company donated $100 to Johnson's 1912 campaign, a move greeted by local lumbermen and other elites as assisting in having "representation for the Harbor in Congress, such as we could not have if Mr. Johnson was not elected."[17]

With his decisive victory in the congressional election, Johnson took his red-baiting, anti-immigrant crusade to the nation's capital. When Johnson

Congressman Albert Johnson addresses a crowd. Penciled notes on the back read "A Congressman Speaks." Photo courtesy of the Polson Museum, Hoquiam, Washington.

moved to Washington, DC, he brought the *Home Defender* along. There, while serving within the minority Republican Party in Congress, he worked to establish the paper as "A National Newspaper Opposed to Revolutionary Socialism."[18] A standard attack against immigrants, particularly those from Southern and Eastern Europe, focused on their allegedly unassimilable and undesirable characteristics, traits that any "patriotic" American should seek to oppose. In one harangue, Johnson suggested that the United States "Put Up the Bars" against immigration:

> The character of immigration has changed and the newcomers are imbued with lawless, restless sentiments of anarchy and collectivism. They arrive to find their hopes too high, the land almost gone and themselves driven to drown into the cities and struggle for a living. Then anarchy becomes rife among them.[19]

Overall, though, the congressman made his mark on Washington—and on America—not primarily through his hateful editorials, but through his political work to enact racist restrictive legislation. During his first term in

Congress, Johnson served on the House Immigration Committee. Northwest newspapers credited his assignment to that committee to the "fact" that "Mr. Johnson has made the immigration problem a matter of special study for many years."[20] Johnson used his first speech on the House floor to assail Asian immigration, giving the public a hint of what was to come. Speaking of the need to retain a tariff, the congressman claimed: "China will send her hordes into this country. They will force the wage-earner and the farmer out.... Until now a protective tariff wall has kept our people of the great Pacific Northwest from too close competition with these Oriental off-scourings."[21]

As a proponent of restriction, Johnson arrived in Washington, DC, at an opportune time, as Congress was considering measures intended to limit immigration. For example, House Resolution 6060 proposed a literacy test for all incoming immigrants over sixteen years old.[22] But Johnson did not believe that the forty-word literacy test went far enough in restricting the number of total immigrants and potential radicals entering the country. Still, he supported the bill in large part because of its clause allowing for the deportation of seditious aliens.[23] During his first reelection bid, the congressman listed four major problems afflicting the country. These included immigration and "dealing firmly with the Industrial Workers of the World." While the two matters were connected, according to Johnson, defeating the IWW "was the greatest and most immediate problem."[24]

Between 1913 and 1918, Johnson continued to serve on the House Immigration Committee, where he pursued the study of various racist ideologies, including eugenics. He was the chief advocate of these beliefs among his congressional colleagues. He also formed friendships with committee members on both sides of the aisle, a fact that certainly aided his crusade against immigrants and radicals when he was appointed chair of the committee in 1919.

Johnson contended that the number of immigrants allowed into the country should be dramatically restricted, essentially arguing for a wall—or, more specifically, bars—to be built to protect the nation's borders:

> Put up the bars against immigration. Enact more stringent laws
> concerning naturalization and enforce these laws to the letter. Let
> citizenship be a privilege to those who live and love the United
> States. Deny citizenship to those newcomers who respect neither our

flag nor our institutions and who have imported a mass of isms that, if not checked must lead to anarchy and revolution.[25]

Johnson's anti-immigrant proposals went too far for many other restrictionists in Congress during the 1910s. In fact, according to historian John Higham, Johnson "alienated other restrictionists by the embarrassing violence of his proposals." As a result, several restrictionist bills proposed between 1903 and 1917 either failed to secure enough votes or were vetoed by the president.[26]

Johnson's proposals centered on the principle of annual quota limits on the number of immigrants able to enter the country. Johnson finally succeeded in these efforts in 1921 after he rose to chair of the House Immigration Committee. On April 11, 1921, Johnson introduced a bill setting up a quota system limiting any nationality to only 3 percent of the number counted during the 1910 census. After two weeks it passed both houses of Congress by resounding margins. President Warren Harding then signed the bill into law. The purpose of this and similar quotas were clear: since most Northern European immigrants had come to the United States in large numbers prior to 1910, the law would have little effect on the future entry of British, German, Irish, or Scandinavian immigrants, whereas many potential immigrants from Southern and Eastern Europe would be barred from entry.

But to Johnson and many of his colleagues, the restrictions seemed too lenient. Building on his public reputation as an immigration "expert," Johnson took up a position as president of the Eugenic Research Association during 1923–1924, a group that pushed for the adoption of public policy based on the pseudo-science of eugenics. The eugenics movement, with Johnson as its chief congressional advocate, pushed for more stringent limits, one that recognized Northern and Western Europeans as more intelligent, democratic, and more readily assimilable into the United States.

On March 17, 1924, Johnson proposed a new bill, one that used the 1890 census as its benchmark. The bill limited European immigrants to 2 percent of each group's population in this country as of 1890. A ceiling of 150,000 immigrants, drawn almost entirely from the eugenicists' favored nations, was placed as the annual ceiling on immigration. The act excluded from entry anyone born in a geographically defined "Asiatic Barred Zone," which included most of the continent of Asia. A final section of the act banned immigration by groups ineligible for naturalization, a category that included the Japanese.

The measure easily passed both houses and received the president's signature on May 26, 1924.[27]

In his short biography of Congressman Johnson, Alfred J. Hillier correctly posited that the 1924 bill was "the most important immigration law to be enacted in the history of the country."[28] Its wide-ranging nature can be seen by looking at its impact on Greeks, who came in their greatest numbers to the United States between 1900 and 1920. Under the limitations placed by the 1921 Act, 3,088 Greeks were allowed to enter the United States per year. After the 1924 Johnson-Reed Act, as the legislation was known, that number dropped to 100, about 3 percent of the earlier figure. The law's success exceeded even its most optimistic supporters' expectations. In part due to the Johnson-Reed Act, from 1924 to 1947, only 2,718,006 immigrants came to the United States.[29]

Johnson was a close ally, and possible member, of the Ku Klux Klan, which was a major proponent of race-based immigrant restriction.[30] During the 1920s, the KKK had a strong following in the Pacific Northwest. Its Seattle-based newspaper, The Watcher on the Tower, listed Klan locals in several Red Coast towns. Klan branches routinely held parades as demonstrations of their local strength. More than sixty Klansmen donned white robes for a 1924 Fourth of July parade in the tiny southwest Washington town of Vader, and an estimated 15,000–20,000 attended a Klan rally at the Lewis County Fairgrounds.[31] "Mainstream" newspapers in Lewis County, including the Centralia Chronicle and Chehalis Bee-Nugget, praised the Klan and ran large advertisements for Klan rallies as late as 1928.[32] The Klan took credit for passage of the Johnson-Reed Act, and indeed, the views on immigration of the KKK and Johnson were indistinguishable.[33]

The 1924 law was the high point of Johnson's career and indeed, as historian Alan Dawley wrote, was the "culmination of decades of nativist agitation going back to the Know-Nothings of the 1850s."[34] After four more terms in office, spent advocating his Republican presidents' agendas and shoring up his restrictionist successes, Johnson was swept out of office in the 1932 Democratic Party landslide victory. Following his defeat, Johnson retired to his home district where he published his memoirs in a series of "Reminiscences" columns in the Washingtonian in 1933 and 1934.[35]

The effects of Johnson's campaigns against immigrants and radicals lasted far beyond his congressional career. By placing race-based quotas on immigration, Johnson succeeded at putting "up the bars" against millions of people who saw the United States, warts and all, as a potential sanctuary against war and persecution. Between 1912 and 1932, the congressman from Hoquiam had advanced from editing a medium-sized-town's daily and fighting radicals in the streets of a Northwest lumber town to playing a major role in building a barrier against most immigrants. He died in 1957 at the age of eighty-seven in American Lake, Washington.

8

Criminal Syndicalism

THE LAW AS A WEAPON OF CLASS WAR

The Washington State Criminal Syndicalism Law of 1919 represented a significant step in the class struggle that raged on the Red Coast and elsewhere in the country. The law can be understood adequately only within the context of the ongoing class war between the employing class and the workers. With this legislation, the Red Coast lumbermen and their allies in the commercial press, private patriotic front groups, and the government targeted, demonized, and criminalized what they saw as the most offensive face of the working class, the Industrial Workers of the World.

One way early twentieth-century industrial capitalists responded to threats to their dominant position was to encourage laws that made it illegal to advocate radical ideas or affiliate with radical groups. For example, during the First World War, the agents of capital passed anti-radical laws such as the Espionage Law (1917) and the Sedition Act (1918). Over twenty states and many municipalities followed suit by passing their own laws aimed at rooting out radical anti-capitalist groups in their own backyard. Such was the case in the state of Washington, where the legislature passed a criminal syndicalism law in 1919 as part of broader package of anti-radical legislation.

The overwhelming majority of the criminal syndicalism laws passed at the state level targeted the IWW, and the Washington State law was no exception. Since the IWW represented the most class-conscious element of the working class, it was the most obvious target for repression. Like the most revered capitalist writer Adam Smith, the Wobblies understood that the capitalists—the masters, Smith called them—and the workers had different self-interests. Smith declared:

What are the common wages of labor, depends everywhere upon the
contract made between those two parties whose interests are by no
means the same. The workmen desire to get as much, the masters to
give as little as possible. The former are disposed to combine in order
to raise, the latter in order to lower the wages of labour.[1]

And in a similar vein but with greater fervor, the IWW proclaimed in its
Constitution's Preamble:

The working class and the employing class have nothing in common.
There can be no peace so long as hunger and want are found among
the millions of the working people and the few, who make up the
employing class, have all the good things in life. Between these
two classes a struggle must go on until the workers of the world
organize as a class, take possession of the earth and the machinery of
production and abolish the wage system.[2]

The struggle between the "masters" and workers to which Smith referred was
central to the Wobbly understanding of society. The IWW Manifesto asserted
that the working-class movement "must be founded on the class struggle, and
its general administration must be conducted in harmony with the recognition
of the irrepressible conflict between the capitalist class and the working class."[3]

Like the Wobblies, members of the employing class possessed a keen
awareness of their own class interests, so they readily combined with other
capitalists to advance that interest. These rugged individualists willingly joined
with others of similar standing when the class enemy was at the door or profits
were threatened. In fact, Smith understood that the employers can form their
class associations much easier than workers. Smith observed:

We rarely hear, it has been said, of the combinations of masters;
though frequently of those of workmen. But whoever imagines, upon
this account, that masters rarely combine, is as ignorant of the world
as of the subject. Masters are always and every where in a sort of tacit,
but constant and uniform combination, not to raise the wages of
labour above its actual rate. To violate this combination is everywhere
a most unpopular action, and a sort of reproach to a master among his
neighbours and equals.[4]

When workers resist employers' actions, Mr. Smith sagely observes, the owners "never cease to call aloud for the assistance of the civil magistrate, and the rigorous execution of those laws which have been enacted with so much severity against the combinations of servants, labourers, and journeyman." Workers' attempts at resistance, however, "generally end in nothing but punishment or ruin of the ringleaders," Smith concludes.[5]

Both the Wobblies and employers, then, possessed a clearly conceived and firmly developed understanding of their positions in the class struggle. Wobblies conceived of themselves not only as a union but also as a revolutionary movement. From their first appearance in the Pacific Northwest to the enactment of the 1919 Criminal Syndicalism Act, the Wobblies sought to organize workers into the One Big Union. Immediately, they had to deal with local ordinances designed to halt their advocacy, and they fought pitched battles to defend their First Amendment rights in the Spokane Free Speech Fight of 1909 and the 1911–1912 free speech fight in Aberdeen. These battles, which involved regular beatings, jailings, and deportations of Wobblies, were succeeded by the 1912 Lumber Strike. Wobbly poet Ralph Chaplin explained the challenges that workers, or "timber beasts," faced:

> The "timber beast" was starting to reap the benefits of his organized power. Also he was about to feel the force and hatred of the "interest" arrayed against him. He was soon to learn that the path of labor unionism is strewn with more rocks than roses. He was making an earnest effort to emerge from the squalor and misery of peonage and was soon to see that his overlords were satisfied to keep him right where he had always been.[6]

Although the struggle assumed lower visibility between 1913 and 1915, that changed dramatically in 1916 when the struggle broke into open class warfare with a free speech fight and a wave of business-class terror that culminated in the famous Everett Massacre on Bloody Sunday, November 5.

The IWW continued its campaign to "organize, educate and emancipate" even while the employing class continued its campaign of class repression. Anti-labor mobs, drawing support from businessmen, police, and vigilantes, raided and wrecked IWW halls and beat and deported workers in Centralia, Aberdeen, Hoquiam, and elsewhere. When called upon by the employing class to intervene on its behalf, the federal government conducted raids and prosecutions against radical labor. And as the United States joined World War I, employers began to play the patriotism card by painting the IWW as not only a thorn in the side of businesses but a threat to the war effort and an affront to American values.

The most significant battle in the class war was the 1917 Lumber Strike, which closed down almost all operations and mills on the Red Coast. The *Industrial Worker* described the action in typical class-conscious terms:

> The Lumber Trust, secure in their power in the past, are now up
> against a new condition. They are learning that the power of the
> "Bums" is a power greater than their own. Any worker in the strike
> area who is not on strike is a traitor to his class. The line is distinct.
> Either a worker stands for his interest or he stands for the interest of
> the industrial overlord.[7]

The Federal Mediation Commission, sent to investigate the strike in the hope of settling it in the interest of the war effort, reported in a tone uncharacteristic of government commissions when it suggested that the lumber interest made use of the war to fight the unions. "The I.W.W.," the report noted, "is filling a vacuum created by the operators. The hold of the I.W.W. is riveted instead of weakened by unimaginative opposition to the correction of real grievances."[8] In short, the government appealed to the patriotism of businessmen and urged them to address grievances and settle the strike, something they were unwilling to do. The businessmen themselves were guilty of the very lack of patriotism—or "paytriotism," as the Wobblies said—of which they accused the IWW.

The Wobblies believed unequivocally that the oppressor was the class with property and that the workers' emancipation would necessitate the fall of the old parasitic order and the creation of a new society, in which the rewards of society would go to those who performed its productive labor. The class-conscious employers, and to some lesser degree, their allies in the mainstream press, patriotic groups, and government were aware of the development of class consciousness among members of the IWW and their attempts to influence other workers. From their position, the truly class-conscious worker was a threat that could not be allowed to go unopposed. When the employers' never-ending campaign to produce false consciousness—which was arguably successful with the craft unions—met with failure with the Wobblies,

Portrait of Washington
Governor Ernest Lister,
the man who vetoed the
1917 Washington State
Criminal Syndicalism Act.
In 1919, with Lister gravely
ill, his replacement Louis
F. Hart became governor,
opening the way for passage
of Washington's criminal
syndicalism law. Photo
courtesy of Washington
State Archives.

employers found it necessary to repress the IWW through criminal syndicalism legislation.

With this object in mind, the 1917 Washington State Legislature convened
amid significant publicity, organizing activity, and economic disruption associated with the Wobblies. The IWW appeared to have gained greater strength
and more adherents, thus posing a potent threat to business interests. The 1917
legislative session passed a criminal syndicalism bill in response to alleged
"Wobbly horrors," but in reality, the bill was an attempt to eliminate the threat
the IWW posed to capitalists in general, and the Lumber Trust in particular,
by criminalizing membership in the IWW.[9]

At the conclusion of the 1917 session, however, employers suffered an
unexpected setback when Governor Ernest Lister vetoed the bill. Lister was
generally considered to be politically progressive, but he had waged his own
war on the IWW through the creation of a secret police organization, the
Washington State Secret Service. He had also appealed to federal law enforcement for action against the IWW. But Lister was uncomfortable signing into
law what he termed "class legislation" and felt that the law violated the civil
liberties of citizens and would add to the appeal of radical organizing.[10]

After two more years of intense class conflict, the legislature reconvened in 1919 determined to fire off a broadside of legislation aimed at the Wobblies. Washington State, in fact, already had a Criminal Anarchy Law dating to 1903. The 1903 law made it a felony to advocate the doctrine of criminal anarchy, "that organized government should be overthrown by force or violence, or by assassination of the executive head or any of the executive officials of government, or by any unlawful means."[11] This law predated the IWW, but it was used mainly to prosecute their members. For example, following the 1919 Seattle General Strike, 27 workers, 22 of whom were Wobblies, were charged with criminal anarchy.[12] As in the later criminal syndicalism cases, the charges against the accused were typically membership in, or association with, an organization that advocated unlawful activity. But in 1919 the employing class and its allies in the legislature wanted more certainty in dealing with their economic enemy, and they moved quickly to pass anti-syndicalism, sabotage, and flag laws to protect their interests.

The legislature's most significant action was to override Governor Lister's veto of the 1917 bill. Later in the session, it superseded that bill with a somewhat altered criminal syndicalism bill. By this time Governor Lister was gravely ill. His replacement, Acting Governor Lewis Hart, signed the bill into law. In short, the law "made it criminal to be an IWW or to advocate industrial change through direct action."[13]

In its war against radicals, the 1919 Legislature also passed a sabotage law "to protect certain industrial enterprises wherein persons are employed for wage, and to prevent interference with the management or control thereof, and to prohibit the dissemination of doctrines inimical to industry."[14] Like its criminal syndicalism companion, the Sabotage Act was directed at the IWW. In a vein similar to the syndicalism law, violent action was not necessary to constitute a crime. Mere advocacy of proscribed activity, signs of support for those who advocated sabotage or direct industrial action, or membership in a group that might have advocated such doctrines was plenty to run afoul of the law.

The wording of the Sabotage Act differed somewhat from the anti-syndicalism legislation. However, its additional value as a class weapon is dubious. In his discussion of the anti-syndicalism law, historian and attorney Tom Copeland clearly addresses the real issue:

Laws to safeguard the public from violent attack against the
government and property already existed, and this new law added
no new protection. The law was directed at radicals who spoke out
against existing laws but who otherwise obeyed them. It was not
directed against those who professed a belief in law and order but who
resorted to lawless practices to enforce those beliefs.[15]

Most any activity or advocacy that might be proscribed under the Sabotage Act
could also fall under the scope of the Criminal Syndicalism Act. Indeed, few
prosecutions were initiated under the sabotage statute. In short, the Sabotage
Act appears redundant. It would appear that the employers wanted simply to
have multiple legal options with which to prosecute the class war.

One example of where this legislative overkill actually may have back-
fired came in the case of Kenneth McLennen.[16] McLennen, a member of
the IWW, was initially convicted in King County Superior Court under the
Criminal Syndicalism Act. But the presiding judge in the case charged the jury
that *sabotage* was a crime under Washington law and recited the definition of
sabotage from the 1919 Sabotage Act. On appeal, McLennan won a new trial
when the State Supreme Court ruled that the county judge had instructed the
jury improperly given that McLennen was charged under the Syndicalism Act.
Ironically, the superabundance of anti-labor legislation seemed to have confused and worked against the prosecution.[17]

During the same session of the legislature that had passed the Syndicalism
and Sabotage Bills, it also passed what was commonly called the "Red Flag"
Law, which was also directed at the IWW. Political scientist F. G. Franklin
observed that Washington's flag law was the broadest in scope of any such law
in the country.[18] The law made it a felony to display, own, or possess a

> flag, banner, standard, insignia, badge, emblem, sign, or device of, of
> suggestive of, any organized or unorganized group of persons who, by
> their laws, rules, declarations, doctrines, creeds, purposes, practices,
> or effects, espouse, propose or advocate any theory, principle or form
> of government antagonistic to, or subversive of, the constitution, its
> mandates, or laws of the United States or of this state.[19]

And, if this torturous language was not enough, the statute further declared
that "every article or thing owned or kept in violation of this act is hereby

declared to be pernicious and dangerous to the public welfare and subject to be searched for, seized, forfeited and destroyed."[20]

These three 1919 anti-radical laws joined the existing Washington State Criminal Anarchy Law of 1903 to round out a powerful legislative arsenal in the war against the Wobblies. However, one distinction of the Syndicalism and Sabotage Laws is that they were specifically designed to counteract the direct action tactics the IWW used on the job.

Direct action was certainly the preferred tactic of the IWW. With its syndicalist influence, the IWW favored economic action over political participation such as voting or working for political reforms.[21] They viewed the political realm as but a mirror of the economic realm and political power as a mere reflection of private wealth. Vincent St. John, one of the organization's founders, captured the Wobbly view when he testified that the capitalist government was "a committee to look after the interests of the employers."[22] The front line of the class war was not political, but economic. It was on the job, at the point of production. As St. John put it, "All peace as long as the wage system lasts is but an armed truce." He advised workers to bring economic pressure to bear against employers. This pressure included strikes, which were not merely to achieve better wages or working conditions, but also a means to achieve working-class solidarity and to weaken the boss. Other tactics workers could employ included propaganda, free speech fights, boycotts, industrial organizing, the general strike, and sabotage.[23]

The issue of sabotage is of paramount interest as a tactic in the class struggle. It involved "the removal of efficiency." A prominent Wobbly, Elizabeth Gurley Flynn provides one of the most frequently cited descriptions of sabotage:

> Sabotage means either to slacken up and interfere with the quality,
> or to botch in your skill and interfere with the quality of capitalist
> production so as to give poor service. It is something that is fought
> out within the walls of the shop. Sabotage is not physical violence;
> sabotage is an internal industrial process. It is simply another form of
> coercion.[24]

The Washington State Supreme Court, considering one Wobbly case, turned to the *Encyclopedia Americana* for a definition of sabotage, and cited it as follows in its opinion:

> Sabotage, a method used by labor revolutionist to force employers to accede to demands made on them. It consists in a willful obstruction and interference with the normal processes of industry. It aims at inconveniencing and tying up all production, but stops short of actual destruction or of endangering human life directly.... Some of the more common forms are waste of material; telling the exact truth to customers; obeying orders punctiliously ... and any number of petty devices for hindering and delaying production.[25]

Sabotage was seldom, if ever, associated with physical violence in IWW writings and propaganda.[26] Not only did the IWW not associate sabotage with physical violence, it also opposed the use or advocacy of violence except in self-defense. It is significant that no member of the IWW was ever convicted of the act of sabotage, only for membership in an organization that advocated it.[27]

The employers and the commercial press, however, utterly misrepresented the Wobblies on the issues of sabotage and violence. This misrepresentation encouraged the public to associate the IWW and radical labor with violence and un-American activity. Even George Creel, President Wilson's Director of Public Information during the First World War, realized just how badly the IWW position on violence was misrepresented. "Just as every untoward incident was credited to the German spy system," he wrote, "so was every disorder, every manifestation of unrest ascribed either to the IWW or to the Bolsheviki."[28] According to Robert Bruere, writing for the *New York Evening Post*, Washington State lumbermen even admitted to the President's Mediation Commission that their own press agents were responsible for giving the IWW its violent reputation.[29]

Probably the most salient point about the Wobblies, with respect to violence, is that they were portrayed as a violent, lawless, and terrorist bunch, but they seldom practiced violence except in self-defense. The Wobblies were loud and disdainful of authority, but they were surprisingly nonviolent. This stands in marked contrast with the actions of the IWW's accusers, the employing class and its allies, who practiced individual and collective violence against the Wobblies on a regular basis. The employing class, touted for its rugged individualism, self-sufficiency, and Hobbesian view of human nature, organized quickly and efficiently as a class in associations and clubs to counter its class enemy. Its libertarianism turned quickly communitarian when its class interest seemed threatened.

Just as the IWW used an array of tactics in its struggle with the Red Coast lumbermen, so too the employers organized to wield a wide range of weapons in their struggle with the working class. Abandoning their libertarian ethos, employers called upon government to criminalize and prosecute radical work- ers under the 1919 Criminal Syndicalism and associated acts. Sabotage and violence—the very charges capitalists leveled against the Wobblies—were also both weapons in the employers' anti-union arsenal. For example, although production slowdowns are generally described by capitalists as adjustments to market conditions—adjustments intended to reduce labor costs and drive up prices—they are in fact a form of work slowdown, which might well be regarded as sabotage. Naturally, legislative attempts to amend the Sabotage Act to make acts of sabotage applicable to employers who profiteered on food prices or who tried to reduce wages failed, once again demonstrating the obvi- ous class nature of this legislation.[30]

In addition to production slowdowns, employers, in their all-consuming desire for profits, also promoted unsafe working conditions, conditions that led to the maiming and deaths of countless workers. They also promoted violence against workers more directly, for example, when they hired private police to spy on, harass, and beat workers, or organized vigilante groups to do the same. The employers could speak with great authority about violence and sabotage because they had mastered their infinite variety of forms.

An early victim of this spate of 1919 class legislation was Mike Hennessy, who in 1920 was convicted in Clark County in southwest Washington. His crime was one of association; he had become a member of the Industrial Workers of the World. By "joining the statutorily prohibited group," the High Court later proclaimed, the "defendant became guilty of the offense whether or not he intended to violate the law."[31] Hennessy appealed his conviction to the Washington State Supreme Court, but the court upheld the conviction and the Criminal Syndicalism Law on January 25, 1921. Hennessy's attorney, George Vanderveer, raised over a dozen issues, one of which claimed that the law amounted to class legislation. The court dutifully waded through the issues raised by the appellant and dismissed them all, thereby setting a prec- edent. When subsequent syndicalism cases came before Washington courts with objections similar to those raised by Vanderveer, the courts referenced Hennessy and dismissed them all.

In dismissing Vanderveer's claim that the Syndicalism Law amounted to class legislation, the court asserted that the law could be applied to any person or group who violated its provisions. "The act is general in its terms and provides that 'whoever' shall do the things there prohibited, shall be guilty of a felony under this language." The court continued, "anyone no matter what his business association or professional calling might be, who did the things prohibited by the act, would be subject to its provisions."[32] So with great ease, and perhaps even with a straight collective face, the court dismissed the class issue. But the anti-syndicalism legislation was clearly directed at the IWW. The Employers' Association of Washington Law, as Vanderveer called it, had been championed by lumber and other business interests. The court, in fact, was entirely disingenuous, since it was commonly understood by friend and by foe alike that the legislation was directed at this radical union organization.

Washington's own governor acknowledged that the legislation was directed specifically at the Wobblies. Governor Lister, in his veto message of the 1917 bill, declared: "By its advocates, it is hoped that its enactment into law will bring about the elimination of the doctrines advocated by members of an organization known as the Industrial Workers of the World from the state, and makes it a felony to discuss or advocate such doctrines."[33] In a letter to Governor Lister encouraging him to veto the bill, H. L. Hughes of the AFL declared, "Senate Bill #264 was introduced and passed the legislature for the purpose of striking at some of the practices of the Industrial Workers of the World." Hughes asserted that the measure passed by an overwhelming vote "because of the intense hatred for and prejudice against the I.W.W. entertained by many members of the Senate and the House."[34] Among the bill's proponents, according to Dorothy Schmidt, "No attempt was made to disguise the fact that the law was directed against the Industrial Workers of the World and most of the legislature considered it was special legislation against that group."[35]

It is also worth pointing out that many of the Washington State legislators who voted in favor of the anti-radical bills were either members of, or associated with, business interests. As Eldridge Dowell, the most comprehensive authority on criminal syndicalism legislation notes, the legislators were "essentially of the employer attitude of mind and had an interest of their own in preserving the existing industrial and economic order. They believed their own welfare was involved in preserving from destruction or substantial restriction those interests which the I.W.W. was fighting."[36]

The 1917 Criminal Syndicalism bill was introduced by Senators E. B. Palmer and E. J. Cleary. Palmer was an attorney with close ties to the lumber industry, and Cleary was an important lumberman. In the House, W. W. Connor and E. H. Guie led the override of Lister's veto. Guie worked on legislative affairs for the Federated Industries of Washington, and Conner was a shipbuilder.[37] Frank G. Barnes, who penned the original draft of the revised criminal syndicalism bill of 1919, was a Red Coast lumberman and farmer from Cowlitz County.[38]

After passage of the 1917 bill, Governor Lister was besieged with telegrams from lumbermen and employers' groups requesting that he sign the bill. Alex Polson, president of Polson Lumber Company, informed Lister of the popularity of the bill by noting that it "is a sabotage bill, and [one] which nearly everyone except the IWWs are in favor of."[39] Centralia lumberman F. B. Hubbard wrote Lister that "we do not believe this law will work a hardship on loyal American citizens." Grays Harbor lumberman Frank Lamb echoed the business line: "We believe Washington Business and Industries are entitled to the protection against illegal and criminal methods afforded by . . . [S.B] 264." A telegram from Fischer Brothers Company informed the governor that if he were to sign the bill "confidence will be in great measure restored in the minds of our Eastern investors."[40]

Two failed amendments to the sabotage bill provide additional evidence that the anti-radical laws of 1917 and 1919 were class legislation. One amendment aimed at including food profiteers within the reach of the bill. Another aimed at businesses that reduced output in order to increase prices, or threatened to close operation to reduce wages. But these proposed amendments received little support. The legislation was aimed at the working class, and the legislature was concerned only with working-class sabotage, not sabotage committed by employers.[41]

Representative George Hodgdon, an outlier as a consistent defender of the working class, introduced legislation titled the "Criminal Patrioteering" bill. Drafting it was easy, since Representative Hodgdon simply used the wording of the 1917 criminal syndicalism bill, but replaced the term "criminal syndicalism" with the term "criminal patrioteering." This was reminiscent of the common Wobbly practice of using the music of popular hymns, but changing the words to fit the workers' message. Not surprisingly, Hodgdon's bill failed to make it out of committee.

However, one interesting change in wording was made in the revised criminal syndicalism bill of 1919. Criminal syndicalism was not mentioned by name; rather the bill targeted "whoever shall advocate, advise, teach or justify crime, sedition, violence, intimidation or injury as a means or way of effecting or resisting any industrial, economic, social or political change." The words "or resisting" were added to the sentence. Historian Albert Gunns notes that liberals and labor leaders hoped that "the inclusion of the words 'or resisting' . . . would make the law as applicable to reactionaries as to radicals." Gunns also observed that the new law "was apparently partially designed to allay criticism that it constituted class legislation."[42] In point of fact, the wording intentionally or unintentionally offered a legal loophole to those who argued that the legislation could be applied to anyone or any group that violated the provision of the law. And that is exactly what the State Supreme Court did by declaring that on its face the law did not single out a group and could be applied to any group. Of course, that claim ignores both the intent and the application of the law, which was written and used only to attack the Wobblies.

The employers' new weapon against the IWW was soon put to use in a crackdown against IWW members in this Washington, and the Wobblies were also targeted elsewhere under similar laws. Since it effectively criminalized association and membership in the organization, it proved to be the weapon of choice in the employers' effort to destroy their enemy. The first arrests came quickly, when injured worker R. E. Eddy and eighteen-year-old Perry St. Louis were arrested in Tacoma and charged with criminal syndicalism. As the *Industrial Worker* reported, the new law would "be used against any worker that has a tendency to cut into the profits of the masters."[43]

In November 1919, after the Centralia Tragedy, the crackdown gained momentum. Historian Robert Tyler reports that "Attorney General Thompson advised the county prosecutors to rush I.W.W. cases under the Washington Criminal Syndicalism law through the courts, to try defendants *en masse* to save taxpayers' money and to insure more convictions, and to keep a close check on jury panels to see that only 'courageous and patriotic' jurors would be chosen."[44] The Employers' Association of Washington reported that seventy-four cases of criminal syndicalism resulted in fifty-two convictions as of May 1, 1920. In his excellent biography of Centralia IWW attorney, Elmer Smith, Tom Copeland noted that Smith defended about twenty criminal syndicalism defendants, and the famous Wobbly lawyer George Vanderveer defended even more.[45] In the Wobbly hotbed of Grays Harbor, authorities rounded up dozens of IWWs, charging them with criminal syndicalism.[46]

Much has been written about IWW strikes and other activities—both violent and nonviolent—which characterized the labor struggle of this period.

But central to any account of the Wobblies must be a clear understanding of something that both the Wobblies and the employers understood all too well: every strike, every free speech fight, every piece of legislation that touched on the workplace, and every involvement of the government on one side or the other was a tactic in the class war that played out on the Red Coast. The Washington Criminal Syndicalism Law, as class legislation, serves to illuminate that struggle.

9

Class War Violence

CENTRALIA 1919

Around Centralia are wooded hills; men have been beaten
beneath these trees and lynched from them. The beautiful Chehalis
River flows near by; Wesley Everest was left dangling from one
of its bridges. But Centralia is provokingly pretty for all that. It is
small wonder that lumber trust henchmen wish to keep it all for
themselves.[1]

The Centralia American Legion and the leading businessmen of that city
had more than a parade in mind when they gathered on November 11, 1919,
to celebrate Armistice Day. Apparently believing that the spectacle of political violence would enhance the patriotic experience, they concocted a plan
to raid the Centralia IWW Hall. IWW halls were of great practical and sym-
bolic importance to workers. As Wobbly activist and historian Ralph Chaplin
explains, the halls were loved by workers, but despised by employers. These
"churches of the movement," as public historian Robert Weyeneth called
them, represented the closest thing to a home for many wandering IWW
members.[2] Chaplin noted:

It is here the men can gather around a crackling wood fire, smoke
their pipes and warm their souls with the glow of comradeship. Here
they can, between jobs or after work, discuss the vicissitudes of their
daily lives, read their books and magazines and sing their songs of
solidarity, or merely listen to the "tinned" humor or harmony of the
much prized Victrola. Also they here attend to the affairs of their

union—line up members, hold business and educational meetings
and a weekly "open forum."[3]

So, as the parading legionnaires passed the hall for the second time, they
paused, then charged the hall, only to be surprised by the spirited defense
they encountered. A volley of gunfire dropped three of the attackers, but the
mob continued to press home its attack, capturing the hall. One additional
legionnaire was killed in pursuit of Wesley Everest, who escaped out the back
but was later captured and dragged by the neck to the jail. Later that night,
he joined the ranks of IWW martyrs when he was lynched at the hands of
Centralia businessmen and patriots, none of whom were ever prosecuted for
his gruesome murder.

The Armistice Day 1919 Centralia event is perhaps the single most written
about event involving the IWW in the entire state of Washington. Analysis of
the event has been extremely polarized, as interests representing the employing class and the working class have contested its meaning. And because of
competing accounts, affidavits, and testimony, even some of the most basic
facts of the case will probably never be established conclusively. What is perfectly clear is that the Centralia story must be understood in the context of
the class struggle that had been raging on the Red Coast for over a decade and
which had surfaced in Centralia since at least 1914. As all of the working-class
accounts of the Centralia event note, violence and lawlessness were defining
characteristics of the employers' approach to this conflict.

The IWW served as the most logical target of employers' violence and
repression because, since its inception in 1905, it represented the most
advanced, class conscious, and revolutionary element of the working class
in this country. The patriotic fervor of the First World War and fear that the
Russian Revolution would heighten class consciousness among American
workers only intensified persecution of the Wobblies. Sensing an opportunity, employers engaged both the state and the public in their efforts to crush
the hated IWW. Nationally, the federal government enforced the wartime
Espionage and Sedition Acts against the IWW and other radicals to imprison
and deport many. In September of 1917, the federal government raided IWW
halls across the country and indicted more than 160 leaders of the organization. At the state and local level, class warfare raged as employers mobilized
both the state and the mob to lash out at class-conscious workers. Washington
State was one of the great theaters of this conflict, as the teens witnessed the

Grays Harbor and Pacific County Lumber Strike of 1912, multiple free speech fights, the 1916 Everett Massacre, and the 1919 Seattle General Strike.

In Centralia, this war against workers effectively merged employers' traditional weapons—a cooperative police, a captive legal system, and vigilante citizens' committees—with the anti-radicalism and patriotism of the American Legion, a veterans' organization at the fore of anti-radical activities. The American Legion described Centralia like this: "The city is the center of a rich timber district and the logging camps of the northwest are infested with bearers of the red card, who boast that in many districts membership in the I.W.W. is a requisite to employment."[4] The leadership of the Centralia Legion read like a roster of Centralia businessmen and the Legion became essentially a front organization, even the vanguard, for Northwest lumber bosses. In the words of Wobbly Ralph Chaplin, "The American Legion began to function as a cat's paw for the men behind the scenes."[5] Indeed, there was nothing secret about the role of the Legion in the class war. The National Commander of the American Legion declared in 1923: "If ever needed, the American Legion stands ready to protect our country's institutions and ideals as the Fascisti dealt with the destructionists who menaced Italy. . . . Do not forget that the Fascisti are to Italy what the American Legion is to the United States."[6]

Representatives of capital did not shy away from class conflict. An IWW organizer was run out of Centralia by the sheriff in 1914, and in early 1915 more Wobblies were "escorted" out of town by police and vigilantes.[7] According to historian John McClelland, the local paper, the *Centralia Chronicle*, applauded anti-Wobbly repression and stated that it was everyone's responsibility to keep rebel workers out of Centralia.[8] Tom Lassiter, a partially blind newsstand operator whose stock included labor and radical papers, was victimized by the business interest on several occasions. At various times, his radical papers were destroyed, he was threatened, arrested, kidnapped, and dumped in a ditch. Yet no one was ever prosecuted for any of these acts of class violence.[9] In Centralia, it was clear, the law was a weapon in the hands of the propertied class.

Perhaps inevitably, class conflict in Centralia came to center on the struggle to establish and defend an IWW union hall. As Chaplin notes, the "union halls were a standing challenge to their [the employers'] hitherto undisputed right to the complete domination of the forests. . . . They were not going to tolerate the encroachments of the One Big Union of the lumber workers."[10] In 1917, an IWW attempt to establish a hall was met with great hostility in the employer-dominated town, and the landlord evicted the Wobblies on learning of their

identity. In the spring of 1918, Centralia employers targeted the town's new
IWW hall. During a Red Cross parade, prominent businessmen, including
members of the Centralia Elks, and political officials attacked and destroyed
it. They beat IWW members and burned hall property and records in a street
bonfire. F. B. Hubbard, the most prominent of the Centralia timber barons
and president of the Washington Employers' Association, stole the desk from
the Wobbly Hall and donated it to the local Chamber of Commerce.[11] Despite
the intimidation of the business leaders, the local IWW secretary, Britt Smith,
opened a new hall on north Tower Avenue on September 1, 1919. It was clear
for all to see that the IWW was not easily intimidated, but neither were their
enemies.

In July 1919, George Russell, secretary of the Washington Employers'
Association, called a meeting of the Centralia Chamber of Commerce to find
a way to destroy the IWW. F. B. Hubbard was picked to head a group designed
to accomplish that objective.[12] Although this was not the first meeting of
Centralia business interests to combat the Wobbly threat, it marked a new
level of organization on the part of capital that would not tolerate the affront
the new IWW Hall afforded to its dominance.

Plans to rid themselves of the enemy intensified with the formation of the
Centralia Citizens Protective Association, the purpose of which, according to
one local paper, was "to combat IWW activities in this vicinity."[13] Local businessmen were members of the Chamber of Commerce, the Centralia Elks,
and the American Legion; many belonged to more than one of these organizations. Although the plans called for greater secrecy as to the specific methods
to rid themselves of the Wobblies, too many people were aware of the plans to
keep it secret. Word began to leak out, and soon it became public knowledge
that the IWW would be driven out of town. Once the Armistice Day Parade
was planned, the Wobblies knew that this was the pretense to attack their hall,
destroy their property, and assault them.[14]

Initially, IWW members acted with uncommon prudence in attempting
to prevent a violent attack on their hall. The owners of the Roderick Hotel,
which housed the union hall and from whom the IWW rented, went to the
local police with information about the planned attack. IWW members
requested police protection. A trusted attorney, Elmer Smith, sought help
from Governor Louis F. Hart in Olympia. The Wobblies even made a desperate appeal to the entire community. They distributed a lengthy handbill "to the
law-abiding citizens of Centralia and to the working class in general," which

said, in part, "The profiteering class of Centralia have of late been waving the flag of our country in an endeavor to incite the lawless element of our city to raid our hall and club us out of town." But Wobbly pleas to avoid violence fell on deaf ears, and the police chief declined protection.[15]

Finally, as a last resort, the Wobblies sought legal advice from attorney Elmer Smith to determine whether they had the legal right to defend their hall with arms. Smith affirmed that they did. This was a major move on the part of the IWW. Although it had usually shown remarkable restraint, the IWW was a defiant and proud group of class-conscious workers, and by November 1919 in Centralia Washington the Wobblies had had enough of the beatings, enough of the tar and featherings, enough of the destruction of their meager property, enough of the humiliation, and enough of the criminally brutal business-patriotic element. They would defend their hall, and plans for its self-defense were laid. Radical historian Harvey O'Conner opined: "Prudent men, valuing their own skins, would have closed the hall in the face of the obvious threat. But prudence was not a Wobbly trait. Rather their shining glory stood out in audacity, courage, and stubbornness in defense of their rights, and for that they are remembered in history."[16]

As the Armistice Day Parade got under way on the drizzly and ill-fated afternoon of November 11, 1919, the Wobblies made ready to defend their hall. They positioned armed men inside the hall and also in three locations outside the hall: in the Avalon and Arnold Hotels on the opposite (east) side of the street, and on Seminary Hill which overlooked the street from some considerable distance away.[17] The parade route took the marchers north on Tower Avenue past the main business district to Third Street, the next side street past the IWW Hall, in a section of town occupied by businesses catering to the working class. At Third Street the marchers reversed direction to return now southbound on Tower Avenue with the Centralia American Legion contingent making up the rear of the parade. In front of the IWW Hall, the marchers paused and then rushed the hall.[18]

Shots rang out from the hall and then from Seminary Hill and the Avalon Hotel. Three Legionnaires—Warren Grimm, Arthur McElfresh, and Ben Cassagranda—received fatal wounds on the streets near the hall, and Dale Hubbard, the nephew of the lumbar baron F. B. Hubbard, was shot by a fleeing Wesley Everest at the edge of the Skookumchuck river. Hubbard died later that night. Several other marchers were injured, and the IWW Hall was smashed and its contents dragged to the street and burned. Wesley Everest was severely beaten and dragged back into town and thrown in a heap on the jail floor. One of the marchers who pursued Everest to the river and presumably helped drag him to the jail was Legionnaire Ed Cunningham, who was picked by the American Legion to become the Special Prosecutor in the trial against the Centralia Wobblies. According to the Legion account, "Cunningham was able to use his first-hand knowledge of the tragedy to telling effect."[19]

In many of their clashes with the working class, employers hired detective agencies or relied on local or state police to combat workers, but in Centralia the American Legion served as the armed guard of the employing class. As news of the event spread, the American Legion assumed control of the town, controlled the flow of information, formed vigilante groups to hunt down suspected Wobblies, and raided establishments and homes. In touting the Legion takeover, the *American Legion Weekly* stated, "Though the office of the Sheriff and the Chief of Police assisted as much as possible, their forces were small and their aid nominal," and "Posses which scoured the country about Centralia in search of fugitives were made up almost exclusively of American Legion men"[20]

That evening, two meetings were held at the Elks Club in which the murder of Wesley Everest was conceivably planned. At about five o'clock a group of men was told to go the armory for weapons and return to the Elks at six o'clock. At the six o'clock meeting, all assembled men who were not members of the Elks or the American Legion were asked to leave. In effect, this left the established business class and the Legion, those that could most be trusted to carry out a class lynching and protect those involved in it. This meeting lasted until about seven o'clock. At seven-thirty, someone visited the city's power station and shut off all the lights in Centralia. Meanwhile, a lynching party entered the jail where Wesley Everest was held. The lynching party—meeting no opposition from the jailer—seized Everest and dragged him to a waiting automobile.[21]

The automobile that held Everest fell in with a procession of automobiles containing Centralia's most prominent citizens, and proceeded to the Chehalis River Bridge. Radical author Harvey O'Conner graphically described the scene:

> At the bridge Everest was dragged out and rope knotted around
> his neck, and his body flung over. Everest clutched at a plank;
> Legionnaires stamped on his fingers, and he fell. Dissatisfied with the

knot, the lynchers pulled the body back up and used a longer rope, and hurled the body over again. Still dissatisfied, they hauled Everest body up a third time—by then he must have been dead—and tied a more professional knot on a longer rope and flung the body over. Then with carlights playing on the scene, they amused themselves awhile by shooting at the swaying body. Satiated at last, the mob left and darkness returned. Next morning somebody cut the rope and the body fell into the Chehalis River.[22]

The next day, Everest's mutilated body was retrieved from the river, dumped on the jail floor, and left for two days in plain view of his imprisoned fellow workers. As Centralia's authorities were no doubt complicit in the lynching, no attempt was ever made to bring the Everest's murderers to justice.

As the Legion-led posses combed the surrounding area for more Wobblies, state authorities interrogated the jailed Wobblies by day as the enraged mobs terrorized them by night. In the woods surrounding Centralia, one posse member was shot and killed when he was mistaken by another for a Wobbly. This shooting, first reported as a murder committed by a Wobbly, was later ruled an accident. As this reign of terror continued in southwest Washington, the commercial press continued to churn out propagandistic accounts of how the Wobblies ambushed and murdered America's finest young men in the streets of Centralia. Characteristic of this treatment was the front-page article in the *Chehalis Bee-Nugget*: "IWW Shoot into Armistice Day Parade in Centralia Tuesday. Warren Grimm, Arthur McElfresh, Dale Hubbard, and Ben Cassagranda Killed by the Assassins."[23] Authorities, businessmen, and Legionnaires combined to attack workers in other parts of the state and in neighboring Oregon. In Seattle, the Department of Justice seized the *Union Record*, the official organ of the Seattle Central Labor Council, and arrested its staff, including Harry Ault and Anna Louise Strong, on charges of sedition.[24]

The passions that this class war engendered were still highly visible on January 26, 1920, when eleven Wobblies, including Elmer Smith, the attorney who advised the IWW members that they had the legal right to defend their hall, were brought to trial in the town of Montesano, the county seat of neighboring Grays Harbor County. The defense faced many obstacles in the trial, beginning with a huge resource disparity. The Wobblies were represented by George Vanderveer with occasional help from his law partner, Ralph Pierce, and attorney Elmer Smith, himself a defendant in the case. Meanwhile, Special

I. W. W. DEFENDANTS IN MONTESANO TRIAL

Top Row—(1) Loren Roberts, (2) Roy Becker, (3) Britt Smith, (4) Elmer C. Smith, Centralia Attorney. Second Row—(5) Eugene Burnett, (center) Mrs. Elmer C. Smith and, her daughter, (6) James Mclnery. Third Row—(7) Mike Sheehan, (8) Bert Bland. Bottom Row—(9) John Lamb, (10) Bert Falkner, (11) O. C. Bland.

The IWW defendants in the trial held in Montesano. In the center is a photograph of "Mrs. Elmer C. Smith and her daughter," wife and daughter of IWW attorney, Elmer Smith. This image appeared in the *Industrial Worker*, February 14, 1920.

Prosecutor Ed Cunningham led a staff of six attorneys, whom Vanderveer referred to as the attorneys for the lumber trust. The Luke May Secret Service, a private detective agency paid for by lumber company funds, aided them. Finally, the American Legion recruited some fifty uniformed veterans to sit in on the trial by day, presumably to influence the jury. They were paid four dollars a day from funds contributed by the lumber companies and the Elks.[25]

The prosecution certainly lived up to its reputation as the counsel for the lumber trust. Special Prosecutor Cunningham was himself deeply involved in the Armistice Day violence. He was one of the members of the mob that pursued Everest to the Skookumchuck River and helped drag him to jail. He watched while the mob broke into the jail and kidnapped Everest, and was alleged to have witnessed his murder.[26] Historian Tom Copeland observed that "as Cunningham built the case against the Wobblies, he was also shielding himself from any potential legal action for his role in the raid and lynching." Cunningham's team successfully fought off a change of venue request, claiming there was no prejudice against the IWW in either Centralia or Montesano. In a clear attempt to intimidate anyone willing to testify for the defense, the prosecution had two defense witnesses arrested for perjury when they finished their testimony. The prosecution called on the governor to have troops from Camp Lewis sent to Montesano to stand guard outside the courtroom, thereby frightening the jury into thinking that an IWW attack was imminent.[27]

The trial was, in fact, a mere extension of the class war, a political trial in which the authorities put the IWW on trial while pretending to adhere to the rule of law. The judge, John M. Wilson, insisted that he could try the case impartially, despite the fact that he had delivered an anti-IWW speech in the nearby town of Bucoda and had addressed the memorial service at the Centralia Elks commemorating the Legionnaires who had been killed during the Armistice Day Parade. Wilson rejected the defense's request for a change of venue from Montesano, disallowed much of the evidence that Vanderveer tried to introduce during the trial, and made numerous prejudicial rulings that favored the prosecution and infuriated the defense.[28] Vanderveer captured the trial's essence in his closing statement. The prosecutors, he told the jury, "have told you this was a murder trial, and not a labor trial. But vastly more than the lives of ten men are the stakes in the big gamble here; for the right of workers to organize for the bettering of their own condition is on trial; the right of free assemblage is on trial; democracy and Americanism are on trial."[29]

"In view of such a charged atmosphere," Albert Gunns contended, "the final verdict of the jury was moderate."[30] The prosecution sought a first-degree murder verdict for all of the defendants, but the jury did not agree. Elmer Smith, the Wobbly attorney, was acquitted, along with one other defendant. Seven defendants were convicted of second-degree murder, and one young defendant was judged legally insane. The jury attached to their verdict a written request for leniency in sentencing, but Judge Wilson rendered stiff sentences ranging from 25 to 40 years in the state penitentiary in Walla Walla. Irish immigrant James McInerney, himself a veteran of the Everett Massacre and victim of torture while in the Centralia jail, died while imprisoned, "murdered," the *Industrial Worker* proclaimed, "by the Capitalist class."[31] Most of the remaining prisoners remained incarcerated until 1933, when Governor Clarence Martin commuted their sentences.[32]

Several jurors were clearly uneasy with their decision, believing that they were not allowed to hear all of the important evidence. "Remarkably, two years after the trial," Robert Weyeneth concludes, "seven of the twelve jurors voluntarily repudiated their verdict."[33] No member of the employing class or its "cat paws" was ever charged or even investigated for Everest's murder or the Armistice Day hall raid that ushered in the Centralia Tragedy.

10

Fellow Worker William McKay

In the early afternoon of May 8, 1923, more than a thousand workers paraded through the streets of Aberdeen, Washington, carrying banners and waving red flags. The workers marched in commemoration of their fallen comrade, William McKay, an Irish-born logger, who had been shot in the back of the head by a company gunman while picketing.[1] Yet although this parade sought to be many things to its participants—a commemoration, a show of solidarity during the still ongoing general strike, and an overall demonstration of power in a town long known for its militant working class—the truth is that McKay's memory did not last. Stories of the shooting appeared in local and regional newspapers, and the radical press pushed for the gunman's conviction.[2] But by the end of May, McKay's killer had escaped any punishment, and the Wobbly's death, like that of so many working people, was forgotten to all but those closest to him.[3]

McKay's murder came in the heat of battle, as thousands of Grays Harbor men and women had joined their fellow workers in many parts of the world in a general strike to free class war prisoners such as those, like James McInerney, imprisoned as a result of the Centralia tragedy. The strike and funeral march that followed were vivid demonstrations of working-class power in the community. Striking Wobblies had closed down logging camps, docks, and lumber mills, including the notorious Grays Harbor Commercial Company in Cosmopolis, the lone mill in Grays Harbor to have never before been closed by a strike.

The Wobblies consistently threatened the power and profits of Grays Harbor lumbermen throughout the 1910s, but much of the IWW program during the 1920s revolved around its defense of those class war prisoners held in the Leavenworth, San Quentin, and Walla Walla penitentiaries. Authorities throughout the Red Coast arrested Wobblies and suspected Wobblies on charges of criminal syndicalism under the notorious 1919 law that criminalized membership in, and support for, the IWW. Dozens of IWWs were arrested in the Red Coast between November 12, 1919, and 1922.[4]

The struggles to free these political prisoners took on many forms. Wobblies wrote propaganda pamphlets, collected donations for the defense fund, and sponsored speaking tours by the likes of long-time militants James Rowan and James P. Thompson.[5] But the IWW preferred direct action to political electioneering or legal maneuvers.[6] Thus, few could have been surprised when, during October 1922, the IWW General Executive Board decided to call for a general strike to free all class war prisoners.[7] This strike, which eventually spread across the nation and affected tens of thousands of workers, became the centerpiece of the Wobblies' struggle to free their fellow workers. As could be expected, however, the Wobbly preference for militant direct action also gave employers reason to bear their fangs. Indeed, once the general strike commenced, this is precisely what happened, and with the assistance of a sympathetic state apparatus, these employers were able to get away with murder.

Meanwhile, organization in Grays Harbor continued in haste. Letters poured in from the towns and camps of the Harbor throughout 1922–1923, and IWW membership around the nation rapidly climbed. In late 1922 the IWW laid an ultimatum at President Warren G. Harding's doorstep: release all class war prisoners held in federal and state penitentiaries or face a general strike beginning May 1, International Workers' Day.[8]

Beginning in the first decade of the twentieth century, Red Coast workers celebrated May Day by parading in the streets. On occasion, as on May 1, 1903, May Day festivities were planned and carried out by branches of the local labor movement with little clear participation by more radical elements. This parade differed little from a traditional Labor Day celebration as unions, including the sailors, longshoremen, tailors, and molders marched alongside the Aberdeen Fire Department Band. The pro-business *Aberdeen Herald* remarked on its "success," but noted that a "general parade" had to be canceled, otherwise participants would have carried out a "much larger street demonstration."[9]

Sometimes workers used May Day as an occasion to strike against local employers. Brewery workers employed at the Aberdeen Brewing Company joined union members throughout Western Washington in declaring a strike on May Day, 1905, to force employers to recognize the closed shop.

Although the six-months-long strike ended in a compromise between workers and employers, the contract included language that incorporated the strikers' demands: "Only union men in good standing who are members of the International Union of United Brewery Workmen of America shall be employed in all breweries and malthouses."[10]

Most May Day events were organized by radical groups, chiefly Grays Harbor socialists, Wobblies, and members of the local communist movement. In the early 1910s, as Harbor socialists grew in membership and influence, they turned out in force to celebrate the First of May. Grays Harbor socialists planned an elaborate series of activities for May Day 1911, including a parade led by the Red Finn band, a series of street meetings and hall orations, a public feast, and an evening of dancing and socializing at the Red Finn Hall.[11] Northwest Wobblies also commemorated the workers' holiday by declaring strikes and making demands on employers and the state. On May 1, 1912, the *Industrial Worker* ran an eight-page commemorative May Day issue calling on Wobblies to "Drop Your Tools—Show Your Power" in a front-page headline.[12]

On April 25, 1923, the *Industrial Worker* ran a giant headline reading: "Strike One—Strike All!" Many workers across the nation had already begun to pour off the job. Three-thousand dock workers struck in San Pedro, California, and striking workers tied up shipping along the East, West, and Gulf coasts. By the end of April, thirty logging camps were closed down in the Portland area alone.[13]

Grays Harbor was one of the centers of strike activity. At the start of May, loggers had shut down at least forty camps. Wobbly James Pezzanis wrote that there were "30 or 40 men in each mill, distributing hand bills and talking to the workers as they come off the job."[14] In all, between four thousand and five thousand Grays Harbor mill workers, loggers, longshoremen, and clam diggers struck in late April and early May 1923 to free class war prisoners.[15]

Among the Wobblies' greatest successes was the aforementioned strike at the Grays Harbor Commercial Company in Cosmopolis. Dubbed the "penitentiary" because of its strict labor discipline and hyper-exploitative hiring practices, this was the lone mill in the region to avoid being closed by a strike during the 1910s. "Penitentiary" management regularly used imported strikebreakers, barbed wire, and armed guards to keep picketers away from the plant. Their violent anti-unionism failed, however, to prevent "penitentiary" workers from shutting the mill down on May 3, when 450 out of the

600 Commercial Company's mill workers walked off the job. Determined to spread the strike, these workers marched en masse to the Bay City Mill, where they set up informational pickets outside the mill gates.[16]

Unlike the Commercial Company, the Bay City Mill had been closed by strikes on numerous occasions during its long history. Formed as the ironically named "Union Mill" (the name referred to the Union side in the Civil War), Harbor lumbermen S. M Anderson, A. W. Middleton, G. E. Anderson, and H. N. Anderson purchased it in February 1912. They reorganized it as the Bay City Lumber Company only a month before the massive IWW lumber strike of that year. In 1914, the mill employed 125 workers and produced 150,000 board feet of lumber per day.[17] Like many Northwest mills, the Bay City produced only lumber, not shingles, and thus had little interaction with the unionized shingle weavers, the lone group of unionists to maintain their organization during the early twentieth century. The firm's owners maintained an intense hostility to unionized workers and strikes. In April 1912, the IWW's *Industrial Worker* described the actions of one of the mill's owners during the Wobbly-led lumber strike: "Mill owner Anderson, swinging a heavy club and brandishing a revolver, urged his thugs to shoot down the workers. . . . He had shot a workingman who had come after his pay and who was leaving the vicinity of violence. Shot from behind. He may recover."[18] The Bay City owners' enmity toward unions extended to AFL organizations as well. A 1915 pamphlet produced by the International Union of Timber Workers separated Northwest lumber operations into categories based on their management's views of unions. Produced to aid union workers in finding jobs, it sorted logging camps, lumber and shingle mills, and other wood products operations into "opposes union," "tolerates union," and "fair to union" groups. The Bay City Mill was solidly in the "opposes union" camp.[19] To keep the Bay City Mill "union free," its owners employed a gunman to guard the plant.

IWW logger William McKay was one of the workers who picketed at the Commercial Company and Bay City mills on May 3, 1923. McKay was an Irish immigrant who came to North America at an early age. Stopping first in Chicago, he found his way west to British Columbia, where he took up logging. Like tens of thousands of Pacific Northwest loggers, McKay was drawn to the radical message of the One Big Union. This message made McKay and other fellow workers potential targets of the wrath of the timber bosses, who themselves organized to fight unionism. James Rowan, another

Irish immigrant logger and one of the founders of the IWW lumber workers' union, in fact, described Pacific Northwest lumbermen as "the One Big
Union of the bosses in the timber industry."[20]

McKay joined the IWW during its first big organizational push in British
Columbia between 1906 and 1910. He was active in the agitation surrounding
the Vancouver Free Speech Fight of 1912, during which numerous Wobblies
were run down and beaten by mounted police. Following the conclusion
of the fight, McKay traveled along the British Columbia coast, working as
a logger and organizing for the IWW. For his agitation during the Canadian
Northern Railroad strike of 1912, McKay was marked an agitator and black-
listed from employment in the British Columbia lumber industry.

McKay was one of the millions of migratory workers who harvested the
fields, cut the trees, and built the railroads of the West. Like most of them, he
changed jobs with the season. But because of his difficulty in securing work
in British Columbia after 1912, William "voted with his feet" and moved to
Washington at the conclusion of the Canadian Northern strike. Tragically,
this move took him away from his family—a wife and two children—who
lived on a farm near Vancouver, BC. Separated from his loved ones for political reasons, McKay sent home his pay to put food on the table for his family, who waited for the happy reunion when their husband and father could
return home. Little is known what became of them after William's death.

In the spring of 1923 his work brought him to Grays Harbor County, the
largest lumber-producing region in the world. Like so many Red Coast workers, McKay was living in a boardinghouse, renting his quarters for a small fee,
when he joined his fellow workers in picketing the Bay City Mill on May 3,
1923. When the picketers arrived at the gate they were met by E. I. Green,
a hired gunman for the Bay City Mill. Green had a long history of violent
activities. He had fought in the Spanish-American War and World War I,
and according to the *Southwest Washington Labor Press* "was known as a man
quick to use a gun and had done time because of it previously."[21] The confrontation immediately bred trouble. C. E. Barton, a non-IWW bystander,
recalled that Green "was standing a short distance away [from the pickets],
loudly taunting the crowd of men with abuse and vile language, including
in his remarks something to the effect that no one belongs to the Industrial
Workers' Union but foreigners who cannot speak English." Outraged at the
taunt, McKay stepped forward, shouting, "Do you mean that for me?"[22] The
scene played out just as the Bay City Mill manager's intended. Green and

McKay met in open battle over political and economic issues. All the while, the employers who exploited their labor and the legislators and judges who condemned the Wobblies to prison sat comfortably in their large, safe homes on Broadway Hill and in the Broadways Hills around the nation.

Accounts of the confrontation vary significantly, and all that is certain is that Green's repeated taunts led to a bitter argument with McKay. During the quarrel, Green pulled his revolver, and McKay, seeing the weapon, attempted to flee. As McKay ran, Green fired two shots. One of the bullets struck McKay in the back of the head. At the coroner's inquest later that day, three doctors and six community members confirmed the horrific details of the murder. According to the autopsy, McKay died from a single bullet that entered two inches above his right ear, "traversed through brain substance," and bounced between many parts of his skull.[23]

The Wobblies celebrated McKay's life on the streets and in print. More than a thousand working people marched from the Elerding funeral parlor in downtown Aberdeen to Fern Hill Cemetery in a massive funeral parade. Photographs of the parade were reprinted as postcards and widely distributed around the United States. Articles on McKay's life and his murder followed for weeks thereafter in the radical and labor press. But the Wobblies did not march or write in McKay's honor merely to celebrate his life, but to attack the arbitrary and authoritarian power of American capitalists that made the murder possible.

At the funeral, two young Finnish girls carried a giant banner reading: "Fellow Worker McKay: Murdered at Bay City Mill by a Co Gunman May 3rd 1923. A Victim of Capitalistic Greed. We Never Forget?"[24] The question mark in their sign appears to be a challenge. Sadly, we have mostly forgotten the lives lost and struggles waged by working people across this nation. After receiving a few short blurbs in the mainstream press, McKay's death went unmentioned in every major history of the IWW, and his name was lost to posterity.

The IWW press pushed fruitlessly against the levers of power for Green's prosecution and urged fellow workers to "be ready for trial" of "the gunman who murdered Fellow Worker McKay." Nonetheless, in a decision that some workers compared with the "Centralia frame-up," members of the coroner's inquest refused to affix blame for the murder and thus "tacitly condoned the killing by holding that Green was 'on duty.'"[25] Reacting callously to McKay's murder, the right-wing *Hoquiam American* opined: "A man who listens to the

Thousands of workers marched through town on their way to the funeral of Fellow Worker William McKay in Aberdeen, Washington. Photo courtesy of Roy Vataja.

talk of an IWW is on a par with the man who looks down the muzzle of a loaded gun while fooling with the trigger."[26] Grays Harbor County prosecutor, A. E. Graham, declared that he would prosecute Green for the murder. Yet after an initial hearing, the gunman was freed on bail and was never tried for the murder.[27]

In looking back for lessons to draw from his life and death, we should not see McKay's murder as a simple mistake. Instead, his death was the result of a series of decisions made and executed by powerful elites, first to declare the IWW illegal and then to toss its members into prison. Even more directly, Grays Harbor lumbermen had made the conscious choice to hire and arm belligerent gunmen to stand watch outside their mills. Showing no sorrow over the tragedy, the practice of hiring and arming gunmen continued to be a mainstay of Grays Harbor labor relations. Shortly after McKay's death, a Grays Harbor Company mill guard named Jackson gained notoriety for strutting about the mill flashing his gun at any man who walked by, proclaiming, "If my son joined the I.W.W. I would shoot him." With this as the context, it is fortunate that more picketers did not end up like McKay.

In memory of McKay, one IWW stated that McKay had once declared, "I would rather die fighting the masters than be killed slaving for them."[28] Indeed, McKay had certainly labored alongside scores of loggers who lost their lives while enriching Pacific Northwest lumbermen. That he died in a struggle to end the exploitative practices of capitalism—to "Dump the Bosses Off our Back"—should not be forgotten.

11
Shingle Weavers and the Six-Hour Day

From mid-July to mid-August 1935, members of the Washington-Oregon Shingle Weavers District Council ratified their contracts with the Red Cedar Shingle Manufacturers' Association. In an era when millions of American workers joined and formed their first unions and signed their first collective bargaining agreements, something about the weavers' contract stood out. The weavers had won a concession that a decade earlier would have been unthinkable, and in the early twenty-first century is believed by many to be the sole province of utopian fiction and the democratic countries of northern Europe. The shingle weavers' contract included provisions for a six-hour workday. In 1966, celebrating both the weavers' victory in their fight for humane working hours and their ability to maintain that achievement, the *Shingle Weaver*, the union's monthly organ, editorialized:

> We, as shingleweavers, are well aware and justly proud of the fact that we have enjoyed a six hour day since 1935. Also for the past several years we have scrupulously guarded our 30 hour week, and we intend to continue that practice. Being a small union, as we are, and perhaps not getting the deserved publicity, results in not many people being aware of our six hour day and thirty hour week. Perhaps if our success for so many years under those conditions was publicized more, it might encourage other unions to go all out for shorter hours.[1]

Born of a group of workers with deep socialist and communist roots, the weavers' six-hour day was the culmination of a decades-long struggle for shorter hours for workers in one of the nation's most dangerous industries.

In the late nineteenth and early twentieth centuries, shingle manufacturing was one of the major industries in the Pacific Northwest. Lumber bosses, some drawn from New England and the Midwest, looked longingly at the great red cedar trees found in the evergreen forests along the Puget Sound on the Olympic Peninsula. By 1900, more than three hundred shingle mills stretched from Whatcom County near the Canadian border to Clark and Cowlitz counties across the Columbia River from Oregon.[2] They also began shingle manufacturing in Hoquiam, Chehalis, and at other points along the Red Coast.

The term "shingle weaver" originally referred to the men—and in the late nineteenth and early twentieth century, practically all shingle industry employees were male—who packed the shingles into bundles after sawyers sawed cedar blocks into the thin strips known as shingles. Their hands moved so rapidly during the packing process that it appeared they wove them into a bundle. By the 1910s, the term itself had broadened to include all workers involved in the shingle-production process.[3]

Shingle weavers lived and worked in a variety of settings, both urban and rural. The largest mills were found in urban locations. Their workers enjoyed the comforts and experienced the conflicts of the early twentieth-century city. They married, had children, lived in single-family dwellings, joined fraternities, visited saloons and cigar stores, and ran for public office. But those who worked in one of the small mills of the rural Red Coast had vastly different experiences. Many of these men lived in tiny company towns or rural hamlets, at times residing in company housing, shopping at company stores, and subject to capitalist authoritarianism that extended well beyond the mill gate. Some idea of the restrictions on these workers' freedom can be gleaned from the town rules of Aloha, Washington, a tiny company town located in northern Grays Harbor and run by the Aloha Lumber Company. In Aloha, where all houses had to be painted white, alcohol and, of course, unions were officially prohibited.[4]

In 1890, shingle weavers in several Puget Sound and Red Coast towns formed the International Shingle Weavers' Union (ISWU). The unionists significantly increased wages at several mills and established a set wage scale before losing a decisive strike in 1893 on the front edge of a major depression that gradually destroyed the organization. In April 1901, after eight years of declining wages in an open shop shingle industry, weavers in Ballard, Washington, struck for increased pay. Soon, shingle weavers' locals formed in towns throughout the Pacific Northwest and Upper Midwest, culminating in January 1903 with the formation of the International Shingle Weavers' Union of America (ISWUA) at Everett.[5]

Weavers in several Red Coast towns took leadership roles in the organizational upsurge that accompanied the return of more prosperous times just after the turn of the century. Unionists formed locals in Elma, Aberdeen, and Hoquiam in 1902. Others followed suit in Cosmopolis in 1906, and Montesano in 1907.[6] By 1910, the union had spread into many small industrial villages and company towns on the Olympic Peninsula.

Shingle manufacturing was dirty, dangerous work, among the most "accident-prone" industries in a country full of workplace injuries and deaths. A reporter writing for *Sunset: The Magazine of the Pacific and All the Far West* documented the shingle weavers' labor:

> Hour after hour the shingle weaver's hands and arms, plain,
> unarmored flesh and blood, are staked against the screeching steel
> that cares not what it severs. Hour after hour the steel sings its
> crescendo note as it bites into the wood, the sawdust cloud thickens,
> the wet sponge under the sawyer's nose fills with fine particles.
>   If "cedar asthma," the shingle weaver's occupational disease, does
> not get him, the steel will. Sooner or later he reaches over a little too
> far, the whirling blade tosses drops of deep red into the air, and a
> finger, a hand, or part of an arm comes sliding down the slick chute.[7]

Weavers lost fingers, hands, arms, and even their lives at frightening rates during the early twentieth century. The swirling saws and the speed at which operations were conducted led Cloice R. Howd to write: "Few men have sawn shingles for any length of time, particularly on an upright machine, without paying toll in a part or all of a hand."[8]

The Washington State Bureau of Labor reported the details of several of these casualties. Typical was the June 1901 injury caused to Dryad, Washington, shingle sawyer Fletch Burnett, whose "hand [was] severely scratched in a saw, resulting in the loss of one of his fingers. Disabled 12 or 14 days."[9] Six months later, at a Centralia shingle mill, "Bert Ammon, a young man, had his arm severely cut in two places by the shingle saw. Amputation was necessary." Later in 1902, Markham shingle weaver "P. P. Porter was accidentally caught in the machinery, receiving a badly broken and crushed arm. Amputation of the arm was necessary."[10]

The real threat of so-called industrial accidents colored the weavers' discussions of practically all issues. In 1917, in response to the Aberdeen City

THE PRICE THE SHINGLE WEAVER PAYS

CLINTON B. FISK, WHO LOST SIX FINGERS IN THE PAST 16 YEARES WHILE EMPLOYED IN SAWMILLS.

Shingle weavers frequently lost fingers, hands, and arms while at work. This image accompanied a *Seattle Star* story detailing the dangers of shingle mills. *Seattle Star*, April 10, 1913.

Council's consideration of an occupational tax, shingle weaver and socialist city council candidate Joe Thomas wrote:

> Who pays a real occupation tax? All you shingle weavers raise your hands so Mr. Phillips [Aberdeen mayor] can see the two or three remaining fingers you have left on them. Breathe, so he can hear your cedar asthma choking lungs. Come forward you mill workers.
>
> Show the mayor your torn flesh, your broken bones, your crippled hands, your smashed legs, your bent backs, your dust-filled joints. Every foot of land in the lumber industry is blood covered and all the machinery is blood stained with your arms and legs, your fingers and toes. Yes! If the blood and flesh of our workers be the price for an occupation, then by the gods, we have paid the occupation tax in full![11]

Weaver unionists used their collective power to mitigate the dangers of their work by fighting for higher wages, improved insurance, and safety improvements to shingle machinery. If the shingle weavers were the most injured group in the lumber industry, they were also the most strike-prone. Grays Harbor weavers struck no less than ten times between 1902 and 1911. They carried out strikes over wages, piece rates, work hours, and control over the work process. Often these were "quickie strikes," intended to surprise employers and force them into making concessions during profitable periods. In one such strike, weavers at the Hoquiam Lumber and Shingle Company mill spontaneously walked off the job after hearing that Jay G. Brown had been fired because of his political commitments. After only a few days, mill manager Lytle retreated, and the weavers returned to their posts.[12]

Throughout their history, though, the weavers' unions remained committed to securing a shorter workday. The commitment centered on a well-known fact: longer workdays led to greater rates of injury. Issued one year after the weavers won their thirty-hour workweek, a 1947 US Department of Labor report stated that during World War II: "Injuries also increased as hours increased, not only in absolute numbers, but also in the rate of incidence. In most observed instances, the number of injuries per million hours worked was very much higher at the longer hours." Leaving little doubt, the report continued: "Work injuries increase disproportionately as daily hours are raised above 8 and weekly hours are raised above 40."[13] As per the norm, the workers themselves understood the realities—including the dangers—of working-class life long before government officials and other elites. In 1918, the Aberdeen shingle weavers' union press committee used sarcasm to make a point about the connection between workday length and workplace injuries: "Alex Fiske had the good luck to lose a finger while working ten hours at the Sylvia Mill. It is reported that he lost his finger between 5 and 6 o'clock. Had he been working only eight hours . . . he would still have his digit."[14]

The ISWUA struck repeatedly during the first two decades of the twentieth century, often including the demand for the eight-hour day. In 1909, weavers unsuccessfully tried to enforce an eight-hour day through a strike.[15] In 1912, a Seattle shingle weaver listed "an eight hour day" first among his list of "needs of wage earners."[16] At several points in the 1910s, members of the ISWUA pressed for the eight-hour day, often using militant direct action.

The most famous weavers' strike came in Everett during 1915–1916. The struggle broke into open class warfare as Wobblies joined the striking shingle weavers attempting to organize workers through a major free speech fight in the streets of Everett. Employers, led by David Clough of Clough-Hartley Lumber, responded by organizing the Commercial Club, commissioning the local sheriff to deputize and arm hundreds of local thugs, and opening a hunting season on the IWW. Vicious clubbings, arrests, and deportations ensued and the terror spread throughout the city during the summer and fall of 1916. While the Wobblies did not seek out violence, neither were they inclined to back down, and they continued to organize. The struggle culminated in the well-known Everett Massacre, Bloody Sunday, November 5, when the *Verona*, a passenger boat, filled with 250 Wobblies from Seattle was met at the Everett dock by the sheriff and armed thugs and ended in a pitched gun battle. The seven dead—five Wobblies and two from the deck—resulted in murder charges against only the IWW men. The not guilty verdict rendered by a Seattle jury vindicated the IWW, but inflamed the lumber interest and its allies.[17]

In July 1917, just three months after the United States entered World War I, weaver unionists joined thousands of other lumber workers in striking for union recognition and the eight-hour day for the same wages paid for ten hours of work.[18] While loggers and sawmill workers fought for a host of improvements, the weavers concentrated on a central demand: the eight-hour day. In a strike notice, ISWUA President Jay G. Brown announced the union's decision to strike on July 16 unless manufacturers switched to the eight-hour day: "Let every one observe the 16th day of July. In time to come we shall celebrate this day even as the miners now celebrate the 1st of April—the day when the eight hours was secured. We are living in a grand and awful time. Everyone must make good this year. All hail the eight-hour day!"[19] Brown clearly saw the historic importance of the strike. In a statement titled "At Death Grip with the Lumber Trust Barons," he declared, "This is our chance to gain the shorter work day."[20] Through the strike, weavers unleashed full-throated attacks on anyone who dared return to work in a ten-hour mill. Shingle weaver M. P. Corbett concluded: "Another plea made by these degenerates is that they have a right to work as many hours as they want to. They have the same right to work ten hours under existing circumstances as their apostle, Judas, had in betraying Christ, and anyone with any brains or honor will no doubt agree on that."[21] Almost immediately, shingle mills began granting the eight-hour day. In 1918, due to state pressure and ongoing militant direct action, lumber workers won the shorter workday.

Despite their victory in the 1917 strike, the shingle weavers' union and the timber workers' unions took major hits in the early 1920s, as aggressive employers utilized blacklists, company spies, lockouts, and paternalistic bonus systems to defeat the unions.[22] But a strike of 1,500 Grays Harbor weavers in February 1927 provided the impetus to rebuild the shingle weavers' movement.[23] Most of the 1,500 strikers did not belong to a union when the strike began. Wobblies contributed advice and publicity to the strikers, but far more assistance came from the Northwest's Communist movement, which was building an impressive following among the weavers.[24] At a strike meeting in Hoquiam on February 20, Communist organizer Aaron Fislerman encouraged the weavers to unionize. The weavers responded to his call for a union, he said, "by a unanimous rising vote . . . [that] decided that shingle weavers union included all workers skilled and unskilled in the union."[25] They named their union the International Shingle Weavers Union (ISWU), the same name carried by its nineteenth-century predecessor, with its headquarters in Aberdeen.[26] Fislerman also succeeded at recruiting O. P. Allison into the Party, and on February 20 the Communist weaver was elected as the first president of the new union. Thus, the Communists gained their first toehold in the region's lumber industry.[27]

A month into the strike the balance of forces was clearly on the workers' side, as mill after mill yielded to their demands. On March 11, the strike ended in total victory for the weavers when the Saginaw, Aloha, and Hoquiam Shingle Companies, three of the largest mills in the region, began operations with the demanded pay increase.[28] Within five months of its formation, the new union had four branches in Grays Harbor alone. The Harbor weavers were, according to Fislerman, "100% organized."[29] The 1927 strike and union organizing drive helped to politicize the weavers, who turned to their union newspaper, the *Shingle Weaver*, to advocate their fellow workers' interests.[30] Celebrating both the Party's organizing achievements and the victory of the striking shingle weavers, Fislerman declared: "We shall not stop there with this single union. But we must proceed with the organization of the rest of the shingle and lumber workers and connect them together."[31]

Echoing the traditions of their predecessors in shingle weavers' unions, the ISWU fought for higher wages and to improve "Conditions bad as Hell," as union president Ralph E. Lovelace described them. But in a poem published in the *Shingle Weaver*, Lovelace spoke to the weavers' understanding of the importance of leisure time, a little freedom from the boss and the machine:

Sneak away to some wild brook,
There feel as free as any man;

> Catch a fish upon a hook,
> And watch it sizzle in the pan.[32]

Unfortunately, the onset of the Great Depression in 1929 had a cata-strophic impact on the lives of shingle weavers, much as it did the entire lumber industry workforce. By 1932, in some regions of the state, the entire industry shuttered for months on end. In April 1930, the *Industrial Worker* gave a taste of the troubles haunting the weavers: "The East Hoquiam shingle mill has closed. The Robert Gray [mill] is reported to be intending to close this week. The Saginaw shingle mill has closed the night shift and men there are wondering if the day shift will be let out 'for a time.'"[33] Lifelong shingle weaver Harold Stilson reacted with horror at being thrown into the reserve army of labor during the early Depression:

> During these hard times, only a small percentage of the labor force
> was able to find any work. Things got so tough that, although I was
> one of the best shingle sawyers and also a good all-around mill hand, I
> along with hundreds of others lived only by catching an odd job here
> and there.[34]

Workers across the United States confronted similar situations. Impressively, though, shingle weavers—led by those on the Red Coast—reacted militantly to the possibility of wage and hours reductions, shutdowns, and other employer threats. Wobbly journalist C. E. "Stumpy" Payne praised the weavers' militancy for stemming the tide of wage cuts: "The shingle weavers have taken organized action to make a fight against any wage reduction. They have elected committees to notify all men in the different mills where notices of wage reductions have been posted, that no reduction can be permitted."[35]

The weavers' unions kept up the fight throughout the Great Depression and crafted a creative solution that promised to alleviate, if not solve, some of their industry's problems. Understanding that there were far more potential shingle workers than jobs available in the early 1930s, the weavers demanded that the industry switch from a ten- or eight-hour workday to six-hour daily shifts. Stilson offered a convincing rationale for the switch:

> At the start of the Great Depression in 1929, we the Shingle
> Weavers Union, began to realize that we were confronted with

something different than had ever happened to us before. So many
of our co-workers were being laid off and thrown on the general
labor market and were having to compete with hundreds of other
ex-workers from other forms of labor. So we decided to ask for a six-
hour day and five-day week.[36]

Praising the unionized weavers' ingenuity for offering up a potential and partial
solution to a problem created by bosses and politicians, the *Industrial Worker*
wrote: "Many of the Grays Harbor workers, Wilson's men included, are talking of the six-hour day. The six hour day, with three hours product going to
the workers in the form of wages, instead of the eight hour day with only two
hours product going to them for wages, can be taken by just a little organization and action."[37]

The weavers found they were not alone in fighting for shorter hours, as the
Depression opened up opportunities to press for new and radical demands. At
the end of the 1920s, long hours were the rule in American industry. "At this
time, by way of contrast," wrote historians Philip Foner and David Roediger,
the industrialized nations of Europe and Australia had shifted to the eight-
hour day, "while the Soviet Union had introduced the seven-hour principle."[38]
In the United States, workers argued that working shorter hours without a cut
in pay marked the surest way to increase employment opportunities. Railway
and metal unionists led the way in the push for shorter working hours, while
the AFL convention in 1930 focused on the five-day workweek. In 1932, AFL
President William Green called for a thirty-hour workweek with no cut in
pay.[39] The *Industrial Worker* concluded: "The six-hour day is the logical immediate objective of labor. . . . Do not DEMAND the six-hour day. Organize on
the job and TAKE the six-hour day. There is no other way."[40]

In December 1932, Senator Hugo Black of Alabama introduced what, in
retrospect, was one of the most radical pieces of legislation to ever pass the
US Senate. His thirty-hour workweek bill was designed to open up jobs to
millions of unemployed workers. It passed the Senate on April 6, 1933, by a
vote of 53 to 30. Eventually running up against determined opponents in the
House and the Roosevelt administration, the Black Bill was quickly defeated.
But throughout the country, workers inspired by this vision of shorter hours
without a decline in pay pushed the issue for themselves. In March 1934, a
large part of the United Mine Workers' bituminous coal miner membership
won a seven-hour, five-day workweek with a wage increase. Seven months

later, 19,000 unionized elevator constructors won a thirty-hour workweek.[41] In July 1934, the city council of Seattle voted to adopt the thirty-hour work-week for all municipal work done within the city limits.[42]

The year 1935 stands as a milestone in the history of the American lumber workers, as they stood united in their demand for union recognition, higher wages, and shorter hours in the face of massive employer opposition. Shingle weavers—historically only a small wing of the lumber labor force, but the most densely unionized of that work group—fought alongside their more numer-ous fellow workers from the logging camps and saw and plywood mills in the great 1935 Lumber Strike, an epic showdown between one of the West's larg-est and most exploited group of workers and the logging and lumber bosses.

In the buildup to this strike, members of the Northwest Shingle-Weavers' Council met at the Olympia Labor Temple in February 1935, issuing demands for a six-hour day, thirty-hour week, time-and-a-half for overtime, and a mini-mum wage of four dollars per day. The weavers also added the important provision that they would be paid the same rate for a six-hour shift as they cur-rently made for their eight-hour shift. The more than one hundred delegates at the meeting elected two Red Coast workers—Bernard Bright and Errol Herr, both of Raymond—to serve as the union's president and executive secretary.[43]

Led by Communists and non-Communist militants, Pacific Northwest lumber workers pressed ambitious demands, hoping to reshape the industry and their work lives in a more humane fashion. When operators refused the demands for union recognition, pay increases, and a thirty-hour workweek, tens of thousands of woodworkers in Washington, Oregon, Idaho, and beyond struck, paralyzing the Pacific Coast's largest industry.

Red Coast shingle weavers joined in the great strike, lending their solidar-ity to a conflict that dominated Northwest news for several weeks. Thirty-four weavers at the Panama Shingle Company in Olympia struck on May 3, three days ahead of the general strike call. On May 6, all of Grays Harbor's shingle weavers struck as part of a force of 5,000 Harbor strikers from the lumber industry. The executive secretary of the Northwest Shingle Weavers' Council explained that employers' unwillingness to bargain caused the strike:

> For the past one and a half years . . . we have held the men on the job
> while attempting an industry-wide conference with employers on
> the subjects now submitted as demands. . . . The unions feel that a
> majority of the manufacturers are in favor of peaceful negotiations but

were unable to agree among themselves as long as the mills and camps were in operation.[44]

Hopes for peaceful negotiations with employers did not last long. By May 13, only twelve shingle mills operated in Washington and Oregon. Representatives from the shingle manufacturers' association refused to improve wages or working conditions, contending that competition from other roofing materials, as well as the ban on red cedar shingles from municipalities concerned about fire dangers, forced red cedar manufacturers to keep their labor costs down. Manufacturers then invited the importation of Canadian shingles into the US market as a way to pressure the weavers into surrendering. Responding with an appropriate amount of indignation at this attempt to pressure his fellow workers, weavers' secretary Errol Herr wrote to the AFL and congressional officials declaring that the union will hold "the administration responsible as strike breakers" if they allowed an increase in Canadian shingles into the United States during the strike.[45]

Throughout mid-May, shingle manufacturers reached temporary agreements with the weavers who returned to work in anticipation of a deal being struck. At the same time, US weavers put pressure on their Canadian counterparts to extend the strike north of the border. On June 2, representatives of 3,000 striking shingle weavers met at Port Angeles, Washington, and voted to continue the strike. Herr celebrated the support of union longshoremen, who, he reported, refused to handle shingles on the Pacific or Atlantic coasts until the strike was settled. The weavers showed that their militancy had the potential to influence the wider timber strike. On June 5, weavers picketed and closed the massive Long-Bell and Weyerhaeuser sawmills at Longview, which had returned to work, because the mills had allowed shipments of "unfair" shingles. The weavers' militancy went further: they threatened to give up their AFL union charters if officers in the Carpenters' Union, an AFL affiliate attempting to direct the timber strike from above, pressured the weavers to accept a compromise forty-hour workweek and smaller-than-demanded wage hike.[46]

Well before the end of the wider lumber strike, workers at several shingle mills signed agreements with manufacturers. In mid-July, unionists at several Northwest mills adopted what became known as the "Ballard Agreement," which created an arbitration board to handle disputes. The board, composed of seven workers and seven employers, was quickly lauded by union executives.

By July 19, 40 percent of shingle manufacturers had agreed to follow the rec-
ommendations of the board's majority. Agreement in hand, some mills began
to reopen.[47]

Buried in much of the news coverage of the shingle strike's end was the
most radical provision of the agreement. Workers demanded, and some manufacturers agreed, that their industry would operate on the basis of a six-hour
day.[48] As the mills reopened, they did so on a six-hour-day, thirty-six-hour week
basis with a minimum wage of sixty cents per hour. Where bosses dug in their
heels, refusing to implement the six-hour day, the strikers steadfastly remained
on the picket lines, refusing to compromise away their chance at greater freedom. On August 12, weavers at two of Grays Harbor's largest mills returned
to work with a six-hour day in hand. By August 19, nearly all Northwest weavers returned to their jobs, among the last Northwest lumber workers to end
their strike in an epic, nearly four-months-long strike for higher wages, better
conditions, and most importantly, shorter hours.[49] With their victory in hand,
thousands of weavers returned to work, among the only American workers to
have ever won a six-hour workday.

The six-hour day and thirty-six-hour workweek were major achievements
for the weavers, ones equaled by only a few groups of American workers.
Following the establishment of this standard workweek in 1935, the six-hour
day became the object of admiration among their fellow lumber workers. In
1937, Federation of Woodworkers President Harold Pritchett spoke of the
need to "lay plans for the accomplishment of a 30-hour week," in the industry,
made necessary "by the rapid growth of unemployment and the installation
within the industry of labor saving devices." "We should make it one of our
first tasks of the future to inaugurate the six-hour day, with no reduction in
pay."[50] Aberdeen worker Fred Siefken wrote to the *Timber Worker* to explain
the connection between shorter hours and working-class liberation from
the machine and the boss: "If we really want to live we will favor a shorter
work week, for the time we spend with our families and friends enjoying the
sunshine, the fresh part of the beauties of nature are truly a part of the good
things of life. They are really ours and can not be taken from us by taxes or
price increases or any other maneuvers of the employer from whom we escape
when we have the shorter work week."[51]

Maintaining the six-hour day was a central mission of the shingle weavers'
union. From 1935 until its dissolution in the 1970s, weavers' unions insisted
that a six-hour day constituted full-time work. In 1946, after the widespread

adoption of a five-day workweek throughout the United States, the weavers took a step further, establishing the thirty-hour workweek, which was maintained for decades. A 1973 shingle weavers' union agreement stated that the shingle weavers' workweek was to be thirty hours.[52] The thought of going back to a longer day was anathema to the weavers once they had tasted that bit of freedom. In 1966, the *Shingle Weaver* reminded readers that: "A worker becomes part of a machine, drugged with work, a slave to the machine that he keeps running eight hours."[53]

Shingle weavers remained justifiably proud of their great achievement and boasted of the length of their workdays and workweeks long after they'd been won. In August 1955, Ray Thompson, editor of the Portland-based *Shingle Weaver* celebrated their two decades of working a six-hour day, a feat he ranked among the greatest in the history of the labor movement. "We have read in the papers of remarks by heads of various unions and economists that a shorter working week is possible in the future. Our Union might have shortcomings, and may be without some benefits enjoyed by others, but, with what we hope is pardonable pride, we point to our 6 hour day." Thompson continued: "In a declining and highly competitive industry, we have for our 20 years had something that other unions have just recently started trying for. Let them have their so called guaranteed wage, their hospital plans, and their vacation. *Give me the 6 hour day.*"[54]

12
Proletarian Novels

As American capitalism teetered and threatened to collapse in the 1930s, a new weapon in the class struggle emerged, the proletarian novel. Proletarian literature aimed to "reflect proletarian values, ... bring the worker to class-consciousness, steel him for the coming revolution, [and] prepare him for the role he would play in the next stage of history. [In them] Art was a form of politics; it was a weapon in the class war."[1] According to a 1939 issue of the *North American Review*, the preceding ten or eleven years had produced in proletarian literature "some fifty novels, several hundred poems, and a dozen plays."[2] Reflecting the Red Coast's history of militant labor struggles, four of these novels were set in Grays Harbor: Louis Colman's *Lumber* (1931), Robert Cantwell's *Land of Plenty* (1934), Clara Weatherwax's *Marching! Marching!* (1935), and William Coldiron and Robert Cochrane's *Disillusion* (1939).

Since these novels were set in and written by authors who lived in Grays Harbor, they provide a fascinating and sometimes terrifying window into the class struggle of workers in one of the most unionized places in America. All of the novels revolve around strikes. The earliest of these, Louis Colman's *Lumber,* might be the most effective at dramatizing the violent opposition that striking workers faced. Colman was a Communist who occasionally contributed proletarian short stories for the communist newspaper *New Masses.*[3] Later, he lived in New York and worked as publicity director for the Communist front International Labor Defense, fighting to free the Scottsboro Boys, to abolish labor peonage, and for the repeal of criminal syndicalism laws.[4] In the 1920s, however, Colman worked at the Wilson Brothers' Mill in Aberdeen, and he wrote *Lumber* while out on strike, so Colman knew his subject firsthand.[5]

Lumber is the story of Jimmie, who left home when he was fifteen after his father died in a logging accident. Jimmie ranged up and down the Red Coast working in the lumber industry, and became a card-carrying Wobbly after seeing a man brutalized by a police officer. The novel is inspired by a number of historical events on the Red Coast, where the violent suppression of workers' movements was part of business as usual. For example, when writing about the 1917 Lumber Strike, Colman drew on historical events from both the 1912 and 1917 strikes in Grays Harbor to produce the most powerful and terrifying moments in the book. At one point Jimmie (whose shipyard has not called a strike) realizes that many of his IWW friends were being lynched with the cooperation of the local authorities, who ruled their deaths suicides, a phenomenon which Wobbly Ralph Chaplin indeed reported happening.[6] In another powerful scene, Jimmie and his wife, Pearl, decide to go downtown to see a movie, but find themselves swept up in a mob of the city's leading citizens, who were rounding up, beating, and deporting striking workers. This scene was also based on real events, from the 1912 strike, when vigilantes from Grays and Willapa Harbors succeeded in forcibly deporting striking workers.

Jimmie is physically strong, extremely capable at his profession, and begins as a sympathetic character, but the novel is a tragedy in the classical sense. Though he belongs to the One Big Union, Jimmie's tragic flaw is that he thinks that he is capable of navigating the working world and protecting his family as an individual. He is hardened by a series of setbacks, which appear to him as a string of bad breaks. But actually we can see that Jimmie has too much faith in individualism, that he abandons collective action at the most inopportune moment, and that he is crushed not by misfortune but by the system itself. Amid job loss and family illness and disintegration, his life falls apart and he dies, at work, while fighting with a coworker.

Robert Cantwell's *Land of Plenty* (1934) is the most famous of the Red Coast novels, and is generally regarded as one of the best proletarian novels ever written, although it certainly had its critics. Cantwell came from a prominent pioneer family, and his father was a mill superintendent at Carlisle, near Grays Harbor. Cantwell entered the University of Washington in 1924 but had to withdraw when his father became ill the next year. He worked at Harbor Plywood for the next four years. His experiences at the plywood mill became the basis of his novel. He published his first novel, *Laugh and Lie Down*, in 1931. He later became a regular contributor to *The New Republic*, and then moved on to a distinguished literary career and an increasingly conservative worldview.[7]

The action in *Land of Plenty* begins when the power goes out during the night shift at a Grays Harbor factory and a man is crushed under a log hoist. According to literary critic T. V. Reed, the power outage at the factory serves as a "Marxian allegory" for the failure of capitalism. But as the novel unfolds, it becomes clear that most of the workers—for whom the factory is a familiar environment—are able to cope with the power outage. The managers, meanwhile, stumble about incompetently and get lost. The workers' competence, paired with the ineptitude of the managers, Reed argues, is more reflective of the "anarcho-syndicalist ideology" of the IWW than of the Communist Party. The novel implies that the workers could run the factory without the managers at all, as the Wobblies themselves proposed.[8]

One worker, Johnny, appears to be based on Cantwell himself: the character and the author had each left the University of Washington to help support his family. Johnny's father, Carl, is an electrician at the factory, and he manages to get the lights back on. But in the course of doing so he manages to offend the incompetent watch foreman, who in his frustration fires Carl and another worker. These and further layoffs, coming on top of previous layoffs and wage cuts, convince workers to take a stand, and they strike and occupy the factory, only to see their strike brutally suppressed, and Johnny's father, Carl, shot by the police.

Like Cantwell, Clara Weatherwax also came from a family of some prominence. She was the granddaughter of a millowner and founding father of Aberdeen, Captain J. M. Weatherwax, for whom Aberdeen High School is still named. However, her father died when she was twelve, and she and her siblings had to work to help her mother get by. By the 1930s most Weatherwaxes were working class, and Clara Weatherwax had the politics to match: her novel *Marching! Marching!* won the proletarian novel contest sponsored by the Communist magazine, *New Masses.*[9]

Despite this victory, *Marching! Marching!* was not well reviewed, partly owing to the book's politics and partly to the unconventional structure of the novel, which had "no hero but half-a-dozen protagonists, each symbolizing some aspect of the proletarian struggle."[10] This was in keeping with the Marxist aims of Weatherwax, who sought to emphasize the power of the collective over individual action, but even to some sympathetic readers, the effect was off-putting. According to Cantwell, "The characters, for the most part, seem to be communist magicians: they appear, get involved in the most intricate and terrifying complications and then, when their troubles have reached a climax, they vanish from the novel, uttering revolutionary statements."[11]

In fact, the novel is both artistically innovative and historically informative. The unconventional structure of *Marching! Marching!* allows its readers to recognize the great diversity among worker-activists, both with respect to ethnicity and gender. Whereas the other novels are narrated through the eyes of white males, the narrative of *Marching! Marching!* advances through the actions of a Filipino labor organizer, Europeans of many ethnicities (and perhaps especially Red Finns), and women, all of whom play an active role in the revolutionary struggle.

Weatherwax also uses another effective device to illustrate the way the capitalist press deceived the public when it reported on the class struggle. One chapter of *Marching! Marching!* is told entirely through rival news articles. In one column, the mainstream press presents the millowners' version of events and depicts strikers as fanatical, bloodthirsty, foreign revolutionaries. In the opposite column, the same events and people are described very differently in the workers' leftist press. To anyone who has looked at the newspapers from this period, and Weatherwax certainly did, this re-creation feels very authentic.

Writing in 1936, and reviewing his own work as well as the work of Colman and Weatherwax, Cantwell suggested that it was somewhat ironic that these novels "pictured strikes that had such unhappy conclusions," since the 1935 Lumber Strike "was won by the strikers, hands-down—the Sawmill and Timber Workers' Union was recognized, a measure of job control was established, the town as a whole was unionized, [and] the Labor Party elected a few people to office."[12] Had Colman, Cantwell, and Weatherwax written their novels after instead of before this victory, perhaps they would have concluded with clear victories for the workers.

Such is, in fact, the case with *Disillusion*, written by Ben H. Cochrane and William Coldiron and published in 1939. This is the least known of the Grays Harbor novels, but the most amazing in some ways, as it is a lightly fictionalized account of the 1935 Lumber Strike, a militant labor novel, written by two former scabs. The material for the novel comes primarily from the experiences of Cochrane, whose own life closely paralleled that of the book's main character, Bill Jackson. Cochrane, like Jackson, decided to scab partially because he lacked class consciousness, and partially because his wife was sick and he needed the money. But as he scabbed, he was drawn deeper and deeper into the company's strikebreaking operations, called the Mohawk Valley Plan, after the region in New York where it was pioneered.

The Mohawk Valley Plan involved grooming workers like Cochrane to undermine organization efforts, circulating propaganda to brand organizers as foreign radicals, encouraging Klan terrorism to frighten workers, blackmailing the public by threatening to move factories, and supporting the creation of a company union that would be controlled by men in the pocket of management. As Cochrane testified in an affidavit, at the behest of Harbor Plywood superintendent Ben Ibsen, he indeed recruited thugs to beat up workers, stoned strikers' houses (who stoned his in retaliation), and channeled money from management to the Ku Klux Klan to fund acts of domestic terrorism against workers.[13] However, like the main character in his novel, and in good capitalist fashion, Cochrane was fired from the company after he had outlived his usefulness. Disillusioned, he switched sides in the strike, becoming a proletarian novelist.

It should come as no surprise that the Depression decade, and 1930s Grays Harbor in particular, proved such fertile ground for proletarian writers. Novelists historically come from middle-class backgrounds, since middle-class writers most often have the education and the leisure to undertake projects such as novels. However, the Depression drove many middle-class writers into the ranks of the proletariat, or at least made them insecure enough to identify with it and produce novels that reflected its concerns and values.[14] Such downward social mobility appears to have shaped the experience at least of Clara Weatherwax and Robert Cantwell.

Grays Harbor was also fertile ground for proletarian writers because the class struggle was especially naked there, creating a high degree of class consciousness among its residents. As Robert Cantwell described it:

> It is almost entirely a working-class community. The major stores are chain stores, and most of the mill officials are hired representatives of Eastern capitalists; the absorbent layer of shopkeepers, small owners and professional people that in other places acts as a sort of cushion to break the clash of class antagonisms—or prevents their being recognized plainly for what they are—is numerically and culturally unimportant. Consequently, class lines are firmly drawn, and the classes can scarcely be said to be in that "state of flux, with a persistent

interchange of their elements" which Marx once observed to be a condition of American society in general.[15]

The overtness of the class struggle on the Harbor, then, provided rich material for proletarian authors, and strengthened their work. Marxist critic Joseph Freeman, writing in the introduction to a 1935 proletarian literature anthology, observed, "Where the class struggle was latent, the Socialist movement was weak; where the movement was weak, the art it inspired was weak. Where the class struggle was sharp, the movement was strong; where the movement was strong, the art it inspired was strong."[16]

Indeed, the class struggle shaped opinions about these revolutionary novels every bit as much as it shaped opinions about bosses, workers, and strikes, and these positions were staked out along ideological lines. Literary critic R. W. Steadman spoke for many in the liberal-bourgeois establishment when he claimed that "most proletarian novelists are what might be called *lumpenliterati*; they can't write and they haven't the shadow of an idea of what constitutes literature." Proletarian novelists wrote about their experiences: oppressive working conditions, workers being attacked and imprisoned, and laborers organizing, and striking, despite great opposition, in the attempt to improve their lives. To Steadman and other critics of proletarian literature this amounted to little more than dreary propaganda. He complained ludicrously that "it is possible for a poor and unemployed worker to rejoice at the sight of a passing cloud on a spring day or to glory in the remembered song of the nightingale."[17] The absence in proletarian literature of such poetic musings on passing clouds and nightingales, for Steadman, meant that proletarian novels did not communicate objective or universal human experiences, and were therefore not art.

To the defender of proletarian literature, however, this kind of critique embodied the decadent and "class-conditioned" nature of the liberal-bourgeois literary establishment Steadman represented. Freeman, the Marxist critic, explained:

What [critics of proletarian literature] are really saying is that *their* experience is experience. They are ignorant of or hate the proletarian experience; hence for them it is not experience at all and not a fit subject for art. . . . Their experience is class-conditioned, but, as has always been the case with the bourgeoisie, they pretend that their values are the values of humanity.[18]

As the proletarian novelists themselves might have pointed out, this critique might equally have been applied to the capitalist press. The mainstream press, like the bourgeois literary establishment, claimed that they were objective and the workers were biased, that they dealt in real experience and the workers dealt in propaganda.

In the workers' press, the proletarian novelists' work was respected precisely because it did reflect workers' lived experience. Melvin P. Levy, reviewing *Lumber* for the Communist *New Masses*, reflected that the novel was not really about Jimmie, "but of every man who works in the lumber mills—even of any man who works—and of his family." Levy continued, "And if [Jimmie's] life and that of his wife and children end with catastrophe, it is not a *personal* catastrophe . . . but a thing that could happen to any man who sometimes works and has money and sometimes can find neither labor nor wages."[19] John Dos Passos, who reviewed *Land of Plenty* for *The New Republic,* observed that it was "written more from the inside than any Russian book about a factory I've read. . . . To tell truly, and not romantically or sentimentally, about the relation between men and machines, and to describe the machine worker, are among the most important tasks before novelists today."[20] Proletarian critic Jack Conroy wrote of *Land of Plenty*: "For one who has worked in a factor from necessity, as I have, it rings as true as a well-tempered bell and is as fresh and strong as it was more than 30 years ago."[21] Emjo Basshe, in his review of *Marching! Marching!* for *New Masses,* also wrote of that work's authenticity. The "wage cuts, stool pigeons, frameups, attacks on workers, suicides, the Law that breaks its very own Law, raids upon peaceful homes" described in the novel were "too deeply engraved upon the minds of those who have lived with seeing eyes and listening ears to be new or startling," he explained. For Basshe, the book's dramatic strength was the effect of workers' experiences "woven into a tapestry at once dreadful in its reality and colorful in its moods, sharp and crisp like slogans on banners and with a constant beat (Marching! Marching!) of sledge-hammer intensity."[22] A review of *Disillusion* published in the "Books for Workers" column of *The Timber Worker* actually suggested that the work was more fact than fiction. Describing Cochrane and Coldiron's work as "living history," the review explained that "it is the kind of fiction that is so real you know it is history as you read it. More than that, 'Disillusion' is thoroughly up to date; for the struggle it describes is actually, today, going on in Grays Harbor."[23]

Proletarian artists, critics, and journalists, while exposing the fallacious and class-conditioned arguments of their bourgeois counterparts, were themselves at least honest enough to not pretend to be "objective." Instead, they clearly sided with the workers. One can get a clear sense of this in the communist announcement in *New Masses* that it would sponsor a proletarian novel contest, the contest won by Clara Weatherwax's *Marching! Marching!* "Unlike the Pulitzer committee," the editors asserted, "we have nothing up our sleeves: far from it, we want to make it perfectly clear. We sponsor this contest because we desire to foster the literature of the American working class. . . . For the purposes of this contest, it is not sufficient that the novel be written from the point of view of the proletariat; it must actually be concerned with the proletariat."[24]

13
Women Who Fought

RADICAL FINNISH AMERICAN WOMEN ON THE RED COAST

On July 19, 1934, Lydia Laukkanen-Sommerville addressed her comrades and supporters at a picnic near Montesano, county seat of Grays Harbor. Hosted by the Grays Harbor local of the Communist Party (CP), the event served to raise funds and awareness for the upcoming county elections. Although no transcript of the speech is available, we can get some idea of its major themes based on Laukkanen's writing—and CP writings about her—from 1934.[1] For years, she had been a leading Red Coast Communist. Two years earlier she led two delegations of unemployed workers from Grays Harbor to Olympia demanding relief in the well-known "Hunger Marches" on the State Capitol.

Neither Laukkanen's political orientation nor her militant forms of activism were unusual among Finnish American women on the Red Coast. Finnish American women like Laukkanen-Sommerville took to the streets to protest anti-labor vigilantes and picket the mills where their family members worked. They also performed the hard work of operating soup kitchens during strikes and depressions, and organized union auxiliaries and activities that connected unions to the wider community. Yet scholars have not appreciated the importance of Finnish American women activists to the labor struggles that so marked Pacific Northwest history between 1910 and 1940. The lives of Wobbly Jenny Sipo, Communist Lydia Laukkanen, and union auxiliary leader Laura Law, in fact, suggest that Finnish culture promoted a much more active role for Finnish women than was the case for non-Finns.

Those acquainted with Finnish American history will not be surprised that Finns took major parts in most of the Northwest's lumber strikes that shook the region's greatest industry during the first four decades of the twentieth century. During the 1910s, a flood of Finnish immigrants entered Grays Harbor,

Cowlitz, and Pacific Counties. Hundreds of the region's Finnish American workers migrated to the Harbor following their experiences in the "mine wars" of Montana, the Upper Midwest, and other parts of the country. Some Red Coast radicals came west after their experiences in the epic 1913–1914 Michigan Copper Country Strike. Many others left the great copper-producing city of Butte, Montana, for Grays Harbor, or Woodland, in southwest Washington. The flow of Red Finns out of "the Gibraltar of Labor" and into the Red Coast provided the coast with many members of its radical community.

Because of the relative absence of women working for wages in the lumber industry—few worked in logging, sawmilling, and shingle work at the time— Finnish women had to find creative ways to influence the lumber workers' union movement. Male unionists commonly held meetings at rural logging camps, in bars and saloons, and other locations where "respectable" women were barred by law or custom. Moreover, male unionists were frequently unwilling to stay home and mind children, which would have allowed their wives to attend union or political activities.

One of the ways that Finnish American women established an activist role for themselves was through their participation in that defining feature of Finnish American life, the Finnish hall. In most cases, these halls were open to both women and men, as was clear from the most common activities housed therein: dances, dinners, dramatic performances, sewing club meetings, and school lessons. These halls, especially the socialist buildings, also housed union meetings, fundraisers, parties, and other activities. These shared spaces proved to be important to Finnish American women as they joined, and often led, local radical political movements and militant union activities. Unlike some other labor and left-wing spaces—including the taverns and cigar shops where union business was sometimes conducted—Finn halls opened their doors to working-class families, and radical women oftentimes led meetings and other activities inside the halls. For example, Aberdeen Party leader Lydia Laukkanen used the hall as a headquarters for the committee that investigated the fiscal malfeasance of Seattle organizer R. P. Forrest during the 1927–1928 Miners' Relief campaign.[2]

A second factor contributing to Finnish American women's labor activism was the history of female political and social activity in Finland and in earlier Finnish North American settlements. By the first years of the twentieth century, Finland had one of the world's most powerful socialist movements.[3] Founded in 1899 as the Finnish Workers' Party, the Finnish Social

Democratic Party (SDP) experienced dramatic growth after the turn of the century, drawing intense support from Finland's tenant farmers, landless agricultural workers, and its small industrial proletariat. [4] Women were active in Finnish workers' societies throughout the 1890s, and formed a key pillar of support for the Party during its early years.[5] In November 1905, many sectors of Finnish society launched a general strike to protest what they considered various forms of Russian oppression and to demand the expansion of civil liberties and a more representative political system. Although striking workers, whose demands included socioeconomic reforms, did not get all that they wanted, the Finns did gain a new and more democratic constitution that included universal suffrage for those twenty-four and older.[6] When they went to the polls in 1907, Finnish women became the first in Europe to vote in a national election.[7] And when the Finnish electorate voted nineteen women into Parliament—the world's first female parliamentarians—nine of them belonged to the Social Democratic Party.[8] To many Finnish Americans, the successes born of the general strike and growth of the SDP demonstrated the clear value of workplace and political organizing.

In a series of strikes between 1905 and 1912 in Grays Harbor, and later Pacific County, Finnish American workers—including Finnish American women—thrust themselves to the forefront of the Northwest's labor movement. Although not confined to Finnish workers, the strikes always centered on the mills that employed large numbers of Finns, and not surprisingly, the strikers used the Finn halls (see chapter 3) as their union headquarters. The great 1912 Grays Harbor and Pacific County Lumber Strike, often called "The War of Grays Harbor" (see chapter 5) was an epic showdown between exploited labor and organized capital. Beginning in March 1912, the strike eventually involved thousands of southwest Washington mill workers organized with the help of the IWW. Capital organized in force to combat the threat posed by workers who dared fight for improved wages and to form their own union.

The strike also gave employers a chance to settle old scores against the immigrant mill laborers and their families who so frequently led these strikes. At first, male strikers took to the picket line. In the first two weeks of picketing, police, strikebreakers, and vigilantes beat, jailed, and kidnapped male strikers. When violence broke out in April 1912 in Grays Harbor, women—the wives, daughters, and female friends of lumber mill strikers—took center stage. After vigilantes deported striking lumber mill worker L. A. Jacobson, he told the *Tacoma Times* that he feared "whether [his wife and five children] are still alive or not."[9] According to J. S. Biscay, editor of the IWW's Grays Harbor strike bulletin: "The women began to help picket the mills. This sudden move on the part of the women practically tied up all the mills which opened Monday, and put the Slade mill in such bad shape that slabs had to be hauled from the outside to keep the fires going."[10] Women held the lines against Grays Harbor police and strikebreakers, who tried to disperse them using fire hoses, clubs, and even axe handles. Many of these women were Finnish American Socialists and supporters of the Wobblies.

The women picketers were acting to defend their families: the strike's main demand—a $2.25 daily wage—would have a direct effect on living conditions. Indeed, low wages, bouts of unemployment, seasonal workplace shutdowns, and so-called "industrial accidents" went hand in hand with substandard housing, malnutrition, and homelessness. The *Seattle Star* ran a story and photograph of three Finnish women, Anna Kaakinen, Fannie Kaarinen, and Sophy Sipela, who stood their ground as police sprayed them with a high-powered fire hose. According to the *Star*, the women "laughed in the faces of the bullies—laughed sturdily, good-naturedly and called upon the quaking 'scabs' to quit work and call the strike."[11]

These picketers were the first Finnish women to gain major attention for their activism on the Red Coast, but for the next three decades, their socialist, IWW, Communist, and militant unionist successors followed similar paths, organizing, boycotting, and striking to challenge the region's oligarchy and improve conditions for the region's working-class majority.

Jennie Sipo, Aberdeen's best-known female Wobbly, came to the Harbor by way of Finland and Butte. Born Jennie Heikkila in Finland, Sipo married Butte miner John Sipo in 1916 at the age of twenty-two.[12] The couple and their son, John Jr., lived in Butte through the tumultuous labor conflicts that shook the mining city during World War I.[13] Frequently led by Finnish radicals and met by employer violence and blacklists, these strikes likely influenced the lives of the Sipos. John, as a miner, and Jennie, as a future IWW leader, left Butte for Aberdeen during the war, perhaps fleeing from the mineowners' blacklists or to escape the dangers of the mines for the ostensibly healthier climate of the Pacific Northwest.

Whatever the reason for their move to Aberdeen's Finntown, the Sipo family met tragedy shortly after their arrival. John Sipo died of pneumonia on January 1919, leaving Jennie as a young widow and mother, a not-uncommon fate for working-class women in lumber country. In fact, judging from the large number of widows who joined or supported the IWW, it appears likely that the movement offered a sense of purpose and belonging to working-class women who had fallen on hard times.[14]

Sipo served as the IWW's Foodstuff Workers' Industrial Union's organizer and headed the list of the union's charter members.[15] Her prominence in the IWW was most visible during the IWW's 1922 free speech fight. During the conflict, local authorities arrested Sipo, Wobbly Hilma Ray, and twenty of their male fellow workers, charging them all with criminal syndicalism.[16] Grays Harbor authorities recorded that Sipo had "in her possession the minute book of the meeting" of the IWW, an indication that she had earned a measure of responsibility within the union. Sipo earned even more respect by refusing early release from jail, an offer accepted by some of her fellow workers. For her commitment to remain behind bars until all IWWs gained their freedom, Sipo acquired the honorary title as a "real rebel girl" from the Wobblies' jail committee.[17]

Like many of her fellow workers, Sipo remained involved in the Grays Harbor IWW for several years. In November 1924, she married Aberdeen IWW longshoreman and union leader Robert Benson, and the couple lived in a working-class section of south Aberdeen.[18] Although Jennie's name does not appear in the *Industrial Worker* following her marriage, it continued to appear in the *Industrialisti* "Greetings" section as late as 1939, signifying a continued support for, if not activism in, the union.[19]

By the 1930s, the Coast's left had taken a dramatic turn as the Communist movement displaced the Wobblies as the leading force for militant labor activism in most locales. Communist youth auxiliaries helped train activists for the international movement. Although the Communist Party boasted several youth groups, the best known were the Young Communist League (YCL) and Young Pioneers. Young Finnish American women led the Aberdeen locals of both the YCL and Young Pioneers. For example, in 1929, Ellen Rautio, a widow and dishwasher at an Aberdeen pool hall, served as secretary for the YCL.[20] But young Finnish women also held leadership posts within explicitly Finnish American Communist organizations. *Toveritar* (Woman Comrade), the Finnish-language socialist weekly published in Astoria, Oregon, between 1916 and 1930, carried its own Children's Section, which regularly featured news, correspondence, and poetry from Red Coast women and girls.[21]

Communist youths engaged in a wide range of activities, including attending CP educational trainings in the Northwest. Labor historian Ottilie

Markholt, who participated in these CP youth events, remembered: "District 12 of the YCL held a two-week school at the Communist Finn Hall at Ninth and Yesler [in Seattle] in August, drawing some twenty students from Seattle and nearby communities, 'red diaper' children from Grays Harbor Communists, and a YCLer from Portland."[22] During the 1920s, the Young Pioneers published political magazines that focused on children's labor and poverty in the United States and the efforts to eliminate these problems in the Soviet Union. The *Young Pioneer* featured visual and literary artwork by and for Communist youths. A frequent target of their cartoons was the capitalist education system in the United States, which, according to Party members, taught obedience and deference to bosses over critical thinking. A common trope of the illustrations was a critical, anti-capitalist child challenging an austere teacher. In the cartoon below, "Billy" shows off his artistic talents.[23]

In Grays Harbor, membership in both the YCL and Pioneers included young Finnish women like Mary Laukkanen, who was active in the Aberdeen branch of the Workers' Party of America during the early 1920s.[24] In the mid-1920s, Mary's role in the movement was eclipsed by her younger sister, Lydia who became one of the most effective Communist leaders in the region's history. Born in 1909 in Aberdeen, Lydia Laukkanen lived with her parents and four siblings in a Finnish neighborhood. Her father, Abel, was a mill hand at Donovan Lumber Company.[25] Even before he died of a stroke, five of the six household members needed to work outside the home for the family to get by.

With Laukkanen's history of working-class struggle, it's perhaps not surprising that, before her twentieth birthday, Lydia was already one of the best-known Communist organizers in the Pacific Northwest, and the Party showed its faith in Laukkanen by awarding her high-level duties. She was a leader of local unemployed groups, a Party candidate for city and county office, and had

A DRAWING LESSON   By Murray

In this cartoon from the *Young Pioneer*, a Communist youth magazine, a leftist student uses his art project to make a point about class and capitalism. *Young Pioneer* (New York), December 1930.

the enormous responsibility of overseeing a high-level investigative committee into one of her comrade's fiscal malfeasance.[26]

Laukkanen grew up immersed in left-wing activity. By age thirteen, she was well-versed in Marxist literature, and served as a prominent salesperson— or "shock brigadier"–for the Finnish CP newspapers, *Toveri* and *Toveritar*. At fourteen, she won a national prize for newspaper subscription sales. Lydia also served as president and organizer for the Aberdeen Young Communist League and was the long-time leader of the Aberdeen Young Pioneers. Like dozens of other Red Coast leftist youths, during the summer of 1927 Laukkanen attended the YCL Summer School in Winlock.[27]

As a young adult, Laukkanen stood at the fore of most Party activities. She became section organizer of the Grays Harbor Section of the CP and secretary of the Grays Harbor unemployed movement. In 1934, she was organizational secretary of the local Party. Her activism put her on the front lines of workplace struggles, as she helped to organize Grays Harbor lumber strikes in 1929 and 1932. Laukkanen expressed her commitment to the class struggle in a straightforward, enthusiastic manner, writing, for example, "We . . . pledge ourselves to fight for the organization of the American toiling youth against bosses wars and the capitalist system of hunger, terror, and wars."[28]

Lydia Laukkanen led a busy life of activism, but she most commonly made headlines for leading actions designed to gain relief for those laid low by the Depression. She served as the leader of both of the large Grays Harbor hunger marches to Olympia.[29] In November 1932, while Grays Harbor was deep in the Great Depression, Laukkanen forced her way into the proceedings of the Aberdeen City Council to demand public assistance for the city's considerable destitute population. Radicals had intruded on the councils' proceedings before, but Laukkanen, with the support of a "large group" of workers, drawn mostly from the local Unemployed Councils, demanded that the municipal government provide two meals per day, clean and neat sleeping quarters, and the use of the Salvation Army chapel as an assembly room for unemployed workers during stormy weather. She harangued the public officials, demanding that they live up to their obligations to the city's vast destitute population.[30] Like many first- and second-generation immigrants, Laukkanen was bilingual. She sold subscriptions for both the Finnish- and English-language leftist press, and wrote for the *Voice of Action*. An August 1934 article warned that "Aberdeen Youths Start Fascist Organization," and condemned the "young men" for "following the footsteps and aims of the Mayor of Aberdeen, whose plans are to crush the activity of the Communist party locally."[31]

Laukkanen and her comrades employed a variety of creative tactics to make the lives of those harmed by the Depression more tolerable. They diverted a water main to provide "free water" to destitute workers at the Aberdeen CP hall, held demonstrations at the Salvation Army to demand higher quality relief, and stormed the Aberdeen City Council chambers to demand greater public relief. In 1934, three hundred workers carrying "United Front banners" marched through downtown Aberdeen to the welfare commissioner's office, where Laukkanen delivered an impassioned speech and the group delivered its demands for a minimum wage, cash relief, free medical and dental care, and free milk for children.[32]

Laukkanen also tried to enter the halls of political office through more orthodox means. In 1932, she ran for Aberdeen City Council to represent a heavily working-class district of south Aberdeen. Two years later, she ran for a position on the Grays Harbor County Commission as a candidate of the Communist Party. Although she didn't receive many votes, the elections did provide Laukkanen with a platform to voice the issues important to working-class radicals. About 350 workers and farmers turned out to a July 1934 picnic hosted by the CP to announce Laukkanen-Sommerville's candidacy for commissioner.[33] A CP congressional election platform featured a photo of Laukkanen alongside appeals to radical voters: "The Communist Party is the only political party which leads in the every-day fight of the masses of the people for improved conditions; it alone offers a practical way out of the appalling misery and suffering brought on by capitalism and capitalist rule."[34] To mobilize voters for the election, Grays Harbor Communists held house parties and a "Red Ball" at the Finnish Workers' (IWW) Hall, while the Seattle-based publishers of the *Voice of Action* printed 20,000 copies of the Grays Harbor Communist Party Platform. Laukkanen delivered frequent talks to her supporters at these meetings.[35]

In the mid-1930s, after adopting her husband's surname, Lydia Sommerville took a position with the *Voice of Action*, the Northwest's Communist newspaper. She served as a field representative for the newspaper and toured Oregon and Washington to raise interest in the radical periodical. She was a prolific fundraiser. In 1935, she raised hundreds of dollars in a fundraising contest to support the *Voice of Action*.[36]

In this undated photograph, Laura Law (fourth from right) stands with a group of women. This image is part of a massive collection of materials related to Law's life and death held at the Southwest Washington Archives in Olympia, Washington. Unfortunately, the image includes no further identifying information.

In the late 1930s, Lydia's path crossed that of Laura and Richard "Dick" Law, a married couple with whom she shared a belief that militant working-class activism was central to revolutionizing American society. The Laws were at the center of the Northwest labor movement. Dick Law was a member of the International Executive Board of the International Woodworkers of America (IWA).[37] Formed in 1937, the IWA was the largest Pacific Coast affiliate of the Congress of Industrial Organizations (CIO). Perhaps more important, he was undoubtedly one of the leading figures in the local left, an unflinching militant in the face of boss oppression.

Laura Law was born Laura Luoma in Finland just three years before the Finnish Civil War. Her mother, ironically, was a battlefield nurse for the Whites, who opposed the Red Finns in the civil War. In 1920, Laura accompanied her aunt, Clara, to the United States, following her mother who made the Atlantic voyage a year earlier.[38] In Washington, Laura Luoma Law became a leading member of the Red Coast's woodworkers' union auxiliary movement. She exerted wide influence in local working-class culture and politics from her elected positions in the Federation of Woodworkers' Union Auxiliary 281 and as founding president of IWA auxiliary 3-2. Between 1937 and 1939, the auxiliary sent resolutions to state and national lawmakers to support progressive legislation; canvassed voters to help defeat the anti-union Initiative 130 that would have required a thirty-day "cooling off" period before calling any strike; wrote letters to President Roosevelt demanding that the embargo be lifted against Spain in order to assist the anti-Franco forces; and lobbied the Aberdeen School Board to allow the play "Waiting for Lefty" to be given in local schools. Discussing the Grays Harbor IWA auxiliary's political activism, the *Timber Worker* ran a front page headline reading: "Grays Harbor Women Fight Side-by-Side With the Men."[39]

Like many others associated with the left in the 1930s, Law framed her activism as a struggle to defend civil liberties and civil rights. Her own hall—Aberdeen's Red Finn Hall—came under attack on several occasions during the 1910s. In December 1939, only a few weeks before her death, the Red hall suffered a nearly fatal blow when anti-Communist vigilantes raided and plundered the space. The Laws spent much of their final month together organizing for the Grays Harbor Civil Rights Committee, a labor-left organization that promised to halt the "reign of terror" against radical unionists on Grays Harbor.[40] Auxiliary 3-2 joined dozens of other organizations in issuing resolutions condemning the acts of a mob that "wrecked a hall owned by the Finnish Federation, demolishing fixtures and equipment to the extent of thousands of dollars worth of damage" while "the law enforcement officers of Aberdeen made no attempt to halt the destruction."[41] Not content to issue mere words, the Laws began an investigation of the hall raid in hopes of convincing authorities to bring charges against the vandals.

The Laws' efforts to investigate the vigilante acts put them squarely in the sights of the same right-wing brutes who destroyed the hall.[42] In response to the Laws' central role in the labor movement, and as part of a larger effort to repress and threaten local leftists, Harbor employers cast a surveillance net around the couple. In 1939, Lydia Laukkanen and Dick Law held private meetings about union and CP issues at her home in Aberdeen. The meetings proved less private than they would have liked because John Vekich, a labor spy in the employ of wealthy Harbor boss Joe Schneider, monitored Law's comings and goings, and reported them to his masters. For years, in fact, labor spies surveilled both Laura Law and her husband, and in 1939, their family began receiving harassing phone calls. Prominent and wealthy Grays Harbor residents also threatened Dick Law's life on several occasions. Johnny Vekich

Interior of the Aberdeen Red Finn Hall following the raid and ransacking at the hands of vigilantes. Photo courtesy of Jones Photo, Aberdeen, Washington.

threatened to "liquidate" Dick Law, while *Washingtonian* editor and future Congressman, Russell Mack, told a gathering of wealthy Harbor residents: "The Dick Laws Must Go."[43]

Still, Laura and Dick could hardly have imagined the horror that awaited her on the evening of one January night while her husband was in town at a series of union meetings. That night, an assailant entered the Laws' home and bludgeoned and slashed Laura Law to death. For those on the right, her murder not only eliminated a powerful voice that advocated for workers, it also provided an opportunity to frame her husband, the man at the center of Harbor employers' campaign against the left. Laura's murder was widely seen by those on the left as an act of political retaliation for her husband's activism in the militant wing of the International Woodworkers of America and Communist Party, but it was never officially solved.

Law's grisly death has captured the attention of Red Coasters for decades. Murray Morgan's sole novel, *The Viewless Winds*, presented a fictionalized version of her murder and the subsequent investigation.[44] But Law's life, and the lives of radical working-class women such as Jenny Sipo and Lydia Laukkanen, also deserve attention. The words penned by Finnish American Wobbly Harri Siitonen in tribute to Law might apply to any of them:

I really don't care whether Laura Law was Methodist, Baptist, red, pink or anarcho-black. As one who's sported a Wobbly card for the last quarter century, I look on her as what the modern Wobs call a "Sister Worker." So come next May First, the historic international workers' holiday, I plan to raise my fist in a salute, holding a red rose, to honor the memory of my Sister Worker and American Finn Laura (Luoma) Law, who gave her life so American working folks "would have enough to eat."[45]

It's likely that the full truth about Law's murder will never be known, especially because those with any involvement in the crime and investigation have long since gone to their graves. But it is significant that her death came during an era of massive red-baiting and anti-radical violence, and that she and her family were in the sights of reactionaries every bit as much as the Wobblies had been three decades earlier. What is certain is that women such as Lydia Laukkanen, Jenny Sipo, and Laura Law lent much strength to the leftist movements on the Red Coast, and their contributions were noticed by both friend and foe.

14
Willapa Longshoremen and the Big Strike

At noon on Monday, July 30, 1934, workers began loading lumber on the ships docked at the mills in Raymond in Pacific County, Washington. Ordinarily an unremarkable event, the start of this workday made the news because it marked the first time Willapa Harbor's longshoremen performed paid labor at the docks in more than ninety days.[1] As members of the International Longshoremen's Association—Pacific Coast District, which, in 1937, became the International Longshore and Warehouse Union (ILWU), they belonged to one of the most radical and militant unions in United States history. During the previous three months, these men and their allies stopped all coastal shipping.

The "Big Strike," as the 1934 Maritime Strike is widely known, shut down the Pacific Coast's ports, from the Canadian border to the Mexican border. Few events in labor history are so significant and oft-remembered as the Big Strike, an event that grew into the San Francisco General Strike and completely transformed Pacific Coast labor relations. The strike was extremely violent, which was hardly unusual of 1930s labor disputes. What differs, however, is the importance that labor activists place on remembering the violence visited upon strikers by police, strikebreakers, and other anti-labor forces in ports up and down the West Coast. To this day, on every July 5, Pacific Coast longshoremen stop work and engage in a one-day labor protest designed to commemorate the lives of strikers murdered by San Francisco police on "Bloody Thursday." Noting the significance and scope of this annual commemoration, also known as Maritime Memorial Day, in June 1935, Harry Lundeberg, president of the Maritime Federation of the Pacific Coast, declared, "Every union man will pay tribute to the martyrs of the strike. They will take their place in history with the martyrs of labor, with the victims of Ludlow, Haymarket, Everett, Centralia, Imperial Valley, San Francisco Preparedness Day, and Modesta."[2]

Unionists engage in these one-day commemorations at all US Pacific Coast ports, ranging from Hawaii and Alaska to southern California and Washington's Olympic Peninsula. No work is performed in the massive ports of San Francisco, Portland, or Tacoma, while workers in the small Red Coast ports of Longview, Grays Harbor, and Raymond likewise engage in the annual work stoppage. Bloody Thursday, like the Big Strike itself, was born of intense class struggle, as militantly class-conscious maritime workers demanded that the world never forget the price their fellow workers paid for their union. Indeed, each year on July 5, observers can see banners reading "We Never Forget" up and down America's West Coast ports.

As was common with lumber ports, Willapa Harbor's docks connected the region's lumber mills to the sea. According to the *American Lumberman*, by 1912, twenty lumber mills, shingle mills, and foundries lined the harbor, employing more than 2,000 workers in a town of only 3,500 residents. A sizable number of men—and they were all men during the early twentieth century—made their living as longshoremen.[3]

Longshore work at lumber ports such as those on the Red Coast consisted primarily of loading lumber onto sail and steam vessels. Work at the Red Coast's lumber ports was dirty, difficult, dangerous labor composed of long days and the foreboding that comes with working in a high-fatality industry. To load a lumber schooner, longshoremen lifted the lumber onto the ship, usually by hoisting the lumber with a winch. Once the loads of lumber were aboard ship, longshoremen stowed them in the ship's hold.[4] Hours were long and wages were low for Pacific Coast longshoremen, but the workers' main complaints surrounded employers' hiring methods. Known as the "shape up," this hated practice involved foremen having potential workers gather before working hours to be selected for work. The humiliating practice caused longshoremen to stand around for hours waiting to work, while foremen chose their favorites—those who most successfully begged or bribed—for the prized positions.

Workplace injuries occurred regularly. These ranged in severity from sprained joints and broken limbs to deadly falls, as stacks of lumber fell on longshoremen or knocked them unconscious causing them to fall and drown in the harbor. In a 1916 report, the Washington State Bureau of Labor reported:

These workmen handle about 3,000 pounds of freight per hour
per man, sometimes a long distance with the result that hernia
is a common disease among these workers and it is not at all an
uncommon thing for men to work 10, 12, 16, and 20 hours with no
let up and then when relaxation comes fatigue almost to exhaustion is
often the case.[5]

Dockworkers also died at work with some regularity. In August 1910,
Swedish American longshoreman Harry Lund drowned while working a ship
at an Aberdeen lumber mill. The *Aberdeen Herald* described the death of H.
Hain, who died in a similar fashion a decade earlier: "H. Hain, a longshoreman, fell overboard and was drowned at the Cosmopolis dock Monday morning. Although seen falling into the river and his comrades ran to his assistance,
he did not rise after first sinking, and it is thought that he struck against the
piling in his fall. . . . The body has not yet been recovered."[6] In 1921, Finnish-
born longshoreman Oscar Roswall died at work on the Raymond docks after
being struck by an iron bar, which ruptured his liver, sending him off the dock
and into the water. He died from his injuries four days later.[7]

Willapa dockworkers had long histories of forming unions and fighting
collectively for work-life improvements. Willapa longshoremen formed their
first union in April 1904, Local 587 of the International Longshoremen's
Association (ILA). It was, according to the *Willapa Harbor Pilot*, "the first
labor union to be organized in South Bend which was affiliated with a national
organization." A month later, these unionists waged the first dock strike in that
city's history. Strikers demanded that unionists be given first priority in loading ships. When a ship captain balked at the authority of ILA Local 587, a
representative of the Aberdeen Sailors' Union of the Pacific traveled to Pacific
County and threatened to refuse to provide sailors for the vessel unless it was
loaded by unionists. This standoff ended rapidly when another ship arrived in
port and hired the available unionists.[8] Despite this example of militancy and
solidarity, by August 1904, the union had dissolved because "of opposition
from master mariners and lumber companies."[9]

Organization on Willapa Harbor continued, but like other dockworkers'
unions along the Pacific Coast, Willapa longshoremen experienced a rocky
early history. On June 21, 1909, fifteen Raymond longshoremen signed their
names on an application for a union charter with the Longshoremen's Union
of the Pacific.[10] In September 1909, international officers from the ILA visited

the Pacific Coast and enrolled independent longshoremen's locals, such as the Raymond union formed earlier in the year, into the ILA, within the Pacific Coast District of that association. During its first year, 1909–1910, thirty-eight Pacific Coast longshoremen's locals joined the ILA.[11] Raymond and South Bend longshoremen formed two new locals in the ILA during 1909–1910 and paid dues up through at least September of 1910. But both locals had difficulty maintaining membership and paying dues, and both disbanded by 1913. Still, the ILA did have some success on the Willapa, as Raymond and South Bend maritime workers formed ILA Local No. 38-56, a "Western Lumber Inspectors' Association," in late 1912 or early 1913.[12]

Building the Willapa ILA and other Pacific Coast longshoremen's locals was a vast project, and in Raymond, left-wing activists, especially Finnish American workers, led this work. In 1910, more than 6 percent of Raymond's 2,450 residents were born in Finland, while many more were second-generation Finnish Americans.[13] In the 1910s, the town's socialists hailed primarily from the Finnish population. The same could be said for Raymond's Communists in future decades. By 1912, Raymond's Finns had formed a branch of the Finnish Socialist Federation and held events such as plays at the group's Finnish hall.[14]

Some Willapa longshoremen, including many Finns, also carried red cards in the Industrial Workers of the World. Raymond workers organized with the IWW beginning as early as 1907.[15] The *Industrial Worker* claimed that in 1912, forty Raymond longshoremen were IWW members. By the end of that year— one full of violent anti-radical persecution—the Wobblies still maintained a timber workers' union in Raymond, with shingle weaver Lee Helper serving as secretary.[16]

Opposition to the Willapa longshoremen's unions came early and often from organized capital. In June 1910, a branch of the Grays Harbor Stevedore Company was formed in Raymond, with Captain Ernest Smith being dispatched from Grays Harbor to run the company on Willapa Harbor. Originally operating only in Grays Harbor, the stevedore firm hired non-union dockworkers to load and unload ships docked in Aberdeen and Hoquiam. In 1908, ten Grays Harbor lumbermen incorporated the Stevedore Company, and in 1909 it came under control of the Rothschilds Company, the largest stevedore conglomerate on the Pacific Coast. On the Twin Harbors, the company demanded an "open shop," refusing to sign contracts with the ILA.[17] Shortly after the firm opened its branch in Raymond, non-union men lined the docks

Parades such as this one in Raymond in 1913 were a regular feature of Labor Day festivities throughout the Red Coast. In this photograph, a horse-drawn float carries unionists and a sign reading "These Cigars Are Union Made." Photo courtesy of Pacific County Historical Society, South Bend, Washington.

looking for work, forced to line up and beg for jobs, much as in other non-union ports. The successful anti-union drive championed by the Willapa Harbor and Grays Harbor stevedore companies served as models for coast lumber manufacturers and shippers. Praising the work done by Twin Harbor employers in this regard, the *Timberman,* print organ of Pacific Coast lumber employers, stated that the Pacific Coast's largest ports planned to operate an explicitly "open shop" stevedore company based on the Willapa and Grays Harbor firm. The Stevedore firm maintained a non-union waterfront in Willapa throughout most of the early and mid-1910s.[18]

The town's Finnish population took a major hit in in the spring of 1912. As seen in Chapter 6, the town's employers and police collaborated during the IWW-led lumber strike to close Raymond's Finnish hall—home to its Finnish socialist and IWW movements—and expel Raymond's Greek and Finnish strikers from town. Certainly, officially sanctioned violence convinced some Finns who escaped deportation to leave on their own. In the decade that followed, Finnish leftists continued to face repression in Pacific County.

Employment on lumber docks and in lumber mills grew dramatically in 1916, spurred in part by the demand for war materials. The Raymond ILA branch boomed, with more than fifty members marching during that city's 1916

Labor Day Parade.[19] In that year, the coast's dockworkers engaged in a lengthy and violent strike for increased wages and the closed shop.[20] The Washington State Bureau of Labor noted the impact of the 1916 dock strike: "The most serious disturbance in the industrial relations of the State of Washington during the years from November 1, 1914, to November 1, 1916—and there was an abundance of them, many of them small moment, however—was that of the members of the International Longshoremen's Association."[21]

The strike broke out on June 1, 1916, and raged for more than four months, shutting down much of the coast's shipping for the entire summer. Spurred on by the strike, Raymond and South Bend organized a new ILA local with forty-seven members, which represented 98 percent of Willapa longshoremen. On June 3, the Willapa union struck and distributed handbills throughout town advertising the strike and calling on workers to refuse to scab.[22] Fighting for their jobs against scab labor in an "open shop" port, Willapa longshoremen turned to creative tactics to push for workplace improvements. Joining their fellow unionists in Grays Harbor, Willapa's union dockworkers formed a union-run stevedore company to compete with the Grays Harbor Stevedore Company. The unionists then claimed that the open shop stevedore firm was violating the Sherman Anti-Trust Act, making illegal restraint of trade.[23]

Red Coast longshoremen at Grays and Willapa Harbors struck alongside workers at larger ports. Weeks into the conflict, the *Aberdeen Herald* expressed a common opinion that the strike had little chance of ending anytime soon: "With the big longshoremen's strike advanced two days in its third week, there seems still but a slight chance of its settlement in the near future. Both sides to the fight apparently have made up their minds to a long struggle."[24] Employers refused to budge on the union's demands, presenting a bold and unified resistance. In San Francisco, employers formed the so-called Open Shop Stevedoring Company, a scab-herding operation designed to "work in harmony with the Grays Harbor, Willapa Harbor, Puget Sound, Coos Bay, Coquille River, and other open shop organizations formed to handle lumber cargoes," according to the *Timberman*.[25] At some ports, employers continued to hire non-union workers throughout the strike. The strike ended in early October. Historian Ronald Magden contended that in Grays and Willapa Harbors, "union men were stuck in the employers' 'peonage system.'"[26]

The failure of the 1916 Longshoremen's Strike, which ended in defeat and fragmentation for the region's longshoremen, dealt a serious blow to the Pacific Coast ILA. The Red Coast's labor movement suffered further setbacks during the First World War, as Willapa Wobblies became targets of government sur-veillance and infiltration. In late 1917 and early 1918, a spy from Governor Ernest Lister's Secret Service—a government spy agency—infiltrated the Raymond IWW, posing as a working-class radical and collecting names of local Wobblies. He was apparently quite effective, as, in January 1918, Raymond IWW leaders asked him to open a Wobbly hall in the city and to serve as sec-retary of the local IWW branch.[27] In April 1920 state authorities convicted a group of Pacific County Finnish Wobblies of criminal syndicalism.[28]

The persistent repression of Raymond's Finns and other leftists no doubt set back the movement's work, but Pacific County Red Finns joined their Red Coast comrades in sustaining the movement throughout the 1920s, generally viewed as a difficult period for labor and the left in America. For example, the Finnish Federation of the Workers' (Communist) Party recorded Red Coast Finnish locals in Pacific County towns of Raymond and Ilwaco, along with those in Woodland, Kalama, Deep River, Aberdeen, and Hoquiam.[29] Members of these locals show up as subscribers to Finnish Communist news-papers *Toveri* and *Toveritar*, based in nearby Astoria, Oregon, as well as the daily *Työmies*, which remained the daily news organ of Finnish Communism throughout the period covered in this book. In fact, the Raymond, Winlock, Hoquiam, and Aberdeen Finnish socialist locals each held ownership shares in *Toveritar*.[30] Records indicate that Raymond's Communist group remained busy throughout the 1920s and 1930s. They hosted national Communist speakers, put on leftist films and plays in both English and Finnish, and con-tributed local news articles to *Toveri* and *Toveritar*.[31]

From the 1910s through the Pacific Coast "Big Strike" in 1934, Finns remained the largest ethnic group on the Willapa docks. Some of these men continued to support the revolutionary industrial unionism of the Wobblies, but a larger group increasingly belonged to or supported the Communist Party, which played a significant role in the Raymond longshoremen's union throughout the 1930s. The membership lists of ILA Local 38-92 and ILWU Local 1 are filled with the names of Finnish Americans, including many with long histories of left-wing activism.[32]

Chartered on October 2, 1933, ILA Local 38-92 was one of the smallest West Coast longshoremen's locals. It initiated only seventeen members at its first meeting and another ten a week later. What the local lacked in size, it more than made up for in militancy. Two weeks after its first meeting, the local voted to inform employees of the Twin Harbor Stevedore Company—based in Grays Harbor—to cease work on Willapa docks, and to keep them from working the docks "by force if necessary."[33] In early November, the local launched an investigation into securing a closed shop for the Raymond docks. By April 1934, the Raymond union had joint control over a hall with a branch of the National Lumber Workers' Union (NLWU), a Communist union in the lumber industry. At a joint meeting of the Raymond ILA and NLWU, Roy Brown, NLWU chairman, called "upon the loggers and mill workers to stand on the side of the longshoremen in case they strike, refusing to allow scabs on the lumber docks nor to produce lumber for scab handlers," according to the *Voice of Action*.[34] With the Big Strike of Pacific Coast maritime workers only a month in the future, Brown's comments made for a timely reminder of the importance of working-class solidarity.

The Big Strike broke out on May 9, 1934. Longshoremen demanding "a closed shop, union control of the hiring halls, a six hour day, and $1.00 per hour" shut down ports stretching from the Canadian border to the Mexican border, involving more than 12,000 workers. A week into the strike, longshoremen got a major boost when the Sailors' Union of the Pacific joined the conflict. As in earlier labor conflicts at lumber ports, the Willapa longshoremen's strike caused a de facto general shutdown in lumber, the region's basic industry. Agitated by the 1,500 Willapa Harbor laborers put out of work by the strike, the *Raymond Herald* wrote of the closure of several mills "for lack of further available storage space" due to the dockworkers' refusal to remove lumber from the struck docks. In an impressive show of solidarity, one ship's crew that struck at Willapa Harbor proclaimed their unwillingness to scab, stating that they joined the strike for the "recognition of the working man and living conditions to make it better for all."[35]

Shippers used their usual methods—anti-labor news coverage, divide-and-conquer tactics, and violent strikebreaking—in an attempt to coerce the longshoremen back to work. On May 28, employers made a "compromise" offer to Pacific Coast dockworkers: recognition of the ILA as the workers' union of choice and "no discrimination in hiring as between union or non-union men." Shippers made the offer knowing that the union would refuse it and thus make the ILA look unreasonable. Employers refused to concede on the union hiring hall, the ILA's most important demand. Offended at the employers' duplicity, ILA locals refused the deal, with Raymond longshoremen stating: "This is not at all what the union men in this strike are after."[36]

Up and down the coast, police and strikebreakers resorted to violence to quell working-class militancy. The first murder came in San Pedro, the port for Los Angeles, on May 14, when police and strikebreakers opened fire on a group of striking workers, shooting a young striker named Dicky Parker through the heart. On July 5, the infamous "Bloody Thursday," San Francisco police opened fire on strikers, killing two men—Howard Sperry and Nick Bordoise—and injuring many more. On July 18, Portland police fired upon a group that included US Senator Robert F. Wagner, who had been sent by President Franklin Roosevelt to the Rose City to seek an end to the strike. In Seattle, a company guard shot longshoreman Shelvy Daffron in the back, killing him.[37]

In response to the San Francisco murders and the refusal of employers to compromise on worker control of the hiring hall, members of the San Francisco Labor Council declared a general strike, bringing one of America's greatest collections of unionized workers out on strike. On July 16, an estimated 100,000 workers took part in the strike, which spread well beyond San Francisco.[38]

Willapa unions had something of an unusual advantage in the strike: a sympathetic, even supportive, mainstream news organ in the *Willapa Harbor Pilot*. Unlike some Red Coast newspapers, which incited violence against strikers, the *Pilot* editorialized that bloodshed would fail to break the strike. "Mayors of these big towns with their police forces, and sheriffs with their regular and special deputies, will be unable to break the strike," it predicted. In fact, In June 1934, the *Pilot* suggested that the "shippers and shipping interests" should "enter agreement with the union, [and] eliminate these stevedoring companies, which are no more than middlemen." At the end of the Big Strike, the *Pilot* even denounced red-baiters: "Unfortunately some of the big metropolitan press, like the Hearst press, keeps hammering away about Moscow, sabotage, and Russian influences. It's the big fellows who do not want to melt in with the Roosevelt 'New Deal,' some of the big industrialists who have refused to do their part in co-operation with President Roosevelt." Later in the 1930s, the *Pilot* emerged as one of the Northwest's chief boosters of labor when Terry Pettus, Communist and founder of the Seattle branch of the American Newspaper Guild, became its editor. In sharp contrast to the long history of anti-labor and anti-radical news coverage throughout southwest Washington, Pettus strongly supported radical politics and militant labor activism. For example, he placed headlines about the famed longshoremen's union leader Harry Bridges visiting Grays and Willapa Harbors on the front page, above the fold, twice in a single month.[39]

Although an impressive show of solidarity, the General Strike was undermined by conservative union leaders who wanted little to do with a strike of this magnitude. On July 20, the fourth day of the conflict, the General Strike Committee voted by a close margin to end the general strike.[40] With its conclusion longshoremen lost much of their bargaining power. Pressured by state officials and conservative labor leaders, dockworkers went back to work at the end of July and accepted arbitration on all issues, including the hiring hall. Until final arbitration concluded in October, a federal government representative supervised the hiring of dockworkers in Raymond, as in other Pacific Coast ports.[41] Pacific Coast ILA members voted by a whopping 81 percent to 19 percent to accept the settlement, with only two locals, including Raymond Local 38–92, voting to refuse the terms. Their refusal, contended historian Ottilie Markholt, was a product of Communist influences on the union branch.[42]

In the final settlement, which came in October, the arbitration committee set union-friendly terms on many issues, including joint union-management control over hiring. Most important, the ILA gained the right to choose its local dispatcher, providing de facto worker control over hiring. Although control over hiring was the most important victory, the ILA also made major strides on "bread-and-butter" issues. They gained increased wages and a shorter workday. The arbitration award read: "Six hours shall constitute a day's work. Thirty hours shall constitute a week's work, averaged over a period of four weeks."[43] ILA unionists had doggedly refused to work alongside scabs, and after 1934 unionists had control over the docks. Realizing the significance of keeping scabs off the docks, the *Western Worker* implied that unionists should use intimidation to make it that way: "We must have good housecleaning on the waterfront and we all know what that will mean should we happen to see a rat on the waterfront."[44] The Raymond ILA did not take long to sweep the scabs off of the docks. As the *Pilot* noted: "None of the strike breakers will be allowed to work with union men."[45]

Pacific Coast longshoremen won the Big Strike largely due to the impressive show of solidarity by dockworkers and their fellow maritime laborers. Other organizations, including the Ilwaco Fishermen's Union, numerous Northwest lumber workers' locals, and Finnish Workers' Federation branches donated to the strike fund, indicating the potential for a united labor front moving forward.[46] Shortly after the strike's conclusion, Willapa longshoremen moved to deepen the local labor movement's power by creating a local Central Labor Council, which they accomplished in August 1934.[47]

Scholars of labor have likewise praised the collective efforts of West Coast workers. Sociologist Howard Kimeldorf concluded: "The three-month walk-out amounted to one big lesson in labor solidarity for the '34 men. . . . The close interpersonal bonds that were forged in the heat of battle endured long after the fighting was over. 'Remember Bloody Thursday' became the rallying cry for an entire generation."[48]

Emboldened by their successes, West Coast ILA locals joined other maritime unions in the Maritime Federation of the Pacific Coast. After years of hardship and oppression, Pacific maritime workers now looked to a brighter future, one with union control over hiring, increased wages, and a shorter, safer workweek. The *Western Worker*, a San Francisco–based Communist newspaper and official organ of that city's ILA, summarized the changes brought about during the Big Strike:

> Since returning to work after the strike things are very different. . . .
> Whereas before the strike they were beaten, docile and meek, they
> are now in a very opposite frame of mind. To state that the men are
> militant and aggressive would be putting it mildly; in fact, it is hard
> to realize that the same body of men could produce such a change of
> attitude in their own ranks.[49]

Bloody Thursday caught national attention and commemorating the martyrs who lost their lives that day became a ritual for Pacific Coast longshoremen and their allies. Photographs of the unionists' funeral filled the labor press, and left-wing illustrators used the murders and their aftermath as subject material for their work. The Maritime Federation of the Pacific Coast declared July 5, 1935, to be Maritime Memorial Day. The *Voice of the Federation* stated that maritime unionists in every Pacific Coast port, along with "thousands of brother trade unionists and supporters," would wage a one-day strike, demanding that the nation focus its attention on those men killed during the Big Strike.[50]

Adding a sense of urgency to their cause, West Coast lumber workers were at that time engaged in the 1935 Lumber Strike, the largest strike of their industry in the nation's history, as thousands of woodworkers shut down the

Northwest's greatest industry. Sporadic bursts of violence marked the strike, but on June 21, 1935, gunmen in Eureka, California, shot and killed two striking lumber unionists, as well as a third man unlucky enough to be in the way of a bullet. The three Eureka victims—all Finnish Americans—joined the long list of Pacific Coast unionists killed during the struggle for workers' rights and union recognition.[51]

The annual one-day strike to commemorate Bloody Thursday—or Maritime Memorial Day—centered on the struggles of longshoremen. Their union, the ILA, took center stage in the planning of the July 5 events. In Raymond, ILA Local 38-92 members created a committee to plan the protest and march. At their July 1, 1935, meeting they resolved to call a one-day strike and protest, complete with "banners made stating [the] reason for [the] parade."[52] The protest featured a march through downtown Raymond by longshoremen, longshoremen's family members, and their supporters.[53]

Historian Bruce Nelson summarized the event in his brilliant history of the Pacific Coast maritime workers' movement: "Even in the small port of Raymond, Washington, where the ILA membership numbered only 107, more than a thousand people participated in the Bloody Thursday memorial, suggesting, in this case as in others, the ability of the maritime workers to galvanize significant numbers of shoreside workers around their activity."[54] As was common for these types of events, the mainstream press failed to give the demonstration much attention and downplayed its political significance. Despite the mass turnout through the downtown streets of Raymond and other Red Coast port towns, none of the Pacific County newspapers or the neighboring Grays Harbor County newspapers printed photographs of the marches. July 5, 1935, likewise goes unmentioned in any published history of Pacific County, a perhaps unsurprising fact given that these works barely mention the maritime and lumber industry, their workers, or their unions.[55]

The *Voice of the Federation*, news organ of the Maritime Federation of the Pacific, provided the most detailed report of the July 5 event in Raymond. A front-page article entitled "United We Stand," reported:

Raymond, Wash.— ILA Local 38-92 of this city, with a membership of 107, displayed the unity and strength of our organization in this port, when in company with other Unions we held our memorial parade on July 5th, in respect to our fallen Brothers.

The parade, over three city blocks long, was participated in by more than one thousand marchers from the various unions here. Our procession was by far the most impressive turnout ever witnessed in the port of Raymond.

We are a small port but our Solidarity is strong. We work for the good of all.

G. Bessinger

Ed. McQueer[56]

The Big Strike stands as one of the most important events in American labor history. It has been subjected to dozens, if not hundreds, of academic and popular history pieces. But in all but a few instances, these histories focus on the major ports of San Francisco, San Pedro, Portland, Tacoma, and Seattle. They rarely turn their gaze toward the small town lumber ports that lay along the Red Coast. To be sure, more maritime laborers worked at the major ports, and these workers played more integral roles in the strike and its aftermath. But they did not wage the strike alone. Workers at smaller Pacific Coast ports laid down their tools and picked up picket signs for the epic 1934 strike. The lives of small town longshoremen changed every bit as much, and in some cases more, than their metropolitan counterparts. Never in their history had Willapa's dockworkers maintained a union for longer than a few fleeting months. But the labor upsurge of the middle 1930s changed that. When the ILA's Pacific Coast District merged into the International Longshore and Warehouse Union (ILWU) in 1937, Raymond's workers stood first in line, taking out their charter for Local 1 in the new union.

15

"On the Front Trench Picket Lines"

COMMUNIST LUMBER WORKERS
IN THE SPANISH CIVIL WAR

In May 1937, L. E. "Red" Johnson, Ernest Kozlowski, and "Idaho Blackie" Chapin set out via bus from their hometown of Aberdeen, Washington, toward New York City. In New York, a ship waited to take them and dozens of others to Normandy, France, where they disembarked, taking their first steps in Europe on a dangerous journey to wage war against fascism. In a letter home, Johnson wrote of his travels:

> So after we travel in buses and ships and train for many thousands of miles, we have landed in Spain healthy and feeling fine. . . . We crossed the border from France. For three days we rode a train and at every station crowds of people met the train and in the world's nations these people are making history for the rest. Democratic countries should take notice.[1]

Johnson, Kozlowski, and Chapin were communist lumber workers and activist members of the Federation of Woodworkers (FOW), the "one union in the wood." Formed in 1936, the FOW was an industrial union in the lumber industry and the largest labor union on the Pacific Coast. They traveled to Europe as part of the International Brigades, a volunteer fighting force committed to fight alongside the Spanish Republicans against the Fascists led by General Francisco Franco. In the summer of 1936, supported by the military, the Catholic Church, and other right-wing forces, Franco sought to overthrow Spain's democratic government. Celebrating the men's willingness to fight on the other side of the world in defense of Spanish democracy, the Seattle-based

Sunday News ran a front-page article praising the lumber union leaders who "arrived in Spain to fight on the side of the democratic government."[2]

Johnson, Kozlowski, and Chapin were three of the six Red Coast lumber workers and FOW members who traveled to Spain to fight against fascism in a conflict seen widely as a dress rehearsal for the Second World War. At least some of the volunteers were open members of the Communist Party (CP). In the middle and late 1930s, during the "Popular Front," Communism enjoyed a period of relative acceptance when the Communist Party allied with other progressive and labor groups to collectively challenge fascism in all its guises.[3] Indeed, during the mid-1930s, Party membership along the Red Coast and the wider Pacific Northwest grew dramatically. As Gordon "Brick" Moir, a leading CP lumber worker, recalled in an interview with historian and journalist John Hughes, much of the militant union leadership was made up of Communists. "Sure [lumber unionist Dick Law] was a member of the Party! . . . We all were. It was a struggle."[4] The Red Coast anti-fascists joined approximately 2,800 Americans—most of them Communists—who volunteered to fight in defense of Spanish democracy in 1937–1938.[5]

Their individual motivations to join the anti-fascist struggle differed, but the leftist lumber workers likely shared Red Johnson's conviction that they "joined the Loyalist government army" because "we believe in democratic forms of government." Ernest Kozlowski viewed the war in similar terms. He saw the war as a struggle against "the forces of world reaction in Germany, Italy, and Japan," a chance to combat these "aggressors" as they "move into Spain, to enslave, terrorize, and smash the heroic, liberty-loving Spanish people."[6] Johnson welcomed the fight, hoping "we soon get to the Front picket lines and put the Franco 'Hitlers' and the 'Mussolini Fascism' on the run."[7]

Red Coast lumber workers like Johnson no doubt made tremendous sacrifices, but they also considered the fight a logical extension of their workplace struggles. Lumber unionists viewed the violently anti-union lumbermen— and their allies in other industries and in the state—as American fascists, repressing workers and suppressing democracy at home in much the same way that Mussolini, Hitler, and Franco did in Europe. Pacific Coast labor and leftist groups frequently made unequivocal comparisons between fascism abroad and anti-unionism at home.

In 1934, a Seattle communist publication, the *Voice of Action,* and an Aberdeen women's Finnish Communist group called Aberdeen Mayor Herbert Horrocks a "Fascist" for shutting off the municipal water supply for the unemployed. They demanded "that an immediate stop be put to [his] Fascist actions" when the council and mayor refused to allow communists to address the council.[8] The *Timber Worker* labeled the American Legion a "Fascist group," voicing a common perspective among leftists, particularly those in the Pacific Northwest who witnessed the Legion violently assault radical union members with impunity.[9] The *Voice of the Federation*, the monthly publication of the Maritime Federation of the Pacific Coast, ran an editorial titled "Industrial Nazis" that made numerous comparisons between Hitler and Mussolini, and Tom Girdler, chairman of the board of Republic Steel. "Hitler and Mussolini gained and kept their power by lies, spies, and thugs. To the best of his opportunities, Tom Girdler has done the same," the *Voice* asserted.[10] In 1938, a Grays Harbor union auxiliary criticized a Washington State citizens' initiative as an outgrowth of global fascism. They described as "fascist-like," Initiative 130, which would have required a thirty-day "cooling off period" before a strike could be called.[11]

The Red Coast anti-fascists likewise saw the war in Spain as an extension of US labor struggles in the Depression decade. Grays Harbor lumber worker Ernest Kozlowski noted that two fundamental elements of fascism were anti-unionism and racism:

> There is one thing that the Timber Workers of the Harbor can rest assured of, when these Spanish people smash fascism and its union busting, labor-exploiting, educational race-hatred program, the cause of the workers of not only Spain, [but also] right in Grays Harbor and the entire world will be tremendously affected, and will take a gigantic stride forward to progress, peace, and security.[12]

After his return from the war, Kozlowski stated that he had "seen a large part of the world during the past two years, having gone to Spain to serve in the International Brigade on the side of the Spanish workers. I feel that one who has seen and felt traitorous attacks on workers' organizations in other parts of the world can helpfully comment on the Communist Party." Kozlowski made explicit comparisons between the anti-Communist aggression of fascists in Europe and the assaults on the Party in the United States: "The fascist aggressors fought Communists in the wilds of Ethiopia, the mountains of tiny Albania, Spain, Austria. Here at home and in our trade unions they see Mr. and Mrs. Roosevelt as Communists. Lewis, Ickes, Justice Black, LaGuardia, right on down the line, national reaction names the staunchest fighters for a democratic America—they call them all Communists."[13]

Red Coast labor militants had spent decades engaged in struggles with violent anti-union employers whose policies and practices closely resembled their fascist counterparts in Europe. Employers, organized in citizens' committees, the American Legion, and the KKK, used a wide range of tactics, including vigilante violence, to fight unions. Like fascists in Italy and Germany, Northwest anti-unionists convinced legislators to pass anti-union legislation, including criminal syndicalism acts that essentially banned membership in certain unions.

American leftists, in fact, performed a tremendous public service, providing early and biting critiques of the threat posed by European fascism. In December 1926, the *Daily Worker* issued an "appeal to all class-conscious workers throughout the world and all enemies of fascism to sound the alarm against the fascist government in Lithuania which is staging a reign of terror against working-class leaders." During the 1920s, Communists held anti-fascist rallies to demonstrate against Mussolini and his Black Shirts.[14] In early 1932, the *Western Worker*, the San Francisco publication of the CP, celebrated the growth in the Socialist and Communist parties in Germany but mourned that the Fascist Party was "now the single largest party."

Like other leftist news organs, the *Western Worker* informed its readers of the tremendous threat posed by German fascism. "The class struggle has greatly sharpened along the entire front. Hitler has acquired a fleet of 25 airplanes to be used especially against militant workers. On December 17 in Berlin, fascists attacked groups of workers returning from a meeting. In the fighting which ensued one Communist was killed and three wounded."[15] The August 17, 1934, issue of the *Voice of Action*, ran a front-page photograph of "Hitler Torture Camp Scene," followed by an article detailing conditions in Nazi Germany: "Wracked by torture, starvation, and disease, jailed opponents of the Nazi regime, Communists, Socialists, Pacifists, Christians, Jews, die like flies." A year later, the *Voice of Action* ran a headline reporting "Mussolini Continues Murder of Ethiopians."[16]

Thus, by the onset of the Spanish Civil War in the summer of 1936, American unionists and leftists were intimately familiar with the threats posed to peace and democracy by European fascism. For some, raising money and writing letters wasn't enough. They needed to be directly involved in stopping the growing menace.

The Red Coast Spanish Civil War volunteers were all activists in the region's Woodworkers' unions. In 1933, after years of union decline and weakness in the Northwest, lumber workers throughout the Pacific Northwest formed union locals affiliated with the American Federation of Labor (AFL). In early 1935, these locals became known as the Sawmill and Timber Workers' Union, a part of the United Brotherhood of Carpenters and Joiners (UBCJ), a powerful international union with deep ties to the AFL.[17] The UBCJ was a vocal defender of the narrow, conservative forms of unionism that had for decades earned the AFL the enmity of leftists, who gave the Federation the derisive nickname "The American Separation of Labor."[18] The UBCJ-Woodworkers was a poor match. Northwest lumber workers had strong preferences for radical labor politics and for industrial, rather than craft, unionism.

Woodworkers' Unions grew dramatically, especially after the 1934 Maritime Strike gave Pacific Coast workers the confidence that they could win a strike against a unified, well-armed group of employers. The Big Strike likewise strengthened the Pacific Coast maritime unions, which gave the Woodworkers an important potential ally on the docks, one capable of halting marine transportation of any non-union-made wood products. In May 1935, Northwest woodworkers struck by the thousands. Their demands included a 75-cents per hour minimum wage, overtime pay, seniority rights, and a six-hour day.[19] Few events shook the Pacific Northwest as profoundly as the 1935 lumber strike. Waged six years into the Depression, the conflict brought the region's most important industry to a grinding halt. More than ten thousand workers in logging, sawmills, shingle mills, and veneer and plywood plants took part in the strike, while longshoremen refused to handle materials made during the conflict. Throughout the Northwest, police and strikebreakers attacked picket lines, and Oregon and Washington governors dispatched the National Guard to intimidate strikers. In response, the *Voice of Action* condemned Oregon Governor Charles H. Martin for ordering "his mercenaries to break up picket lines," and accused both him and Clarence Martin, the Washington State governor, of using "terror" to break the strike.[20]

In response to efforts by the conservative Carpenters' Union to commandeer control of the strike, rank-and-file unionists met at Aberdeen's American Legion Stadium and established the Northwest Joint Strike Committee (NWJSC).[21] Composed primarily of militant unionists and a fair number of Communists, the NWJSC took control of the strike, removing power from the conservative Carpenters' Union leaders. Two of the most active members of the Joint Strike Committee were Red Johnson and Ernest Kozlowski, Grays Harbor Communists, militant union members, and future volunteers in the Spanish Civil War. Johnson planned and acted as chairman at the meeting where the NWJSC was formed.[22] Kozlowski served as associate editor of the *Timber Worker* during its early days as a strike bulletin, and served with Johnson on the Harbor's strike committee, acting as liaison to the crew at a Polson Lumber Company mill.[23] A letter sent by the committee to Governor Martin of Washington gave a good idea of their militant, class-conscious views: "We call on all union men and women and friends of the labor movement to repudiate and protest the prostituting of the Governor's high office to aid the mill owners to break our strike and to support the striking lumber workers."[24]

The 1935 Lumber Strike ended in compromise: workers gained higher wages, shorter hours, and union recognition. But, only the shingle weavers succeeded in their efforts to obtain the six-hour workday. Still, the strike was among the most important events in the history of the Pacific Northwest. It birthed a large and militant lumber workers' movement that had demonstrated its ability to shut down the region's largest industry. In September 1936, the region's locals left the conservative Carpenters' Union and formed the Federation of Woodworkers (FOW), with an estimated 100,000 members, making it the largest labor union on the Pacific Coast. The union elected Communists Harold Pritchett of British Columbia and Mickey Orton of Aberdeen, Washington, as president and vice president of the new organization.[25]

The FOW was a short-lived institution. As an industrial union with leftist leadership, it fit poorly with the policies of the AFL. In 1935, eight industrial unions of the AFL formed the Committee on Industrial Organizations within the Federation. Led by United Mine Workers' President John L. Lewis, the organization sought to push the AFL toward organizing the millions of unorganized American workers, including those who worked in mass industries such as auto and steel. Lewis, the CIO's founding president, initially welcomed the assistance of Communist organizers, believing they were often the most committed and effective union activists. In July 1937, the FOW's membership voted overwhelmingly to form the International Woodworkers of America (IWA), a CIO affiliate.[26]

In the wake of the 1935 Lumber Strike, the eyes of Red Coast leftists turned hopefully toward Spain where, in 1936, a liberal-left Popular Front coalition won elections, promising to enact political and social reforms. The elected government included numerous anarchists, socialists, and communists, and had the backing of the international communist movement. Strongly opposing the elected government was a coalition of right-wing groups backed by the military. In July of 1936, General Francisco Franco, stationed in Spanish-controlled Morocco, launched a coup with the support of the Spanish Army of Africa and most of the country's military. Supporting Franco were the European fascist powers of Germany, Italy, and Portugal.[27]

In 1937, the US Congress passed, and President Franklin Roosevelt signed, the Neutrality Act, which banned the sales of arms, ammunition, or implements of war to belligerent states, including nation-states engaged in civil wars. Throughout the war, the US State Department enforced an embargo on military equipment to the Spanish government and Franco's fascist rebels. Still, the US company Texaco sold oil to the fascists, helping to fuel Franco's coup.[28] With the fascist powers in Europe supplying troops and military equipment to Franco, only the Soviet and Mexican governments sold arms to the elected government in Spain.[29] In March 1938, long after realizing that the fascist war machine was too powerful for militias and international volunteers to withstand, the *Spanish Labor Bulletin* condemned the United States and other countries for their uninterested neutrality in the face of right-wing aggression: "Some of these nations who would not lift a finger to defend international law, let along justice and right, may finally realize the danger this situation entails for their own national interests."[30]

To recruit volunteers for the war, the Communist International (Comintern) appealed to supporters from around the world. The Soviet Union gave local CP branches recruitment quotas. Various sources reported that between 35,000 and 50,000 fighters joined the International Brigades, with 30,000 arriving in Spain by February 1937. In the United States the CP recruited in secret, and eventually transformed one of the international battalions that formed the XVth International Brigade into a mostly American force.[31] The Communist Party also formed at least fifteen front organizations in the United States, including the Friends of the Abraham Lincoln Brigade and the American Society for Technical Aid to Spanish Democracy. The CP formed front organizations—Communist groups, whose CP affiliations were masked—to pursue leftist aims and broaden the Party's appeal among non-Communist progressives. The Friends placed advertisements in the media to recruit volunteers and donations to aid the war effort.[32]

In Washington State, the two largest Popular Front organizations were the Washington Commonwealth Federation (WCF) and the Federation of Woodworkers-IWA. The Washington Commonwealth Federation was a progressive caucus within the state's Democratic Party.

On the Red Coast, the most important Popular Front organization was the Federation of Woodworkers, which had local and international Communist leadership. Communist woodworkers such as Brick Moir and Dick Law led efforts to support their comrades fighting in Spain. Moir corresponded with the volunteers and coordinated fundraisers within the union. On September 25, 1937, the Aberdeen IWA raised money to purchase an ambulance for the Republicans, or Loyalists. To raise money, the local sponsored a showing of the film *Heart of Spain*, a documentary about the war. That the union chose to show the film at the massive Olympic Arena was a good indication of the support for the forces fighting fascism in Spain.[33]

The Commonwealth Federation and the IWA both had newspapers that wrote widely of the situation in Spain. The news coverage served at least three purposes: to pull at readers' heartstrings with the intention of inciting activism on behalf of the Spanish Loyalists, to serve as propaganda pieces about the good work being done by the Popular Front government in Spain, and to educate and warn of the growing global fascist menace. Typical of these stories was one that appeared in the January 10, 1937, *Sunday News*, the Seattle-based WCF newspaper: "The Sunday News takes sides in the Spanish war. We are for the Republic of Spain. We are for the defense of democracy and popular government. We declare THE GREATEST TASK AMERICANS CAN HELP ACCOMPLISH IN 1937 IS DEFEAT OF THE FASCIST INVASION OF SPAIN."[34] In news articles and stories about Spain, the Communist Party also issued none-too-subtle hints that supporters of democracy should join the war effort. In a November 1937 article in the Communist monthly *The Fight Against War and Fascism*, James Lerner told of his experiences during a visit to the Spanish front. "Sooner or later," he wrote, "every country has its 1776. Give me liberty or give me death is not an outworn slogan. If you think so go over to Spain and see for yourself."[35]

It's likely that the Red Coast volunteers, like others across North America, gained their perspective on the situation in Spain from news organs of this type. From Spain, Herman Goff, a Seattle volunteer, wrote to a Northwest comrade, informing him, "If you want to get the truth about Spain read the *Daily Worker*."[36] Red Coast residents also heard speakers, such as Anna Louise

Strong, the famed Pacific Northwest Communist journalist. After her return from the Spanish Republic in March 1937, Strong embarked on a Northwest tour that took her to Seattle, Portland, and the Red Coast radical hotspot Aberdeen.[37] Her book, *Spain in Arms*, published in early 1937, gave a good idea of the subject of her talks. The book called upon the forces of democracy to aid the Spanish people. She quoted a nineteen-year-old Catalan Republican soldier whose comment about the need to confront the fascist menace was hauntingly prescient: "Wherever you are, you'll have to fight fascism. You help us now, we'll help you then."[38]

From the front, the Red Coast volunteers maintained a regular correspondence with their fellow unionists. The *Timber Worker*, the Aberdeen-based publication of the FOW and IWA, reported on the volunteers' experiences in Spain. On July 2, 1937, a front-page *Timber Worker* headline read "Kozlowski, Chapin, Johnson in Spain," and honored their efforts. "Three members of Local 2639 of Aberdeen who are demonstrating that they 'practice what they preach' are now in Spain fighting against Fascist Franco," it reported. "Two of them," it continued, "L. E. 'Red' Johnson and Ernest Kozlowski, known the length and breadth of the Federation for their leadership in the 1935 strike and in organizing lumber workers, have written of their trip to Spain and their experiences 'training for the Front Trench Picket Lines.'"[39] The unionists' involvement in the Spanish Civil War was big news, both within the labor movement and to the wider American public. Even the *Grays Harbor Washingtonian*, edited by the notorious red-baiter Russell Mack, reported that "at least six Aberdeen citizens are now fighting with loyalist troops in Spain. . . . Recent letters from Spain report Johnson released from a field hospital and on the way to the front again. In letters received here from Johnson, he says the brutalities at Teruel would make the average man's hair turn gray."[40]

Details of the Red Coast volunteers' involvement in battles are scant, but the veterans and their comrades on the home front did what they could to boast of the soldiers' valor. Shortly after their return to the Northwest, one veteran recalled: "Those Italians. They were lousy. They couldn't shoot and they couldn't fight. Wirta here, and five other men captured forty-six of them, all loaded down with machine guns and ammunition."[41]

Receiving a letter from Spain was a major event for Grays Harbor unionists. The January 22, 1938, meeting minutes of IWA Local 3-2 mention Ernest Kozlowski sending season's greetings from the front. Later at the same meeting, unionists passed a motion instructing their local secretary "to send a communication to acknowledge receipt of this communication and wishing the Abe Lincoln Brigade complete success in their efforts to defeat the barbaric Fascist invaders in Democratic Spain."[42]

The *Timber Worker* greeted the letters enthusiastically, reporting that "we regard these letters as highly educational, with first-hand, authentic information of what is going on." Indeed, the letters provide a bottom-up history of the Civil War from the perspective of American anti-fascists fighting on the front lines. Shortly after arriving in Spain, the Red Coast lumber workers received their first taste of military training. Red Johnson reported that he had "for two months been going through training into different formations, drilling, etc. Now we are waiting to be called to maneuver to the front line."[43] In a letter to union leader Dick Law, James "Pat" Hassett wrote: "Just got back from the front lines where I was stationed for a week. . . . Tough detail but I am supposed to be tough people."[44] Northwest volunteers spent a great deal of time together in Spain. Herman Goff wrote home, reporting:

> I am sitting here with two other Northwest boys, writing. These boys are two swell lumber jacks of the timber workers union. They are number one soldiers. Their names are "Red Johnson" and "Idaho Blacky Chapin." I used to hear of these boys during the great lumber strike. We know of them as leaders in the rank and file movement of the workers.[45]

James "Pat" Hassett praised the work of Spanish Loyalist women, whom he referred to as a "godsend," writing: "The SRI [Socorro Rojo Internacional, or International Aid, a Communist aid organization] does repairing of our clothes and laundry of repaired clothes and functions in a thousand and one ways—This shows you a very small part of what the women of Spain are doing for the men at the front—Besides taking their place in industry."[46]

It took time for the volunteers to adjust to the new climate and cuisine of southern Europe, and to the scenes of civilians struggling with wartime deprivation. Aberdeen IWA Local 3-2 reported: "Brother Johnson tells of many women, children, and old men who are left to die after being injured in air raids by the Fascists, and . . . medical facilities are far too inadequate to properly care for any of the aforesaid cases."[47] The volunteers also fell victim to wartime injuries and illness, fighting in a new terrain against the vast war machine commanded by the Fascists. "Red" Johnson, for one, was injured in early 1938,

Ernest Kozlowski and "Red" Johnson during the Spanish Civil War in 1938. Both men were Communist lumber workers dedicated to fighting the global menace of fascism. Photo courtesy of Tamiment Library & Robert F. Wagner Labor Archives, NYU Special Collections.

and spent time in a Loyalist field hospital before returning to the fight.[48] Bill Shifferly, a Grays Harbor resident who had close relations with some of the Red Coast volunteers, remembered that Paul Wirta's "middle finger on his left hand was damaged by a Fascist bullet."[49]

Despite the dangers they faced, their letters mentioned time and again the hope that supporters would send American cigarettes to them in Spain. It was the most common subject of their letters! After being deluged with these requests, the *Timber Worker* urged unionists to "write to you often and send lots of smokes and snoose."[50] One letter included in the Spanish Civil War Special Collections at the University of Washington remarked, "The Aberdeen area sent many large bundles of cigarettes to the boys in Spain, but there was a shortage, notwithstanding."[51]

Both the *Timber Worker* and Grays Harbor IWA Local 3-2 meetings regularly featured discussions of the war in Spain and the efforts of their comrades fighting on the front lines. The Grays Harbor IWA aided the war effort with both moral and material assistance. Local 3-2 raised money to support the Spanish Republican side and urged members to send American cigarettes. In June 1937, Grays Harbor unionists raised $125 and "a large truckload of clothes" in an Aid for Spain drive. In a letter to the Red Coast volunteers, one Harbor unionist promised, "Soon we will make a big cleanup to send cigarettes, send cigarettes, send cigarettes, and more cigarettes, and a hell of a lot of other things to you boys."[52]

Red Coast unionists replied to their comrades' letters from Spain not only with promises of cigarettes but also with news of their own struggles against fascists on the home front. Shortly after Chapin, Kozlowski, and Johnson arrived in Spain, a Grays Harbor unionist wrote a colorful summary of local union activities to "Blacky and Comrades":

> A two-day strike at Polson was won pronto. The Western camp has
> been shut down since you left as the cedar market went blooey, but
> all others are running strong. . . . The Blagin Mill had a two-day strike
> over wage raises, which was won hands down. R.N. sure took it hard
> about his defeat; the reactionaries came out with a big red-baiting
> scare just before the election, but it only helped win for us.[53]

In addition to corresponding with the Spanish volunteers, IWA Local 3-2 passed several resolutions related to the conflict in Spain. Its members expressed the common thinking at the time that the Spanish government and the international brigades stood a much better chance of defeating the fascists if the United States were to lift its embargo on the sale of arms to Spain. A December 1938 resolution called on President Roosevelt to lift the embargo.[54] Later that month, Spanish Civil War veteran Paul Wirta told his fellow unionists that he returned to the United States mainly to advocate for an end to the embargo.[55]

Despite the challenges, in their letters home, volunteers expressed a hopeful optimism about their prospects for winning the war. On June 1, 1937, Pat Hassett concluded that "the fight now is being carried to the enemies' camp—and so be it till the termination of this war."[56] With more than a little swagger, Kozlowski boasted that a sizable battalion of loggers "could whip General Franco's whole army."[57] Red Johnson expressed much the same belief, writing that if "there was more of those militant loggers here, the war would be over in a short time."[58]

Unfortunately, the war was not over in a short time, and at least two of the militant loggers from the Red Coast, Red Johnson and Robert Pettyjohn, perished in the conflict. *The Sunday News* revealed what few details were available about Pettyjohn's death, concluding that he likely died shortly after a battle, as he "attempted to elude the fascists by swimming a river."[59] Approximately

25 percent of American volunteers died during the war. Those who returned to the States were greeted as heroes by their fellow leftists. The IWA treated Kozlowski and Wirta to a heroes' welcome when they returned to Grays Harbor, and paid silent tribute to Johnson and Pettyjohn, who died fighting against fascism.[60]

Blacky Chapin returned to the United States in June 1938 as a stowaway, along with Randall Williams, a seaman from Tacoma.[61] Still, uncertainty surrounded the fates of many Northwest volunteers. The *Sunday News* reported: "Fates of N.W. Youths Unknown," and "Fate of these valiant northwest youths who went to Spain to offer their lives in the fight for democracy was unknown this week."[62] Eight months later, James (Pat) Hassett fled Spain. The *Grays Harbor Washingtonian,* reported that Hassett escaped under the most dire of circumstances, by "successfully running a gauntlet of almost incessant insurgent aerial bombardment."[63]

"Brick" Moir knew some of the Spanish Civil War fighters and remained in contact with them during their duty abroad. Moir provided the following biographical information about the Red Coast volunteers:

Ernie Kozlowski—I.W.A. activist, became an Officer in Abraham Lincoln Brigade, came back from Spain—Was in World War II in the Philippines, was commissioned to Captain in the field, decorated for Heroism, and Killed in Leyte.

Milford Blackie Chapin—I.W.A. activist and shop steward— Abraham Lincoln Brigade—came back from Spain—Drafted in World War #2—Para Troopers—action Italy North Africa. Flown to Germany, dropped behind Bulge. Came back to the Harbor—again Shop Steward in Logging Camps. Finally went to work _____ [unreadable]. Here he was badly injured in a spill of hot concentrate ore and finally died as a result of these injuries.

Red Johnson—I.W.A. activist—Went to Spain—Abraham Lincoln Brigade—was made a machine gunner—was to be advanced to a Leadership role but refused to stay with his Machine Gun Crew—was killed in the last day of the War.

Wilfred Chapin, one of
the Red Coast Communist
lumber workers who served
in the Spanish Civil War.
Photo courtesy of Tamiment
Library & Robert F. Wagner
Labor Archives, NYU
Special Collections.

Bob Pettyjohn—Student and I.W.A. member—Went to Spain—
Abraham Lincoln Brigade—Was shot and killed while swimming in
Ebro River in the Big Retreat.

Pat Hassett—I.W.A. Mill Worker—Went to Spain—Abraham Lincoln
Brigade assigned to the John Brown Artillery Battery. On returning to
U.S., stayed in New York.

Saul Wirta—Was from Woodland, Wash. Went to Spain—Abraham
Lincoln Brigade. When he returned, he stayed in Aberdeen, WA,
carried on his work as a merchant seaman.[64]

Although physically far removed from the Red Coast, the Spanish Civil
War—which pitted global forces of fascism against democracy—profoundly
affected the lives of the Red Coast volunteers and the wider Red Coast labor
movement. Johnson and Pettyjohn died in the war, but Kozlowski returned to
Grays Harbor in late 1938 before joining the Allied war effort in the Pacific,
which took his life. A 1985 issue of the *Volunteer*, a journal for veterans of the
Spanish Civil War, included the text of a letter written by General Douglas
MacArthur to Kozlowski's widow, Mary Husa Kozlowski, after Ernie's death.
It read: "His service under me was characterized by his complete devotion
to our beloved country and his noble death integrates him with its imperish-
able glory. I have lost a gallant comrade-in-arms and you mourn a splendid

gentleman."[65] As Moir wrote, only two of the six Red Coast IWA activists who went to Spain returned to the region to wage the class war at home.

Most of the Red Coast labor struggles were waged on local terrain and concerned local demands like higher wages or the repeal of an odious municipal ordinance. But as the involvement of the "militant loggers" in the Spanish Civil War demonstrated, the Red Coast left was only one part of an international working-class movement connected by global forms of communication and migration. Although workers had long understood that they confronted a global form of industrial capitalism, during the 1930s they faced a new and dire threat: the rise of international fascism. Workers, particularly leftists, made explicit comparisons between European fascism and the right-wing movements that had long dominated Pacific Northwest politics and labor relations. For them, the battlefront in Spain was an extension of a decades-old class struggle with its own battles and casualties in the United States.

In their own ways, many members of the American left participated in the struggle to save Spanish democracy by donating money or attending a meeting. But for some working-class radicals, including Kozlowski, Johnson, Chapin, Hassett, Pettyjohn, and Wirta, the threat posed by rapidly expanding fascism was so dire and so odious that it needed to be confronted and defeated on the battlefield. Red Johnson and Bob Pettyjohn paid the ultimate price for defending their principles, joining Wesley Everest, William McKay, James McInerney, and Laura Law on the list of Red Coast martyrs to the cause of working-class freedom.

Conclusion

Our goal in the preceding pages has been to write a social and labor history of the working people of the Red Coast, those often forgotten men and women who labored—for the most part anonymously—in the forests and on the fishing boats, in the cities and in the mills in southwest Washington. In telling their story, we have, of necessity, told a story of class struggle. One of the takeaways of our study should be that the intensity and extent of the Red Coast's class war was a product of the high level of class consciousness on the part of both the worker and the boss. The gillnetter, the longshoreman, and the logger of this era understood that the laborer and capitalist had opposing values and interests, and that gain for one meant loss for the other. Thus, very often, these workers joined radical organizations based on the premise that class struggle was fundamental to the lives of all people who worked for wages. Employers likewise organized along class lines into employers' associations and citizens' committees to depress wages, divide workers, and harass, imprison, and expel radicals and militants from town. When high levels of class consciousness and class organization on the part of both workers and bosses combined with raw and exploitative working conditions, as they did on the Red Coast, class conflict was intense.

Several important and related themes emerge clearly from the various stories of class conflict we tell. Employers depicted working-class radicalism as the product of outside agitation, but the history of the Red Coast demonstrates that class consciousness was rooted organically in the communities from which it sprang. A common form of anti-union activity was for employers and their allies to depict labor radicals as "outside agitators," who "invaded" local communities and thus threatened the "peaceful, harmonious" relations that normally exist between workers and employers. This accusation was particularly leveled at the Wobblies, who were routinely depicted as rootless, itinerant men, social outcasts with no ties to family or community. However, the contention that Wobblies and other radicals were not integrated into local communities is disproved by the existence and role of their numerous labor halls, which acted as both community centers and organizing points for labor activism. Employers themselves tacitly acknowledged the relationship between local communities and labor radicalism when they raided these halls, as they did during the 1912 Lumber Strike, when employers' citizens' committees attacked and closed down IWW and Red Finn halls in the Wobbly strongholds of Raymond, Aberdeen, and Hoquiam. The radicals and their movements, then, were much more a product of Red Coast communities than employers admitted or historians have often recognized.

One striking feature of the class war was the sharpness of its demographic divide. Many examples of Red Coast class struggles featured native-born white men acting in concert to protect their employing-class privileges, whereas a more representative sample of America's population combined to pursue reformist or radical aims. Almost all scholarship on Pacific Coast labor looks at the vast majority of wage laborers in the lumber industry who were male. But the class struggle was waged not only by men; women's experiences were also shaped by class, and they too engaged in the class struggle in a variety of ways. On the employers' side of the class struggle stood white men, and on the other stood both men and women, whether immigrants or native-born, skilled or unskilled. A useful illustration of this can be found in the book's opening pages, as dozens of Finnish-born women took to the streets to picket the sawmills and lumber docks where their male relatives and comrades were employed and on strike. Not long after beginning their protests, these women encountered an organized force of white male employers and anti-union state officials, organized as a citizens' committee, which used fire hoses to disperse the picketers and end their protests.

Outnumbered in their struggle against immigrant and native-born workers, bosses drew on a variety of techniques to oppose workers' movements, and several chapters suggest the breadth of these techniques. Employers used the tools traditionally at their disposal, such as the police, politicians, and courts, along with newspapers and other capitalist institutions. Boss efforts to depict radicals as "outsiders" and to play on workers' prejudices are examples of wider patterns of employing-class activity. Employers also organized at the point of production, in community-based organizations, and on the streets to protect their class interests. But when these methods failed, they readily resorted to other methods, including violence, vigilantism, and sabotage. Thus both employers and workers on the Red Coast repeatedly demonstrated their class consciousness in a variety of ways. An interesting illustration of this involves the Centralia story and its aftermath, an episode in which the employing class used a creative mix of the law—including the newly passed criminal syndicalism law—employer organizations, violence, and vigilante activism. The alacrity with which employers resorted to violence is particularly ironic, given their propensity to depict Wobblies and other radicals as a dangerous menace. As *The Red Coast* demonstrates, Wobblies and other radical workers were, in fact, much more likely to be the victims than the perpetrators of violence.

Despite the challenges that radical workers faced, they nonetheless continued to pursue radical aims, which in the case of the Communists and the Wobblies, included the overthrow of the capitalist system itself. Although they clearly did not achieve this revolutionary outcome, they did win meaningful improvements in their working conditions. Although the Wobblies failed to secure their much-publicized four-hour day, they did secure the eight-hour day. And some of the victories of this era might even, by today's standards, appear downright utopian. The shingle weavers' success was perhaps most remarkable. From working an average of ten hours per day, with a six-day workweek in 1900, unionized weavers fought for, and gained, first, an eight-hour day, then a six-hour day and six-day work week, and finally, in 1946 a thirty-hour work week, with five six-hour days.[1] Workers thus demonstrated that although not all of their revolutionary goals and aspirations were achieved, the struggle meant something; lives and working conditions could and did improve.

But the gains that workers made came at a cost, as the 1940 murder of Laura Law demonstrates. Law's murder was not the last act of anti-labor violence, nor were the struggles that she and her husband led the final battles waged by workers on the Red Coast. However, from the perspective of historians of the labor movement, the postwar period differs substantially from the first four decades of the twentieth century. In short, the postwar period was marked by significantly fewer radical and militant struggles than the prewar period. Several factors help account for the changing nature of the movement. In the first place, by the postwar period, the immigrant restrictions of the 1920s began to have telling effect. As the preceding chapters have demonstrated, immigrants and especially Red Finns were at the forefront of labor radicalism. This made them the target of anti-labor legislators such as Albert

Johnson, and their exclusion denied the movement the benefit of their radical traditions. This exclusion coincided with the decline in membership and
influence of the IWW. As the Second World War approached, the Red Coast
lost many other labor organizers, whether they went to fight fascism in Spain,
as in the case of "Red" Johnson and Ernest Kozlowski, or whether they were
murdered, as Laura Law was.

Second, and in a similar vein, with the emergence of the Cold War, openly
left-wing workers such as Communists, who were at the heart of several of
our chapters, were purged from unions. The Red Scare purge of Communists
deprived Red Coast unions of their most skilled and dedicated organizers.

Third, by World War II, workers won recognition of their unions and real
material gains in the form of increased wages, health care, and social insurance. But part of the price for this postwar settlement between capital and
labor was the institutionalization and moderation of their unions. It seems
that the labor movement's successes undermined more radical expressions
of class consciousness. The increased prosperity that followed unionization
no doubt weakened workers' sense of class consciousness. Moreover, unions
that began in the early twentieth century as organic and democratic movements arising from the class consciousness of local communities, became
in the postwar period professional, bureaucratic organizations. As a consequence, decision-making power was taken out of the hands of workers and
put in the hands of labor bosses, who were legally required to have union
members abide by their contracts, which often included no-strike clauses in
this latter period. Labor bosses had a vested interest in taming the militancy
of their members because their jobs depended, in part, on their ability to
enforce the contract.[2]

In telling this story, we have not attempted to present an "objective" history. We reject the idea that the arguments of those who advocate for workers'
rights and those who advocate for workers' oppression deserve equal consideration. Like the proletarian novelists of the 1930s, we side with the workers
who fought for just pay, workplace democracy, and humane working conditions. We hope that the election of 2016 does not prove to be a depressing
coda to the history of the Red Coast. In 2016, for the first time in eighty-four
years and sixty-four years, respectively, the voters of the Red Coast's Grays
Harbor and Pacific Counties went for a Republican presidential candidate. No
doubt, absent the class consciousness of their forebears, many a grandson and
granddaughter of Wobbly immigrants voted—along with their bosses—for

a billionaire who campaigned on pledges to cut taxes for the rich and attack America's most vulnerable workers, immigrants.

It is perhaps more apparent than ever that the American class war continues. But although bosses, despite their occasional squabbles, always manage to rally together in class solidarity, class consciousness among the working class has dramatically diminished. The employing-class's old bag of tricks— dividing workers by race and ethnicity, through control of right-wing media propaganda and pseudo-patriotic nationalistic flag-waving—has not outlived its usefulness. In 2018, anti-labor politicians control all branches of the federal government; not since the 1920s has momentum in the class war so favored the rich. To reverse this momentum, workers may need to relearn the lessons of their Red Coast forebears: they are not partners with their bosses on a team; the immigrant is not the enemy; and workers must organize at the point of production if they wish to improve their lives.

Notes

INTRODUCTION

1   *Day Book* (Chicago), April 27, 1912; *Spokesman-Review*, April 8, 11, 1912; *Seattle Star*, 9, 10, 12, 13; *Raivaaja* (Fitchburg, MA), April 15, 1912.

2   *Seattle Star*, April 13, 1912.

3   Ibid.

4   Agnes C. Laut, "Revolution Yawns!" *Technical World Magazine* (October 1912): 142.

5   *Strike Bulletin* (Aberdeen, WA), April 9, 1912.

6   *Shingle Weaver* (Ballard, WA), June 1905; Philip S. Foner, *History of the Labor Movement in the United States*, vol. 4, *The Industrial Workers of the World, 1905–1917* (1965; reprint, New York: International Publishers, 1997); Charlotte Todes, *Labor and Lumber* (New York: International Publishers, 1931), 152–161; Vernon Jensen, *Lumber and Labor* (New York: J. J. Little and Ives, 1945; New York: Arno Press, 1971), 117–119; State of Washington, *Seventh Biennial Report of the Bureau of Labor Statistics and Factory Inspection*, 1909–1910 (Olympia: E. L. Boardman, Public Printer, 1910), 180–182.

7   On the history of women and the IWW, see Heather Mayer, *Beyond the Rebel Girl: Women and the Industrial Workers of the World in the Pacific Northwest, 1905–1924* (Corvallis: Oregon State University Press, 2018).

8   John Hughes and Ryan Teague Beckwith, ed., *On the Harbor: From Black Friday to Nirvana* (Aberdeen: Daily World, 2001), 72.

9   Bradley Dale Richardson, "'The Forgotten Front: Gender, Labor, and Politics in Camas, Washington, and the Northwest Paper Industry, 1913–1918," (MA thesis, Portland State University, 2015).

10 Ben Weatherwax, "Hometown Scrapbook—No. 71—The Wobblies," Oct. 29, 1953, radio script for Station KBKW, Aberdeen, recorded in the 1950s, Pacific Northwest History Collection, Aberdeen Timberland Library, Aberdeen, Washington"; *Grays Harbor Post*, May 3, 20, 1905; June 10, 1905; Dec. 2, 1905.

11 Alan Dawley, *Struggles for Justice: Social Responsibility and the Liberal State* (Cambridge, MA: Belknap Press of Harvard University Press, 1993), 100.

12 "Preamble of the Industrial Workers of the World," in *Rebel Voices: An IWW Anthology*, ed. Joyce L. Kornbluh, new and exp. ed. (Chicago: Charles H. Kerr, 1998), 12–13.

13 Ibid.

14 See Elizabeth Jameson, *All that Glitters: Class, Conflict, and Community in Cripple Creek* (Urbana, University of Illinois Press, 1998); Melvyn Dubofsky, *We Shall Be*

All: A History of the Industrial Workers of the World (New York: Quadrangle, 1973), 47–54.

15 William Millikan, A Union Against Unions: The Minneapolis Citizens' Alliance and Its Fight Against Organized Labor, 1903–1947 (St. Paul: University of Minnesota Press, 2001).

16 Industrial Worker, Nov. 20, 1911; Jan. 4, 1912; Solidarity, Dec. 23, 1911.

17 Solidarity, March 2, 1912.

18 United States Bureau of the Census (Hereafter USBC), Thirteenth Census of the United States Taken in the Year 1910, Washington State, Pacific County, City of Ilwaco; USBC, Thirteenth Census, Grays Harbor County, Grayland.

19 Industrial Worker, Jan. 5, 1918.

20 Walter L. Stout to Spruce Production Division, Signal Corps, USA, Nov. 27, 1917, Record Group 165, Box 2, File 573, Records of the War Department General Staff, Military Intelligence Division, Plant Protection, Portland District, National Archives and Records Administration, Pacific Alaska Region, Seattle, WA.

21 Industrial Worker, May 14, 1924.

22 Chehalis Bee Nugget, Aug. 1, 1924.

23 Timber Worker (Aberdeen, WA), Feb. 5, 1937; Aberdeen Daily World, May 6, 11, 1938; R.L. Polk and Co.'s Kelso and Longview Cities Directory (1940), 465–466; Polk's Vancouver City Directory (1940), 398–401; R.L. Polk and Co.'s Grays Harbor Cities Directory (1939), 670–672; Polk's Centralia City Directory (1940), 307–308.

CHAPTER 1: THE GILLNET WARS

1 Daily Morning Astorian, May 25, 1887; Washington Standard (Olympia, WA), June 3, 1887.

2 Daily Morning Astorian, May 27, 1887.

3 Courtland L. Smith, Salmon Fishers of the Columbia (Corvallis: Oregon State University Press, 1979), 95–99.

4 Bill Gulick, A Traveler's History of Washington (Caldwell, ID: Caxton Printers, 1996), 235. The conflicts have also been called "fish fights." See, for example, Courtland L. Smith, Oregon Fish Fights (Corvallis: Oregon State University, Sea Grant College Program, 1974).

5 Columbia River Fishermen's Protective Union (CRFPU), Columbia River Fisheries (Astoria, OR: G. W. Snyder, 1890), http://digitalcollections.lib.washington.edu/cdm/compoundobject/collection/salmon/id/417.

6 See Michael Passi, "Fishermen on Strike: Finnish Workers and Community Power in Astoria, Oregon 1880–1900," in The Finnish Experience in the Western Great Lakes Region: New Perspectives, by Michael G. Karni, Matti E. Kaups, and Douglas J. Ollila (Turku [Duluth]: Institute for Migration; Immigration History Research Center, University of Minnesota, 1975).

7 CRFPU, Columbia River Fisheries, 8–9; W. A. Jones, Salmon Fisheries of the Columbia River, 50th Cong., 1st sess., 1888, Ex. Doc. No. 123, 46–47; Courtland L. Smith, Fish or Cut Bait (Corvallis: Oregon State University, Sea Grant College Program, 1977), 5–6.

8 CRFPU, Columbia River Fisheries, 16–17.

9 Ibid., 14–15.

10 *Scientific American*, Sept. 19, 1896, 232.

11 Gulick, *Traveler's History of Washington*, 235.

12 Joseph William Collins, "Salmon Fishing on the Columbia," *Frank Leslie's Popular Monthly* 44 (July–December 1897), 427.

13 David F. Arnold, *The Fishermen's Frontier: People and Salmon in Southeast Alaska* (Seattle: University of Washington Press, 2008), 61; Daniel L. Boxberger, "Ethnicity and Labor in the Puget Sound Fishing Industry, 1880–1935," *Ethnology* 33, no. 2 (Spring 1994): 183.

14 Joseph Cone, *A Common Fate: Endangered Salmon and the People of the Pacific Northwest* (New York: H. Holt, 1995), 109.

15 Jones, *Salmon Fisheries of the Columbia River*, 6.

16 CRFPU, *Columbia River Fisheries*, 8.

17 "Lorntsen Exhibit," in *Industrial Relations: Final Report and Testimony*, vol. 23 (Washington, DC: Government Printing Office, 1916), 4764.

18 Smith, *Salmon Fishers of the Columbia*, 91.

19 CRFPU, "Constitution and By-Laws of the Columbia River Fishermen's Protective Union and Affiliated Cannery Employees," n.d., 3.

20 Ibid., 4, 7–8; CRFPU, *Columbia River Fisheries*, 5.

21 Chris Friday, *Organizing Asian American Labor: The Pacific Coast Canned-Salmon Industry, 1870–1942* (Philadelphia: Temple University Press, 1994), 68–69.

22 CRFPU, *Columbia River Fisheries*, 13–14; "Lorntsen Exhibit," in *Industrial Relations: Final Report and Testimony*, 4764.

23 Ibid.,; Charles C. Dalton, *Salmon Fisheries on the Columbia River* (Ilwaco, WA [1893?]), 4; *Seattle Post-Intelligencer*, May 1, 1890.

24 See *Daily Morning Astorian*, May 1, 1890; *Seattle Post-Intelligencer*, May 1, 1890.

25 *Daily Morning Astorian*, May 1, 1890.

26 Ibid.

27 *Seattle Post-Intelligencer*, May 1, 1890.

28 "Lorntsen Exhibit," in *Industrial Relations: Final Report and Testimony*, 4764.

29 Ibid.

30 *Washington Standard*, April 10, 1896.

31 *Daily Morning Astorian*, April 4, 18, 1896; *Albany States Rights Democrat*, April 10, 1896; State of Washington v. State of Oregon, court decision published by Judd and Detweiler, 121–123 (1907

32 *Oregon Mist*, April 10, 1896; *Daily Morning Astorian*, April 14, 1896.

33 *Daily Morning Astorian*, April 11, 14, 1896.

34 "Gillnet Rebellion of 1896 Threatened Columbia River War," *Sou'wester* (Spring 1979): 15–17.

35 *South Bend Journal*, April 10, 1896.

36 *Seattle Post-Intelligencer*, May 26, 1896.

37 *Daily Capital Journal*, June 9, 1896.

38 *Seattle Post-Intelligencer*, June 16, 17, 1896.

39 *Islander* (Friday Harbor, WA), June 25, 1896; *Seattle Post-Intelligencer*, June 30, 1896.

40 Cone, *Common Fate*, 117; Andrea Larson Perez, *Astoria* (Charleston, SC: Arcadia Publishing, 2016), 18; Richard H. Engeman, *The Oregon Companion: An Historical*

Gazetteer of the Useful, the Curious, and the Arcane (Portland: Timber Press, 2009), 28.

41 Smith, *Salmon Fishers of the Columbia*, 95.

CHAPTER 2: THE ABERDEEN OUTRAGE

1   Throughout the book, we use the terms "deport" and "expel" from town interchangeably to refer to the removal of a person or group from town.

2   Denis Kearney, President, and H. L. Knight, Secretary, "Appeal from California. The Chinese Invasion. Workingmen's Address," *Indianapolis Times*, Feb. 28, 1878.

3   Art Chin, *Golden Tassels: A History of the Chinese in Washington State, 1857–1977* (Seattle: Chin, 1977), 58.

4   *South Bend Journal*, Sept. 19, 1890.

5   Letter from Tsui Kwo Yin, of the Chinese Legation in Washington, DC, to James Blaine, Secretary of State, Sept. 14, 1890, Elisha P. Ferry Papers, Box 2a-1-2, Folder Title: "Anti-Chinese Activities in Aberdeen," Washington State Archives, Olympia, WA (hereafter WSA).

6   *Seattle Post-Intelligencer*, Sept. 16, 1890; Nov. 12, 1890.

7   According to the *Daily Morning Astorian*, some participants grew nervous that the order would be evaded and held a second meeting, in which they gave the Chinese only forty-eight hours to leave. *Daily Morning Astorian*, Sept. 18, 1890.

8   State of Washington v. John Wing, No. 182, 1890, Court Docket of Civil Cases, State Superior Court of Chehalis County, Washington, Southwest Washington Archives, Olympia, Washington (hereafter SWA); *Seattle Post-Intelligencer*, Nov. 12, 1890.

9   *Daily Morning Astorian*, Sept. 17, 1890

10 William F. Wharton to Tsui Kwo Yin, Sept. 16, 1890, Elisha P. Ferry Papers, Box 2a-1-2, Folder Title: "Anti-Chinese Activities in Aberdeen," WSA.

11 The information in this sentence comes from the same letter as above. William F Wharton to Tsui Kwo Yin, Sept 16, 1890, Elisha P. Ferry Papers, Box 2a-1-2, Folder Title: "Anti-Chinese Activities in Aberdeen," WSA.

12 *Seattle Post-Intelligencer*, Sept. 18, 21, 25, 1890.

13 *Chehalis Nugget*, Nov. 21, 1890.

14 *Seattle Post-Intelligencer*, Sept. 12, 1890.

15 State of Washington v. John Wing, Case 182.

16 *Seattle Post-Intelligencer*, Nov. 10, 1890.

17 Superior Court Affidavit, Francis R. Wall v. John Wing, No. 177, 1890, Court Docket of Civil Cases, State Superior Court of Chehalis County Papers, Washington, SWA.

18 *Washington Newspaper: A Publication Dedicated to the Study and Improvement of Journalism in Washington*, October 1916, 31; *Seamen's Journal* (San Francisco), Oct. 15, 1919.

19 *Aberdeen Herald*, March 5, 1896; September 17, 1896.

20 *Seattle Post-Intelligencer*, Nov. 9, 1890.

21 Ruth Kirk and Carmela Alexander, *Exploring Washington's Past: A Road Guide to History*, rev. ed. (Seattle: University of Washington Press, 1995), 496.

22 Database: 1892 Grays Harbor County Census. Online 2009. Washington Secretary of State. Transcribed by Jarlee McCormick, Chehalis, WA; Stan Staniforth, Bellevue,

WA; and Peggy Booth, Seattle, WA. Proofreading by Joshua Matthews, Olympia, WA; Ann Stroupe, Federal Way, WA; and Frances Baker-Spuler, Otis Orchards, WA.

23 Ed Van Syckle, *The River Pioneers: The Early Days on Grays Harbor* (Seattle: Pacific Search Press, 1982), 243.

24 Database: 1889 Grays Harbor County Census. Online 2008. Washington Secretary of State. Transcribed by Judy Mc Millan, Portland, OR; Lorie Parkhurst, Taholah, WA; Linda Smyth, Silverdale, WA; and Jill Kelleman, Tucson, AZ. Proofread by Cyndi Sandahl, Kent, WA; Jarlee McCormick, Chehalis, WA; Joshua Matthews, Olympia, WA; and Ann Stroupe, Federal Way, WA.

25 *Aberdeen Herald,* Nov. 13, 1890; Jan. 1, 1891.

26 *Northwest Magazine,* January 1890, 18; Herbert Hunt, and Floyd C. Kaylor, *Washington, West of the Cascades: Historical and Descriptive; the Explorers, the Indians, the Pioneers, the Modern* (Chicago: S. J. Clarke, 1917).

27 *Morning Oregonian* (Portland), Aug. 8, 1888; April 9, 1890; *Aberdeen Herald,* Dec. 25, 1890.

28 *Aberdeen Herald,* Oct. 23, 30, Dec. 25, 1890; Jan. 15, May 7, 1891; Feb. 12, 1892; Nov. 30, 1893; Dec. 6, 1894; Jan. 3, 1895. Before 1915, Grays Harbor County was known as Chehalis County.

29 *Seattle Post-Intelligencer,* Nov. 10, 1890.

30 *Seattle Post-Intelligencer,* Nov. 29, 1890.

31 *Seattle Post-Intelligencer,* Nov. 12, 1890.

32 *Aberdeen Herald,* Nov. 13, 27, 1890.

33 Cited in *The Seattle Post-Intelligencer,* Nov. 15, 1890.

34 *Morning Oregonian,* Dec. 1, 1890.

35 *Seattle Post-Intelligencer,* Nov. 19, 1890.

36 *Seattle Post-Intelligencer,* Nov. 29, 1890.

CHAPTER 3: RED FINN HALLS

1 Peggy Dennis, *The Autobiography of an American Communist* (Westport, CT: Lawrence, Hill, 1978), 13.

2 House of Representatives, *Investigation of Communist Propaganda, Hearings before A Special Committee to Investigate Communist Activities in the United States of the House of Representatives,* 71st Congress, 2nd Session (Washington, DC: Government Printing Office, 1930), 909.

3 Ibid., 910.

4 Dennis, *Autobiography of an American Communist,* 15.

5 House of Representatives, *Investigation of Communist Propaganda,* 915.

6 Dennis, *Autobiography of an American Communist,* 15.

7 For background on Finnish American labor and left-wing movements, see Michael Karni and Douglas J. Ollila Jr., *For the Common Good: Finnish Immigrants and the Radical Response to Industrial America* (Superior, WI: Työmies Society, 1977); Auvo Kostiainen, ed., *Finns in the United States: A History of Settlement, Dissent, and Integration* (East Lansing: Michigan State University Press, 2014); Paul George Hummasti, *Finnish Radicals in Astoria, Oregon: A Study in Immigrant Socialism, 1904–1940* (New York: Arno Press, 1979); and Gary Kaunonen, *Challenge Accepted: A Finnish Immigrant Response to Industrial America in Michigan's Copper Country* (East Lansing: Michigan State University Press, 2010).

8   Paul George Hummasti, "Fighting for Temperance Ideas," in *Finns in the United States: A History of Settlement, Dissent, and Integration*, ed. Auvo Kostiainen (East Lansing: Michigan State University Press), 91–106.

9   USBC, *Thirteenth Census*, Washington State, Pacific County, City of Ilwaco.

10 Merle A. Reinikka, *Ilwaco's Early Finns, Pacific County, Washington* (Finnish American Historical Society of the West, 1992), 32–33.

11 *Toveri*, March 23, 1915.

12 Reinikka, *Ilwaco's Early Finns*, 33, 38.

13 Helen A. Basso, "Wedding Dances," *Cowlitz Historical Quarterly* 22, no. 1–2 (Spring/Summer 1980): 22; House of Representatives, *Investigation of Communist Propaganda*, 892–902.

14 House of Representatives, *Investigation of Communist Propaganda*, 27.

15 *History of Aberdeen USKB&S Lodge No. 9*, United Finnish Kaleva Brothers and Sisters Lodge 9 Collection, Aberdeen History Museum (AHM), 3–4; Elis Sulkanen, ed., *Amerikan Suomalaisen Työvaenliikkeen historia* (Fitchburg, MA: Amerikan Suomalainen Kansanvallen Liitto ja Raivaaja Publishing Company, 1951), 466–469; Charette, "Finns in Aberdeen"; Smits, "The Finns in Hoquiam."

16 *Aberdeen Daily World*, April 17, 1912.

17 *Toveritar* (Astoria, OR), May 21, 1918.

18 *Industrialisti*, Aug. 30, 1928.

19 On the use of Finn halls as strike headquarters during Grays Harbor labor conflicts, see *Aberdeen Daily World*, March 24, 1912; Oct. 9, 1925; July 26, 1933; *Grays Harbor Post*, Oct. 10, 1925; *Daily Washingtonian*, July 26, 1933.

20 *Grays Harbor Post*, April 6, 1912.

21 *Aberdeen Daily World*, April 17, 1912.

22 *Industrial Worker*, April 4, 1912.

23 Ralph Chaplin, *Wobbly: The Rough-and-Tumble Story of an American Radical* (Chicago: University of Chicago Press, 1948), 290; Melvyn Dubofsky, *We Shall Be All: A History of the Industrial Workers of the World* (New York: Quadrangle, 1973), 435–437.

24 Dennis, *Autobiography of an American Communist*, 15–16.

25 Ibid., 16.

26 Ottilie Markholt, *Maritime Solidarity: Pacific Coast Unionism, 1929–1938* (Tacoma: Pacific Coast Maritime History Committee, 1998), 36.

27 Reinikka, *Ilwaco's Early Finns*, 38.

28 Walter Mattila, ed., *The Lewis River Finns*, 5, no. 5 (Portland: Finnish American Historical Society of the West, 1970), 11–13; Reino Hannula, *An Album of Finnish Halls* (San Luis Obispo, CA: Finn Heritage, 1991), 57.

29 Mattila, *Lewis River Finns*, 11–14.

30 Claim in the matter of Finnish Socialist Society, Claimant, to the Comptroller of the City of Aberdeen, File 8, Box 7, John Caughlan Papers, *University of Washington*, Seattle (UW); Jerry Lembcke and William H. Tattam, *One Union in Wood: A Political History of the International Woodworkers of America* (New York: International Publishers, 1984), 69.

31 Hughes and Beckwith, *On the Harbor*, 105.

32 Statement of Harland L. Plumb, Feb. 29, 1940, Laura Law Records, Box 2, Folder 2-1jj, *Southwest Washington Archives*, Olympia, Washington (SWA).

33 Hughes and Beckwith, *On the Harbor*, 107; Lembcke and Tattam, *One Union in Wood*, 69.

34 James W. Loewen, *Lies Across America: What American Historic Sites Get Wrong* (New York: Simon and Schuster, 2007), 62.

35 Ibid., 63.

CHAPTER 4: THE ABERDEEN FREE SPEECH FIGHT

1 *Aberdeen Herald*, Oct. 12, 1911; Ben Weatherwax, "Hometown Scrapbook," "Hometown Scrapbook—No. 71—The Wobblies," Oct. 29, 1953, radio script for Station KBKW, Aberdeen, recorded in the 1950s, Pacific Northwest History Collection, Aberdeen Timberland Library, Aberdeen, Washington.

2 *Aberdeen Herald*, Oct. 12, 1911; *Aberdeen Daily World*, Nov. 22, 1911.

3 Weatherwax "Hometown Scrapbook."

4 *Industrial Worker*, Feb. 1, 1911, Dec. 14, 1911; *Aberdeen Daily World*, Nov. 22, 1911.

5 Philip S. Foner, *History of the Labor Movement in the United States*, vol. 4, *The Industrial Workers of the World, 1905–1917* (1965; reprint, New York: International Publishers, 1997), 174.

6 *Aberdeen Herald*, Nov. 23, 1911.

7 *Industrial Worker*, Nov. 30, 1911, Feb. 1, 1912; *Daily Washingtonian*, Nov. 24, 1911; *Aberdeen Daily World*, Nov. 24, 1911.

8 Charles Pierce LeWarne, "The Aberdeen, Washington, Free Speech Fight of 1911–1912," *Pacific Northwest Quarterly* 66 (January 1975): 1.

9 *Industrial Worker*, Feb. 1, 1912.

10 *Industrial Worker*, Feb. 1, 1912, Nov. 30, 1911; *Daily Washingtonian*, Nov. 24, 1911.

11 *Industrial Worker*, Feb. 1, 1912.

12 *Industrial Worker*, Nov. 30, 1911; *Aberdeen Daily World*, Nov. 25, 1911.

13 *Aberdeen Herald*, Nov. 27, 1911.

14 *Aberdeen Daily World*, Nov. 24, 1911; Weatherwax, "Hometown Scrapbook."

15 *Aberdeen Daily World*, Nov. 24, 1911.

16 Ibid.

17 *Aberdeen Daily World*, Nov. 25, 1911; *Industrial Worker*, Feb. 1, 1912.

18 LeWarne, "Aberdeen, Washington, Free Speech Fight," 5.

19 *Daily Washingtonian*, Nov. 25, 1911; *Aberdeen Daily World*, Nov. 25, 1911; *Industrial Worker*, Feb. 1, 1912.

20 Tracy Newell, Sworn Testimony given to Pierce County Notary Public, Dec. 16, 1911. Governor Marion E. Hay Papers, Judiciary, 1911-Labor Conflicts/I.W.W, Box 2G-2-19, Labor Conflicts-Aberdeen, Raymond, Spokane, 1910–1912, WSA.

21 *Industrial Worker*, Feb. 1, 1912; Weatherwax, "Hometown Scrapbook."

22 *Daily Washingtonian*, Nov. 25, 1911; *Industrial Worker*, Nov. 30, 1911.

23 *Aberdeen Daily World*, Nov. 25, 1911.

24 Foner, *History of the Labor Movement in the United States*, vol. 4, 191.

25 *Industrial Worker*, Feb. 1, 1912.

26 Joyce L. Kornbluh, ed., *Rebel Voices: An IWW Anthology*, new and exp. ed. (Chicago: Charles H. Kerr, 1998),102; *Industrial Worker*, Oct. 23, 1963.

27 *Industrial Worker*, Dec. 14, 1911, Jan. 11, 1912.

28 *Industrial Worker*, Dec. 14, 1911.

29 *Industrial Worker*, Dec. 21, 1911.

30 *Industrial Worker*, Dec. 14, 21, 1911.

31 Dana Frank, *Purchasing Power: Consumer Organizing, Gender, and the Seattle Labor Movement, 1919–1929* (Cambridge: Cambridge University Press, 1994), 108–109.

32 *Industrial Worker*, Jan. 11, 1912.

33 Ibid.

34 *Industrial Worker*, Dec. 14, 1911.

35 The full text of the Hoquiam Socialists' resolution appeared in the *Industrial Worker*, Dec. 14, 1911.

36 *Industrial Worker*, Dec. 14, 1911.

37 Ibid.

38 *Industrial Worker*, Nov. 30, 1911; Dec. 7, 1911.

39 *Industrial Worker*, Feb. 1, 1912.

40 *Industrial Worker*, Dec. 14, 1911; Dec. 21, 1911, Feb. 1, 1912.

41 Ordinance No. 1154 appeared in the *Grays Harbor Post* (Aberdeen, WA), Jan. 6, 1912.

42 *Daily Washingtonian* (Hoquiam, WA), Jan. 4, 1912; *Aberdeen Herald*, Jan. 11, 1912.

43 *Aberdeen Herald*, Jan. 8, 1912.

44 *Agitator* (Home, WA), Jan. 15, 1912.

45 C. E. Payne, "The Mainspring of Action," in *Fellow Workers and Friends: I.W.W. Free-Speech Fights as Told by Participants*, ed. Philip S. Foner (Westport, CT: Greenwood Press, 1981), 126–128.

46 Henry McGuckin, *Memoirs of a Wobbly* (Chicago: Charles H. Kerr Press, 1987), 38.

47 *Industrial Worker*, Jan. 25, 1912.

48 Payne, "The Mainspring of Action," 128–129.

49 *Industrial Worker*, Jan. 25, 1912; Feb. 1, 1912; LeWarne, "Aberdeen, Washington, Free Speech Fight," 10–11; Payne, "The Mainspring of Action," 128–129.

50 Payne, "The Mainspring of Action," 128–129.

51 *Industrial Worker*, Jan. 18, 1912; Jan. 25, 1912; Feb. 1, 1912.

52 *Industrial Worker*, Jan. 25, Feb. 1, 1912.

53 *Grays Harbor Post*, Feb. 5, 1910; Sept. 2, 1911.

54 LeWarne, "Aberdeen, Washington, Free Speech Fight," 11.

55 Ibid.

56 *Industrial Worker*, Feb. 1, 1912.

57 *Industrial Worker*, Jan. 25, 1912; LeWarne, "Aberdeen, Washington, Free Speech Fight," 11.

CHAPTER 5: THE WAR OF GRAYS HARBOR

1 *Aberdeen Herald*, Jan. 15, 1911; Feb. 15, 1912.

2 Fred Thompson, *The I.W.W.—Its First Fifty Years* (Chicago: Industrial Workers of the World, 1955), 68; *Aberdeen Daily World*, March 14, 1912; Robert L. Tyler, *Rebels of the Woods: The I. W. W. in the Pacific Northwest* (Eugene: University of Oregon Books, 1967), 57.

3 *Aberdeen Daily World*, March 14, April 4, 1912.

4 *Industrial Worker*, March 15, 28, 1912; *Morning Oregonian* (Portland, OR), March 15, 1912.

5 *Morning Oregonian*, March 15, 1912; *Aberdeen Daily World*, March 15, 1912.

6 *Daily Washingtonian*, March 15, 1912.

7 *Aberdeen Daily World*, March 15, 1912.

8 Ibid.; *Daily Washingtonian*, March 16, 1912.

9 *Aberdeen Daily World*, March 15, 16, 1912.

10 Bruce Rogers, "The War of Gray's [*sic*] Harbor," *International Socialist Review* 12, no. 11 (May 1912): 749–753. Reprinted in *The Agitator* (Jan. 15, 1912): 1.

11 *Industrial Worker*, March 28, 1912.

12 *Labor Journal* (Everett, WA), March 29, 1912.

13 *Labor Journal*, April 26, 1912.

14 *Labor Journal*, May 31, 1912.

15 *Industrial Worker*, April 4, 1912.

16 Ibid.; Philip S. Foner, *History of the Labor Movement in the United States*, vol. 4, *The Industrial Workers of the World, 1905–1917* (1965; reprint, New York: International Publishers, 1997), 223–224.

17 *Industrial Worker*, April 18, 1912.

18 Ibid.

19 *Aberdeen Herald*, April 4, 1912.

20 *Industrial Worker*, May 9, 1912.

21 *Industrial Worker*, April 4, May 16, 1912.

22 *Morning Oregonian*, March 21, 1912; *Industrial Worker*, April 4, 1912.

23 "Cosmopolis in 1908," City of Cosmopolis Papers, Special Collections, Aberdeen Timberland Library Archives, Aberdeen, Washington.

24 *Industrial Worker*, April 4, 1912.

25 *Aberdeen Daily World*, March 27, 1912; *Industrial Worker*, April 4, 11, 18, 1912; *Aberdeen Herald*, March 28, 1912.

26 *Aberdeen Daily World*, March 18, 1912.

27 Cited in Robert Walter Bruere, *Following the Trail of the IWW: A First-Hand Investigation into Labor Troubles in the West, A Trip into the Copper and Lumber Camps of the Inland Empire with the Views of the Men on the Job* (New York: New York Evening Post, 1918), 19.

28 *Morning Oregonian*, April 1, 1912.

29 *Tacoma Times*, March 28, 1912.

30 *Industrial Worker*, March 28, April 4, 1912.

31 Philip J. Dreyfus, "The IWW and the Limits of Inter-Ethnic Organizing: Reds, Whites, and Greeks in Grays Harbor, Washington, 1912," *Labor History* 38, no. 4 (Fall 1997): 458.

32 *Seattle Union Record*, April 27, 1912.

33 *Industrial Worker*, Dec. 21, 1911.

34 *Morning Oregonian*, March 27, 28, 1912.

35 *Morning Oregonian*, March 30, 1912.

36 *Tacoma Times*, March 29, 1912; *Daily Capital Journal* (Salem, OR), April 1, 1912.

37 *Industrial Worker*, April 11, 1912.

38 *Aberdeen Herald*, April 15, 1912.

39 *Aberdeen Daily World*, March 22, 1912.

40 *Aberdeen Herald*, April 1, 1912.

41 *Morning Oregonian*, April 2, 1912.

42 Thompson, *The I.W.W.—Its First Fifty Years*, 69.

43 *Aberdeen Herald*, April 1, 4, 1912; *Grays Harbor Post*, April 6, 1912; USBC, *Thirteenth Census*, Washington State, Harbor County, City of Aberdeen.

44 *Grays Harbor Post*, April 6, 1912.

45 *Aberdeen Daily World*, March 15, 23, 1912.

46 Dreyfus, "The IWW and the Limits," 462–463.

47 *Daily Washingtonian*, April 6, 1912.

48 *Aberdeen Herald*, April 8, 15, 1912.

49 *Industrial Worker*, April 18, 1912.

50 *Aberdeen Herald*, April 15, 1912.

51 *Industrial Worker*, May 23, 1912.

52 Cloice R. Howd, *Industrial Relations in the West Coast Lumber Industry*, Bulletin of the United States Bureau of Labor Statistics, No. 349 (Washington, DC: Government Printing Office, 1924), 66–76; Thompson, *The I. W. W.—Its First Fifty Years*, 146–147; John Hughes and Ryan Beckwith, eds., *On the Harbor: From Black Friday to Nirvana* (Aberdeen: Daily World, 2001), 42; Tyler, *Rebels of the Woods*, 202–204; *One Big Union Monthly* (Chicago), April 1920.

CHAPTER 6: MOVING DAY IN RAYMOND

1 *Aberdeen Herald*, April 1, 1912.

2 *Tacoma Times*, April 1, 1912. The *Times* spells the Raymond millman's name "Lytle," but it has confused millman A. C. Little of Raymond with Hoquiam millman R. F. Lytle.

3 *Tacoma Times*, April 1, 1912; *Morning Oregonian*, April 2, 1912.

4 Robert C. Bailey, Dianne Bridgman, and the Washington State Oral History Program, *Robert C. Bailey: An Oral History* (Olympia: Washington State Oral History Program, Office of the Secretary of State, 1996).

5 *Industrial Worker*, May 1, 1912.

6 *South Bend Journal*, March 29, 1912; *Industrial Worker*, April 4, 1912.

7 *South Bend Journal*, March 29, 1912.

8 *Toveri* (Astoria, OR), March 29, 1912, trans. Matti Roitto.

9 *Willapa Harbor Pilot* (Raymond, WA), March 29, 1912; *Industrial Worker*, April 11, 1912.

10 *South Bend Journal*, April 5, 1912.

11 *Toveri* April 3, 1912, trans. Matti Roitto.

12 *Industrial Worker*, May 1, 1912; April 4, 1912; April 18, 1912.

13 *Willapa Harbor Pilot*, March 29, 1912; *South Bend Journal*, April 5, 1912; *Industrial Worker*, May 1, 1912; April 4, 1912; April 18, 1912.

14 *Industrial Worker*, May 1, 1912.

15 *Industrial Worker*, April 11, 1912.

16 *Willapa Harbor Pilot*, April 5, 1912.

17 *Industrial Worker*, March 28, 1912.

18 *Aberdeen Herald*, March 18, 1912.

19 *Industrial Worker*, May 1, 1912.

20 *The Agitator*, April 15, 1912.

21 *Aberdeen Herald*, April 1, 1912.

22 *Tacoma Times*, April 2, 1912.

23 *Aberdeen Herald*, April 8, 1912.

24 *Industrial Worker*, April 18, 1912.

25 *Industrial Worker*, June 20, 1912.

26 *Industrial Worker*, May 1, 1912.

27 Bailey, Bridgman, and the Washington State Oral History Program, *Robert C. Bailey*.

CHAPTER 7: "THE HOME DEFENDER"

 1 Albert Johnson, "Some Reminiscences," *Grays Harbor Washingtonian*, July 29, 1934;
     Alfred J. Hillier, "Albert Johnson, Congressman," *Pacific Northwest Quarterly* 36, no.
     3 (July 1945): 199.

 2 Hillier, "Albert Johnson, Congressman," 196–199.

 3 *Daily Washingtonian*, Feb. 4, 1910.

 4 *Aberdeen Herald*, Jan. 11, 1912; *Grays Harbor Post*, Jan. 20, 1912.

 5 *Aberdeen Daily World*, Nov. 24, 25, 1911.

 6 A. B. Walmsley, "The Home Defender," *Home Defender*, May 12, 1912.

 7 "Gives Warning of Nation's Danger," *Home Defender*, August 1913.

 8 "Albert Johnson as a Campaigner," in Johnson Scrapbooks, Nov. 22, 1913, Albert
     Johnson Scrapbooks, Washington State Library, Tumwater, WA.

 9 "Predicts Johnson Will Be Next Congressman," *Daily Washingtonian*, Sept. 3, 1912.

10 Steve Willis, "Henry McCleary and the Land of the Rising Sun," *McCleary Museum
     Newsletter* 11, no. 3 (September 2001).

11 Johnson, "Reminiscences," July 29, 1934, 4.

12 Hillier, "Albert Johnson, Congressman," 199.

13 *Typographical Journal* 52, no. 2 (February 1918): 169.

14 *The Bricklayer, Mason, and Plasterer* 17, no. 12 (December 1914): 290.

15 "Gompers' Birthday Party Attended by Notables," in Johnson Scrapbooks, Jan. 28,
     1914; *Grays Harbor Washingtonian* (Hoquiam), Aug. 5, 1934.

16 Johnson Scrapbooks, 2–6; *Aberdeen Herald*, Feb. 1, 8, 1912.

17 L. H. Brewer to E. G. Ames, Oct. 16, 1912, Edwin Ames Papers, Acc. No 3820, Box
     4, Folder 21, University of Washington Special Collections, Seattle, WA (Hereafter
     UW).

18 *Home Defender*, March 1914.

19 *Home Defender*, September–October 1913.

20 Johnson Scrapbooks, July 10, 11 1913; *Independent* (Yakima, WA), July 11, 1913.

21 "Coolie Labor vs. American," in Johnson Scrapbooks, April 28, 1913.

22 Mee-ae Kim, "It Is Time to Put Up the Bars: Albert Johnson and the Immigration
     Act of 1924" (MA thesis, Washington State University, 1995), 29.

23 *Home Defender*, March 1914.

24 Johnson Scrapbooks, 82.

25 *Home Defender*, September–October 1913.

26 John Higham, *Strangers in the Land: Patterns of American Nativism* (New Brunswick,
     NJ: Rutgers University Press, 1988), 178 and 202.

27 On the 1924 Immigration Bill, see ibid., 318–325 and Matthew Frye Jacobson, *Whiteness of a Different Color: European Immigrants and the Alchemy of Race* (Cambridge, MA: Harvard University Press, 1998).

28 Hillier, "Albert Johnson, Congressman," 208.

29 Jacobson, *Whiteness of a Different Color*, 83–88; 112–113.

30 Linda Gordon, *The Second Coming of the KKK: The Ku Klux Klan of the 1920s and the American Political Tradition* (New York: W.W. Norton, 2017), 164, 195.

31 *Chehalis Bee-Nugget*, July 11, Aug. 1, 1924.

32 *Centralia Daily Chronicle*, Oct. 4, Dec. 11, 12, 1928; *Chehalis Bee-Nugget*, Feb. 23, 1923; Oct. 5, 1928.

33 Gordon, *Second Coming of the KKK*, 164, 195; Thomas R. Pegram, *One Hundred Percent American: The Rebirth and Decline of the Ku Klux Klan in the 1920s* (Chicago: Ivan R. Dee, 2011), 210.

34 Alan Dawley, *Struggles for Justice: Social Responsibility and the Liberal State* (Cambridge, MA: Belknap Press of Harvard University Press, 1993), 278.

35 *Grays Harbor Washingtonian*, Dec. 31, 1933–Sept. 9, 1934.

CHAPTER 8: CRIMINAL SYNDICALISM

1   Adam Smith, *An Inquiry into the Nature and Causes of the Wealth of Nations* (New York: Modern Library, 1937), 66.

2   Industrial Workers of the World, *The I.W.W. In Theory and Practice*, 5th rev. ed. (Chicago: Industrial Workers of the World, 1937), 124.

3   Ibid., 122.

4   Smith, *Wealth of Nations*, 68.

5   Ibid.

6   Ralph Chaplin, *The Centralia Conspiracy*, in *The Centralia Case: Three Views of the Armistice Day Tragedy at Centralia Washington, November 11, 1919*, by Ralph Chaplin and Ben Hur Lampman, Federal Council of the Churches of Christ in America, Department of Research and Education (New York: Da Capo Press, 1971), 22.

7   *Industrial Worker*, July 21, 1917.

8   Cited in Joyce L. Kornbluh, *Rebel Voices: An IWW Anthology*, new and exp. ed. (Chicago: Charles H. Kerr, 1998), 255.

9   Robert Ficken, "The Wobbly Horrors: Pacific Northwest Lumbermen and the Industrial Workers of the World," *Labor History* 24 (1983): 325–341.

10 "Governor's Veto Message," *Washington State, 16th Legislature. Senate Journal, January 13, 1919* (Olympia, WA: Frank M. Lamborn, Public Printer, 1919).

11 *Session Laws of the State of Washington, 1903* (Tacoma, WA: Allen & Lamborn Printing Company, 1903), 52–53.

12 *Industrial Worker*, May 24, 1919.

13 Albert F. Gunns, *Civil Liberties in Crisis: The Pacific Northwest 1917–1940* (New York: Garland, 1983), 38.

14 *Remington's Compiled Statues of Washington Annotated. Vol 1. Sessions Laws, 1919*, 517.

15 Tom Copeland, *The Centralia Tragedy of 1919: Elmer Smith and the Wobblies* (Seattle: University of Washington Press, 1993), 90.

16 State of Washington v. McLennen, 116 Wash, 612, 200 Pac 319 (1921).

17 Ibid.

18 F. G. Franklin, "Anti-Syndicalism Legislation," *American Political Science Review* 14, no. 2 (May 1920): 293.

19 *Remington's Compiled Statues of Washington Annotated*. Vol 1. *Sessions Laws, 1919*, 555–556.

20 Ibid., 555.

21 See Paul F. Brissenden, *The I.W.W.: A Study of American Syndicalism* (New York: Columbia University Press, 1920); Howard Kimmeldorf, *Battling for American Labor: Wobblies, Craft Workers, and the Making of the Union Movement* (Berkeley: University of California Press, 1999).

22 United States Commission on Industrial Relations, Industrial Relations Final Report, Senate Executive Doc. No 415 64th Congress 1st Session 2 (Washington, 1916), 1452. Cited in Kornbluh, *Rebel Voices*, 35.

23 Vincent St. John, *The I.W.W.: Its History, Structure, and Methods* (Chicago: IWW Publishing Bureau, 1917, 1919), 17. Cited in Kornbluh, *Rebel Voices*, 35.

24 Elizabeth Gurley Flynn, *Sabotage: The Conscious Withdrawal of the Workers' Industrial Efficiency* (Cleveland: I.W.W. Publicity Bureau, 1915), 5. Quoted in Kornbluh, *Rebel Voices*, 37.

25 State v. McLennen.

26 Kornbluh, *Rebel Voices*, chap. 2.

27 Eldridge Dowell, *A History of Criminal Syndicalism Legislation in the United States* (Baltimore: Johns Hopkins University Press,1939), 30; *State v. Kowalchuk*, 116, Wash, 592, 200 Pac. (1921).

28 Dowell, *History of Criminal Syndicalism Legislation*, 37–38.

29 Robert W. Bruere, "Following the Trail of the I.W.W.," *New York Evening Post*, Feb. 16, 1918. See Kornbluh, *Rebel Voices*, 38.

30 See Dorothy Neil Schmidt, "Sedition and Criminal Syndicalism in the State of Washington—1917–1919" (MA thesis, State College of Washington, 1940), 57–58.

31 State of Washington v. Hennessy, 114 Wash., 351, 195, Pac 211 (1921).

32 State v. Hennessy.

33 "Governor's Veto Message," 1919.

34 Letter from H. L. Hughes, Legislative Agent of the Washington Federation of Labor to Governor Lister, "Re Senate Bill #264, Governor Ernest Lister papers, Industrial Workers of the World, Judiciary Files, Box No. 2H-2-112, 1917–1919, WSA.

35 Schmidt, "Sedition and Criminal Syndicalism," 12. Schmidt cites the *Tacoma Daily Ledger*, Feb. 27, 1917, 7.

36 Dowell, *History of Criminal Syndicalism Legislation*, 55.

37 Ibid., 52.

38 *Senate Journal of the Extraordinary Session of the Sixteenth Legislature of the State of Washington* (Olympia, WA: Frank M. Lamborn, Public Printer, 1920), 4.

39 Alex Polson to Mr. Irvin W. Ziegans, Secretary to Governor, March 12, 1917, Governor Ernest Lister Papers, State Secret Service Correspondence Files, 1917–1921, Acc. No. AR2-H-5, WSA.

40 The telegrams are in the Governor Lister Papers, Industrial Workers of the World-Judiciary Files, Box No 2H-2-112, 1917–1919, WSA.

41 Schmidt, "Sedition and Criminal Syndicalism," 58.

42 Gunns, *Civil Liberties in Crisis*, 40.

43　*Industrial Worker*, May 4, 1919.

44　Robert L. Tyler, "I.W.W. in the Pacific N.W.: Rebels of the Woods," *Oregon Historical Quarterly* 55, no. 1 (March 1954): 30–31.

45　Copeland, *Centralia Tragedy of 1919*, 92, 126.

46　*Aberdeen Daily World*, Nov. 12, 13, 1919; Feb. 10, 1920; *Grays Harbor Post*, Nov. 4, 1922; Chehalis/Grays Harbor County Jail Record—Civil/Criminal, 1913-1922, Acc. No. 86-1-19, Box 245D, Southwest Washington Archives, Olympia, WA (SWA).

CHAPTER 9: CLASS WAR VIOLENCE: CENTRALIA 1919

1　Ralph Chaplin, *The Centralia Conspiracy*, in *The Centralia Case: Three Views of the Armistice Day Tragedy at Centralia Washington, November 11, 1919*, by Ralph Chaplin, Ben Hur Lampman, Federal Council of the Churches of Christ in America, Department of Research and Education (New York: Da Capo Press, 1971), 32. All references to Chaplin, *The Centralia Conspiracy* that appear in this chapter refer to the edition of *The Centralia Conspiracy* that appeared in the combined *Three Views of the Armistice Day Tragedy* publication.

2　US Department of Interior, National Park Service, *National Register of Historic Places, Multiple Property Documentation Form*, July 5, 1991, 4.

3　Chaplin, *Centralia Conspiracy*, 33.

4　Jerrold Owen, "The Inevitable Clash between Americanism and Anti-Americanism," *American Legion Weekly*, Dec. 5, 1919.

5　Chaplin, *Centralia Conspiracy*, 46.

6　Quoted in Mark Weber, "America's Changing View of Mussolini and Fascism," *Journal of Historical Review* 15, no. 3 (May–June 1995): 6–7.

7　Tom Copeland, *The Centralia Tragedy of 1919: Elmer Smith and the Wobblies* (Seattle: University of Washington Press, 1993), 23–24; John McClelland Jr., *Wobbly War: The Centralia Story* (Tacoma: Washington State Historical Society, 1987), 1–3.

8　McClelland, *Wobbly War*, 2.

9　Copeland, *Centralia Tragedy of 1919*, 42.

10　Chaplin, *Centralia Conspiracy*, 36–37.

11　McClelland, *Wobbly War*, 52.

12　Ibid., 49–50.

13　Cited ibid., 59.

14　Harvey O'Conner, *Revolution in Seattle: A Memoir* (New York: Monthly Review Press, 1964), 174.

15　Ibid., 174–175.

16　Ibid., 174.

17　Wesley Everest, Britt Smith, Ray Becker, James McInerney, Tom Morgan, Bert Faulkner, and Mike Sheehan were in the IWW Hall; O. C. Bland, and John Lamb were in the Arnold Hotel; John Doe Davis was in the Avalon Hotel; Eugene Barnett was most likely in the lobby of the Roderick Hotel, although the prosecution at the later trial tried to place him in the Avalon Hotel with Davis; and Loren Roberts, Bert Bland, and Ole Hanson were stationed on Seminary Hill.

18　The Joint Report by representatives of churches composed of Protestant, Catholic, and Jewish conferences concluded with respect to the question of whether the rush on the hall or the shots from the Wobblies came first that "while a prior rush toward the hall is not conclusively shown, it appears more probable that this occurred than that the shooting took place first." *A Joint Report on the Armistice Day Tragedy at Centralia, Washington, November 11, 1919,* 17, in *The Centralia Case: Three Views of the Armistice Day Tragedy at Centralia Washington, November 11, 1919* (New York: Da Capo Press, 1971).

19 Ben Hur Lampman, *Centralia Tragedy and Trial,* in *The Centralia Case: Three Views of the Armistice Day Tragedy at Centralia Washington, November 11, 1919,* by Ralph Chaplin, Ben Hur Lampman, Federal Council of the Churches of Christ in America, Department of Research and Education (New York: Da Capo Press, 1971), 20; Owen, "Centralia," 3.

20 Owen, "Centralia," 2.

21 Copeland, *Centralia Tragedy of 1919,* 5, 79.

22 O'Conner, *Revolution in Seattle,* 178.

23 *Chehalis Bee-Nugget,* Nov. 14, 1919.

24 Albert F. Gunns, *Civil Liberties in Crisis: The Pacific Northwest 1917–1940* (New York: Garland, 1983), 44; *Seattle Times,* Nov. 13, 1919.

25 Copeland, *Centralia Tragedy of 1919,* 66–68.

26 McClelland, *Wobbly War,* 74–75; Copeland, *Centralia Tragedy of 1919,* 67–68.

27 Copeland, *Centralia Tragedy of 1919,* 68, 76.

28 *A Joint Report,* 21.

29 Cited in Copeland, *Centralia Tragedy of 1919,* 82.

30 Gunns, *Civil Liberties in Crisis,* 45.

31 *Industrial Worker,* Aug. 23, 1930.

32 McClelland, *Wobbly War,* 224; Copeland, *Centralia Tragedy of 1919,* 185.

33 Department of the Interior, *National Register,* 21.

CHAPTER 10: FELLOW WORKER WILLIAM MCKAY

1 *Industrial Worker,* May 16, 1923.

2 *Aberdeen Daily World,* May 8, 1923; *Seattle Times,* May 6, 1923; *Bellingham Herald,* May 9, 1923; *Tacoma Ledger,* May 5, 1923; *Daily Washingtonian* (Hoquiam, WA), May 5, 1923.

3 *Industrial Worker,* May 23, 1923, July 28, 1923.

4 Chehalis/Grays Harbor County Jail Record: Civil/Criminal, Jail Record, 1913–22, SWA; *Grays Harbor Post,* Nov. 4, 1922.

5 Eugene Nelson, *Break Their Haughty Power: Joe Murphy in the Heyday of the Wobblies* (San Francisco: ISM Press, 1993), 207–216; Walker C. Smith, *Was It Murder? The Truth About Centralia* (Seattle: Northwest General Defense Committee, 1922).

6 The debate over political versus direct action is well chronicled in IWW literature. For example, see Joyce L. Kornbluh, *Rebel Voices: An IWW Anthology,* new and exp. ed. (Chicago: Charles H. Kerr, 1998), 35–64; William E. Trautman, *Direct Action and Sabotage* (Pittsburgh: Socialist News Company, 1912); Melvyn Dubofsky, *We Shall Be All: A History of the Industrial Workers of the World* (New York: Quadrangle, 1973), 146–170.

7 John S. Gambs, *The Decline of the I.W.W.* (New York: Russell & Russell, 1966), 69.

8 Ibid.

9 *Aberdeen Herald,* May 4, 1903.

10 State of Washington, *Fifth Biennial Report of the Bureau of Labor Statistics and Factory Inspection*, 1905–1906 (Olympia: C. W. Gorham Public Printer, 1906), 180.

11 *Aberdeen Herald*, May 1, 4, 1911; *Grays Harbor Post*, May 3, 1913.

12 *Industrial Worker*, May 1, 1912.

13 *The Strike Call for April 25, 1923*, Industrial Workers of the World Collection, Box 46, Folder 28, Walter Reuther Library, Wayne State University, Detroit, MI (WSU); *Industrial Worker*, April 25, May 5, 1923.

14 *General Strike Bulletin*, Seattle District, 7 May 1923, Industrial Workers of the World Collection, Box 162, Folder 1, WSU.

15 *Industrial Worker*, May 5, 16, 1923.

16 *Seattle Union Record*, May 3, 1923.

17 *Aberdeen Herald*, Feb. 8, 1912; Oct. 27, 1914.

18 *Industrial Worker*, April 4, 1912.

19 *State of Washington Timber Workers' Employment Guide* (Seattle: Timber Workers' Publishing Company, 1916), 3–9.

20 James Rowan, *The IWW in the Lumber Industry* (Seattle: Lumber Workers Industrial Union No. 500, 1919), 8.

21 *Southwest Washington Labor Press*, May 11, 1923.

22 *Industrial Worker*, May 16, 1923.

23 Coroner's Inquest into the Death of William McKay, Aberdeen, Washington, May 4, 1923. Grays Harbor County Coroner's Record, SWA; Washington; *Daily Washingtonian*, May 5, 1923.

24 John Hughes and Ryan Beckwith, eds., *On the Harbor: From Black Friday to Nirvana* (Aberdeen: Daily World, 2001), 42; *Industrial Worker*, May 16, 1923. A photograph of these two girls beside this sign has appeared in several different publications, including Elis Sulkanen, ed., *Amerikan Suomalaisen Työvaenliikkeen historia* (Fitchburg, MA: Amerikan Suomalainen Kansanvallen Liitto ja Raivaaja Publishing Company, 1951), 205.

25 In a handbill distributed on the night of McKay's murder, the Wobblies wrote, "Everyone is urged to watch this case and compare it with the Centralia frameup." Cited in the *Tacoma Ledger*, May 4, 1923.

26 *Hoquiam American*, May 10, 1923.

27 *Seattle Union Record*, May 5, 1923; *Aberdeen Daily World*, May 8, 1923.

28 *Industrial Worker*, May 16, 1923.

CHAPTER 11: SHINGLE WEAVERS AND THE SIX-HOUR DAY

1 *Shingle Weaver* (Portland, OR), April 1966.

2 State of Washington, *Second Biennial Report of the Bureau of Labor Statistics and Factory Inspection, 1899–1900* (Olympia: Gwin Hicks, State Printer, 1901), 89.

3 The ISWUA was given jurisdiction over all Pacific Northwest lumber workers in 1913. See Charlotte Todes, *Labor and Lumber* (New York: International Publishers, 1931), 155; Vernon Jensen, *Lumber and Labor* (New York: J. J. Little and Ives, 1945; New York: Arno Press, 1971), 122.

4 *Aloha Lumber Company: Aloha, Wash., 1906–2006: Environment, People, Industry, Concerns* (Aloha Lumber Corporation, 2007).

5 Cloice R. Howd, *Industrial Relations in the West Coast Lumber Industry*, Bulletin of the United States Bureau of Labor Statistics, No. 349 (Washington, DC: Government Printing Office, 1924), 55–57; *Shingle Weaver*, Feb. 8, 1913.

6 *Shingle Weaver*, January, February 1903; November 1905; October 1907.

7 Walter V. Woehlke, "The I.W.W. and the Golden Rule: Why Everett Used Club and Gun on the Red Apostles of Direct Action," *Sunset: The Magazine of the Pacific and of All the Far West* 38, no. 2 (February 1917): 16.

8 Howd, *Industrial Relations in the West Coast Lumber Industry*, 37.

9 State of Washington, *Third Biennial Report of the Bureau of Labor Statistics and Factory Inspection*, 1901–1902 (Seattle: Metropolitan Press, 1903), 124, 128.

10 Ibid., 127.

11 *Shingle Weaver*, March 17, 1917.

12 *Shingle Weaver*, March 1906; *Grays Harbor Post*, Feb. 3, 17, 1906; State of Washington, *Fifth Biennial Report of the Bureau of Labor Statistics and Factory Inspection*, 1905–1906 (Olympia: C. W. Gorham Public Printer, 1906), 194; *Hoquiam Sawyer*, Oct. 13, 1905.

13 United States Department of Labor, *Hours of Work and Output*, Bulletin No. 917 of the United States Department of Labor (Washington, DC: US Government Printing Office, 1947), 2, 5.

14 *Shingle Weaver*, Aug. 25, 1917.

15 *Seattle Times*, March 5, 1934.

16 State of Washington, *Eighth Biennial Report of the Bureau of Labor Statistics and Factory Inspection*, 1911–1912 (Olympia: E. L. Boardman, Public Printer, 1912), 96.

17 Walker C. Smith, *The Everett Massacre—A History of the Class Struggle in the Lumber Industry* (Chicago: I.W.W Publishing Bureau, 1917); Walker C. Smith, "The Voyage of the Verona," *International Socialist Review*, Dec. 17, 1916, 341–46; Anna Louise Strong, "Everett's Bloody Sunday: A Free Speech Fight That Led to a Murder Trial," *Survey* 37 (Jan. 27, 1917): 475–476; Robert L. Tyler, "The Everett Free Speech Fight," *Pacific Historical Review* (Feb. 1954), 19–30.

18 *Labor Journal* (Everett, WA), July 20, 1917.

19 *Shingle Weaver*, July 7, 1917.

20 *Seattle Union Record*, July 21, 1917.

21 *Shingle Weaver*, Sept. 15, 1917.

22 Howd, *Industrial Relations in the West Coast Lumber Industry*, 101.

23 *Aberdeen Daily World*, Feb. 4, 1927; *Daily Washingtonian*, Feb. 5, 1927; *Montesano Vidette*, Feb. 4, 1927.

24 *Industrial Worker*, Feb. 12, 19, 1927; *Daily Washingtonian*, March 1, 1927; *Aberdeen Daily World*, March 1, 1927. Much of the analysis regarding Red Coast Communist activity comes from our research in the Communist Party of the United States collection held at the Russian Center for the Preservation and Study of Documents of Recent History, Tamiment Library, New York University, New York, NY (hereafter RtsKhIDNI). Workers' Party of America, District Twelve, POLCOM Session of Feb. 14, 21, 1927, RTsKhIDNI, f. 515, op. 1, d. 1166; Acting General Secretary to A. Fislerman, May 18, 1927, RTsKhIDNI, f. 515, op. 1, d. 1042.

25 Workers' Party of America, District Twelve, POLCOM Session of Feb. 21, 1927, RTsKhIDNI, f. 515, op. 1, d. 1166; *Daily Washingtonian*, March 12, 1927.

26 *Daily Washingtonian*, March 3, 1927; *Aberdeen Daily World*, March 3, 1927; Workers'
   (Communist) Party of America, District Twelve, Report of District Organizer,
   Aaron Fislerman to the District Convention held Sunday, Aug. 21, 1927,
   RTsKhIDNI, f. 515, op. 1, d. 1166.

27 Aaron Fislerman to C. E. Ruthenberg, General Secretary, Feb. 25, 1927,
   RTsKhIDNI, f. 515, op. 1, d. 1042; Workers' Party of America, District Twelve,
   POLCOM Session of Feb. 21, 1927, RTsKhIDNI, f. 515, op. 1, d. 1166.

28 Aaron Fislerman to C. E. Ruthenberg, Feb. 25, 1927, RTsKhIDNI, f. 515, op. 1, d.
   1042; Workers' Party of America, District Twelve, POLCOM Session of March 14,
   1927, RTsKhIDNI, f. 515, op. 1, d. 1166; *Daily Washingtonian*, March 11, 12, 1927;
   Aberdeen Daily World, March 12, 1927.

29 Workers (Communist) Party of America, District 12, Report of District Organizer,
   Aaron Fislerman, to the District Convention held Sunday, Aug. 21, 1927,
   RTsKhIDNI, f. 515, op. 1, d. 1166.

30 *Shingle Weaver* (Aberdeen, WA), May 1929; Activities of the TUEL, District 12,
   1929, RTsKhIDNI, f. 515, op. 1, d. 1790; Resolution Calling upon the Governor
   and the Parole Board to Release the Eight Centralia Victims, Unanimously Adopted,
   Dec. 2, 1928, Governor Roland Harley Papers, 2K-1-28, Insurance Commission –
   IWW, Folder: "IWW (Centralia Massacre) 1927–1928," WSA.

31 Workers' Party of America, District Twelve, POLCOM Session of Feb. 21, 1927,
   RTsKhIDNI, f. 515, op. 1, d. 1166; Trade Union Educational League National
   Conference," Dec. 3, 1927, RTsKhIDNI, f. 515, op. 1, d. 1192.

32 *Shingle Weaver*, May 3, 1929.

33 *Industrial Worker*, April 19, 1930.

34 Elwood R. Maunder et al., "Red Cedar Shingles & Shakes: The Labor Story," *Journal
   of Forest History* 19, no. 3 (July 1975): 112.

35 *Industrial Worker*, June 7, 1930.

36 Maunder et al., "Red Cedar Shingles," 112.

37 *Industrial Worker*, March 15, 1930.

38 Philip S. Foner and David R. Roediger, *Our Own Time: A History of American Labor
   and the Working Day* (London: Verso, 1989), 243.

39 Ibid., 244–246; *Industrial Worker*, June 14, 1930.

40 *Industrial Worker*, July 19, 1930.

41 Foner and Roediger, *Our Own Time*, 249–250.

42 *Seattle Times*, July 17, 1934.

43 *Aberdeen Daily World*, Feb. 20, 1935. Herr sometimes also appears in the record as
   "Earl" Herr.

44 *Aberdeen Daily World*, May 4, 7, 1935.

45 *Aberdeen Daily World*, May 14, 15, 23, 1935.

46 *Aberdeen Daily World*, May 22, June 3, 5, 1935.

47 *Tacoma News-Tribune*, July 19, 1935; *Chehalis Bee-Nugget*, July 19, 1935.

48 *Tacoma News-Tribune*, July 19, 1935.

49 *Aberdeen Daily World*, Aug. 10, 14, 19, 1935.

50 *Timber Worker* (Aberdeen, WA), Feb. 26, 1937.

51 *Timber Worker*, Sep. 11, 1937.

52 1973–1975 Shingle Agreement between Timber Operators' Council, Inc., and the Washington-Oregon Shingle Weavers' District Council, Museum of the North Beach Archives, Moclips, Washington.

53 *Shingle Weaver*, Feb. 1962.

54 *Shingle Weaver*, Aug. 1955.

CHAPTER 12: PROLETARIAN NOVELS

1   Walter Rideout, *The Radical Novel in the United States, 1900–1954* (Cambridge, MA: Harvard University Press, 1956), 169–70.

2   R. W. Steadman, "An Objective Appraisal of Recent Radical Writing in America," *North American Review* (Spring 1939): 144.

3   Louis H. Colman, "The Oiler," *New Masses* (March 1928): 20; "The Marker," *New Masses* (April 1928): 26.

4   *New York Times*, May 6, 1934; *New Republic*, Dec 5, 1934; *Chicago Defender*, March 9, 1940; "Repealing Repression," *Nation*, May 15, 1937.

5   John Hughes and Ryan Teague Beckwith, eds., *On the Harbor: From Black Friday to Nirvana* (Aberdeen: Daily World, 2001), 91.

6   Ralph Chaplin, *The Centralia Conspiracy* (Chicago: Industrial Workers of the World, 1924), 16–17.

7   Merrill Lewis, *Robert Cantwell* (Boise, ID: Boise State University Press, 1985), 8–9.

8   T. V. Reed, *Robert Cantwell and the Literary Left: A Northwest Writer Reworks American Fiction* (Seattle: University of Washington Press, 2014), 67–68.

9   Chaplin, *The Centralia Conspiracy*, 94; Jon Christian Suggs, Introduction to *Marching! Marching!*, by Clara Weatherwax (Detroit: Omni Graphics, 1990), iv.

10 *Time*, Dec. 30, 1935.

11 Robert Cantwell, "A Town and Its Novels," *New Republic* (Feb. 19, 1936): 51–52.

12 Ibid., 51.

13 Pleadings, State v. Richard Law, 1940 John Caughlin Papers, Acc. No. 704, University of Washington Special Collection, Seattle, Washington (hereafter UW).

14 Joseph Freeman, Introduction to *Proletarian Literature in the United States: An Anthology*, ed. Granville Hicks et al. (New York: International Publishers, 1935), 13, 19–20.

15 Cantwell, "A Town and Novels."

16 Freeman, Introduction to *Proletarian Literature in the United States*, 23–24.

17 Steadman, "An Objective Appraisal," 152.

18 Freeman, Introduction to *Proletarian Literature in the United States*, 12.

19 Melvin P. Levy, Review of Louis Colman's *Lumber*, *New Masses*, May 1931.

20 John Dos Passos, Review of Robert Cantwell's *Land of Plenty*, *New Republic*, May 16, 1934.

21 Jack Conroy, "Robert Cantwell's Land of Plenty," in *Proletarian Writers of the Thirties*, ed. David Madden (Carbondale: Southern Illinois University Press, 1968), 83.

22 Emjo Basshe, Review of Clara Weatherwax's *Marching! Marching! New Masses*, Jan. 7, 1936.

23 Review of Cochrane and Coldiron's *Disillusion*, *Timber Worker* (Seattle), July 22, 1939.

24 *New Masses*, June 5, 1934.

CHAPTER 13: WOMEN WHO FOUGHT

1 *Voice of Action*, July 20, 1934.

2 Report of Central Commission on the Miners Relief Case to the Polcom, Dec. 4–7, 1928, 1–4, Communist Party of the United States collection held at the Russian Center for the Preservation and Study of Documents of Recent History, Tamiment Library, New York University, New York, NY (RTsKhIDNI), f. 515, op. 1, d. 1433.

3 Varpu Lindström-Best, *Defiant Sisters: A Social History of Finnish Immigrant Women in Canada* (Toronto: Multicultural History Society of Ontario, 1988), 139.

4 Jason Lavery, *The History of Finland* (Westport, CT: Greenwood Press, 2006), 75; David Kirby, "The Workers' Cause": Rank-and-File Attitudes and Opinions in the Finnish Social Democratic Party, 1905–1918," *Past and Present* 111 (May 1986): 130–138.

5 Riitta Stjärnstedt, "Finnish Women in the North American Labour Movement," in *Finnish Diaspora II: The United States*, ed. Michael G. Karni (Toronto, Ontario: Multicultural History Society of Ontario, 1981), 260; Irma Sulkunen, "The Mobilization of Women and the Birth of Civil Society," in *The Lady with the Bow*, ed. Merja Manninen and Päivi Setälä; trans. Michael Wynne-Ellis (Helsinki: Otava Publishing, 1990), 49–53.

6 Carl Erik Knoellinger, *Labor in Finland* (Cambridge, MA: Harvard University Press, 1960), 48; Sulkunen, "The Mobilization," 51–52; Toivo U. Raun, "The Revolution of 1905 in the Baltic Provinces and Finland," *Slavic Review* 43, no. 3 (Autumn 1984): 463–464.

7 Lavery, *History of Finland*, 77.

8 Irma Sulkunen, "Suffrage, Gender, and Citizenship in Finland: A Comparative Perspective," *NORDEUROPAforum* (2007): 29.

9 *Tacoma Times*, April 1, 1912.

10 *Industrial Worker*, April 18, 1912.

11 *Seattle Star*, April 13, 1912.

12 Marriage Record of John Sipo and Jennie Heikkila, Nov. 28, 1916, Butte-Silver Bow County Marriage Records, Butte-Silver Bow Public Archives, Butte, Montana.

13 Birth Record of John Sipo, May 5, 1917, Butte-Silver Bow County Birth Records, Butte-Silver Bow Public Archives, Butte, Montana.

14 *Industrialisti*, Dec. 14, 1935.

15 Charter, Aberdeen Branch of Industrial Union 460, Industrial Workers of the World Papers, Oct. 26, 1923, Box 17, Folder 4, Industrial Workers of the World Collection, Walter Reuther Library, Wayne State University, Detroit, Michigan (WSU); USBC, *Fourteenth Census of the United States Taken in the Year 1920*, Washington State, Chehalis County, Aberdeen.

16 Chehalis/Grays Harbor County Jail Record – Civil/Criminal, 1913–1922, Acc. No. 86-1-19, Box 245D, Southwest Washington Archives, Olympia, Washington (SWA).

17 *Industrial Worker*, June 10, 24, 1922.

18 *Polk's Cities Directory for Grays Harbor County*, 1930, 1935, 1937; *Industrialisti*, Dec. 14, 1935; *Third Annual Convention of the Maritime Federation of the Pacific Coast*, June 7–July 9, 1937, Portland, Oregon, microfilm, University of Washington Library.

19 Robert Benson and Jennie Sipo, Certificate of Marriage, State of Washington, County of Clark, Nov. 3, 1924, Marriage Records, Grays Harbor Genealogical

Society, Aberdeen History Museum (AHM); USBC, *Fifteenth Census of the United States Taken in the Year 1930*, Washington State, Chehalis County, Aberdeen; *Industrialisti*, Dec. 14, 1935; Dec. 13, 1939.

20 Resolution to Governor Roland Hartley on behalf of Centralia Prisoners, April 15, 1932, Young Communist League, Aberdeen, Wash., Governor Roland Harley Papers, Accession No. 2K-1-28, Insurance Commission-IWW, 1929, WSA; Resolution Calling upon the Governor and the Parole Board to Release the Eight Centralia Victims, Unanimously Adopted, Dec. 2, 1928, Governor Roland Harley Papers, 2K-1-28, Insurance Commission–IWW, Folder: "IWW (Centralia Massacre) 1927–1928," WSA. USBC, *Fifteenth Census*, Washington State, Chehalis County, Aberdeen.

21 *Toveritar*, Aug. 21, 1917; May 21, Oct. 29, 1918; Dec. 6, 1921; Aug. 15, 1922.

22 Ottilie Markholt, "Against the Current: A Social Memoir," unpublished manuscript, chap. 4, p. 14. University of Washington, Digital Archives, http://digitalcollections. lib.washington.edu/cdm/ref/collection/pnwhm/id/837, [Accessed June 10, 2018].

23 *Young Pioneer* (New York), Dec. 1930. See *The Young Comrade* (Chicago), Jan. 1925.

24 *Työmies*, Dec. 16, 1923; *Toveritar*, Aug. 28, Sept. 11, 1917.

25 USBC, *Fifteenth Census*, Washington State, Grays Harbor County, Aberdeen; Merle A. Reinikka, "Death Certificates of Finns in Chehalis [Grays Harbor] County, 1907–1947," Aberdeen History Collection, AHM.

26 Report of Central Commission on the Miners Relief Case to the Polcom, Dec. 4–7, 1928, 1–4, RTsKhIDNI, f. 515, op. 1, d. 1433; Resolution Calling upon the Governor and the Parole Board to Release the Eight Centralia Victims, Unanimously Adopted, Dec. 2, 1928, Governor Roland Harley Papers, 2K-1-28, Insurance Commission – IWW, Folder: "I.W.W. (Centralia Massacre) 1927–1928," WSA; "Congressional Election Platform of the Communist Party," issued by the Grays Harbor Section Committee Communist Party, RTsKhIDNI, f. 515, op. 1, d. 3605; RTsKhIDNI, f. 515, op. 1, d. 1433.

27 House of Representatives, *Investigation of Communist Propaganda*, 892; *Voice of Action*, Aug. 31, 1934.

28 Resolution against Bosses Wars, submitted to Governor Roland H. Harley, April 15, 1932, Governor Roland Hartley Papers, Accession No. 2K-1-28, Insurance Commission-IWW, 1930-32, WSA.

29 *Voice of Action*, Aug. 31, 1934.

30 *Grays Harbor Post*, Nov. 5, 1932.

31 *Voice of Action*, Aug. 31, 1934.

32 *Voice of Action*, May 8, 1933; July 6, 1934.

33 *Voice of Action*, July 20, 1934.

34 Congressional Election Platform of the Communist Party, 1934, RTsKhIDNI, f. 515, op. 1, d. 3605, 1, 3.

35 *Voice of Action*, Aug. 17, 24, 1934.

36 *Voice of Action*, March 8, April 26, 1935.

37 Todd Goings, "Battles on the Harbor: Inter-Labor Conflict, Anti-Communism, Women's Auxiliaries, and the Murder of Laura Law," (MA thesis, Central Washington University 2014), 1, 43.

38 Ibid., 91.

39 *Timber Worker*, July 16; Aug. 28, 1937; May 28, 1938; Jan. 14, 21; Feb. 11, 1939.

40 John Hughes and Ryan Teague Beckwith, eds., *On the Harbor: From Black Friday to Nirvana* (Aberdeen: Daily World, 2001), 107.

41 Resolution of IWA Ladies Auxiliary #2, Aberdeen, Wash, Adopted Dec. 14, 1939, Box 11, Folder 2Y, Laura Law Collection, SWA.

42 Statement of Norman Mason, Jan. 9, 1940, file 1t, box 2, Laura Law Collection, SWA; Hughes and Beckwith, *On the Harbor,* 109.

43 *Washington New Dealer,* June 6, 1940; Hughes and Beckwith, *On the Harbor,* 109.

44 Murray Morgan, *The Viewless Winds* (Reprint, Corvallis: Oregon State University Press, 1990).

45 Harri Siitonen, "The Ballad of Laura Luoma Law: A Forgotten Face in Finnish America Finally Resurfaces," *Finnish American Reporter,* Oct. 1, 1994.

CHAPTER 14: WILLAPA LONGSHOREMEN AND THE BIG STRIKE

1 *Willapa Harbor Pilot,* Aug. 2, 1934; Minutes of the Meeting of ILA Local 38-92, July 30, 1934, ILWU Local 1–Raymond Records, Acc. No. 4307-001, Box 1, UW.

2 *Voice of Action,* June 14, 1935.

3 *American Lumberman* (Chicago), Feb. 24, 1912.

4 *Bulletin of the US. Bureau of Labor Statistics, No. 550 Cargo Handling and Longshore Labor Conditions* (Washington, DC: US Bureau of Labor Statistics, 1932), 48.

5 State of Washington, *Tenth Biennial Report of the Bureau of Labor, Statistics and Factory Inspection* (Olympia, WA: Frank M. Lamborn, Public Printer, 1916), 215.

6 *Aberdeen Herald,* Aug. 15, 1910; Oct. 25, 1900.

7 Fatal Accident Card for Oscar Roswall, Dec. 6, 1921, Washington State Department of Labor & Industries, Fatal Accident Cards, 1915–1928, Washington State Archives, Digital Archives, http://digitalarchives.wa.gov. Accessed March 20, 2018.

8 *Willapa Harbor Pilot,* April 8, May 13, 1904.

9 *Aberdeen Herald,* Aug. 4, 1904.

10 Application for Charter, Raymond, Longshoremen's Union of the Pacific, June 21, 1909, Pacific Northwest Labor and Civil Rights Projects, http://depts.washington. edu/labpics/zenPhoto/albums/The-ILWU-and-Longshore-Workers/Documents- from-the-ILWU-Archives/Longshoremens%20Union%20of%20the%20Pacific%20 Charters/Raymond_AllLongshoreandLumber.jpg. Accessed March 15, 2018.

11 *Proceedings of the Eighteenth Convention of the International Longshoremen's Association,* (July 11–16, 1910), 23, 32–33.

12 *Proceedings of the Twenty-First Convention of the International Longshoremen's Association* (July 14–19, 1913), 46–47.

13 USBC, *Thirteenth Census,* Washington State, Pacific County, Raymond.

14 Aku Rissanen, ed., *Suomalaisten sosialistiosastojen ja työväenyhdistysten viidennen eli suomalaisen sosialistijärjestön kolmannen edustajakokouksen, Pöytäkirja,* 1912, 51.

15 *Industrial Union Bulletin* (Chicago), May 18, 1907.

16 *Industrial Worker,* May 16, Dec. 26, 1912; USBC, *Thirteenth Census,* Washington State, Pacific County, Raymond.

17 *Aberdeen Herald,* Oct. 12, 1908; Sept. 27, 1909; June 27, 1910. Grays and Willapa Harbors are frequently termed "The Twin Harbors."

18 *Timberman* (July 1916), 32; *Raymond Herald,* June 9, 1916.

19 *Willapa Harbor Pilot,* Sept. 8, 1916; *Biennial Report,* 1915–16, 211

20 Ronald Magden, *The Working Longshoreman* (Tacoma, WA: R-4 Typographers, Inc, 1991), 70–83.; *Coast Seamen's Journal* (San Francisco), June 7, 1916.

21 State of Washington, *Biennial Report*, 1915–16, 244.

22 *Raymond Herald*, June 9, 1916.

23 *Morning Oregonian*, Nov. 24, 1916.

24 *Aberdeen Herald*, June 16, 1916.

25 *Timberman* (August 1916), 63.

26 Magden, *Working Longshoreman*, 80–81.

27 Report No. 567 by E.B., Jan. 30, 1918, South Bend, WA, Governor Ernest Lister Papers, Secret Service Files, Correspondence – 1917–1921, WSA.

28 State v. Passila, 117 Wash. 295, 201 Pac. 295 (1921)

29 List of Workers' Party Branches in District #12, Sept. 20, 1924, RTsKhIDNI, f. 515, op. 1; Auvo Kostiainen, *The Forging of Finnish-American Communism, 1917–1924: A Study in Ethnic Radicalism* (Turku: Turin Yliopisto, 1978), 220.

30 *Toveritar*, Oct. 3, 1922.

31 *Työmies*, May 6, 1937.

32 Meeting of International Longshoremen's Association, Local 38-92, Oct. 11, 18, 23, 1933, Acc. 4307-001, Box 1, ILWU Local 1 – Raymond Records, UW.

33 Charter, International Longshoremen's Association, Local 38-92, Oct. 2, 1933, Acc. 4307-001, Box 1, ILWU Local 1 – Raymond Records, UW; Meeting of ILA, Local 38-92, Oct. 11, 18, 23, 25, 1933, Acc. 4307-001, Box 1, ILWU Local 1 – Raymond Records, UW.

34 *Voice of Action*, April 3, 1934.

35 *Raymond Herald*, May 18, June 1, 1934; Ottilie Markholt, *Maritime Solidarity: Pacific Coast Unionism, 1929–1938 (Tacoma: Pacific Coast Maritime History Committee, 1998)*, 77–78, 91, 104–109.

36 *Raymond Herald*, June 1, 1934; Markholt, *Maritime Solidarity*, 104–109.

37 Michael Munk, *The Portland Red Guide*, 2nd ed. (Portland: Ooligan Press, 2011), 70–73; *Voice of Action*, July 13, 1934; Howard Kimeldorf, *Reds or Rackets: The Making of Radical and Conservative Unions on the Waterfront* (Berkeley: University of California Press, 1992), 102–105; Bruce Nelson, *Workers on the Waterfront: Seamen, Longshoremen, and Unionism in the 1930s* (Urbana: University of Illinois Press, 1990), 128–132; Markholt, *Maritime Solidarity*, 187; Ronald Magden, *A History of Seattle Waterfront Workers, 1884–1934* (Seattle: ILWU Local 19, 1991), 221.

38 Nelson, *Workers on the Waterfront*, 137.

39 *Willapa Harbor Pilot*, June 14, 21, Aug. 2, 1934; March 31, April 14, 1938; Ross Rieder, "Pettus, Terry (1904–1983)," http://www.historylink.org/File/2682. Accessed May 1, 2018.

40 Mike Quin, *The Big Strike* (Olema, CA: Olema, 1949), 176; Nelson, *Workers on the Waterfront*, 149–150.

41 Minutes of the Meeting of ILA Local 38-92, July 30, 1934, ILWU Local 1 – Raymond Records, Acc. No. 4307-001, Box 1, UW.

42 Markholt, *Maritime Solidarity*, 195. Markholt makes numerous references to the Raymond ILA having a strong Communist presence.

43 National Longshoremen's Board, In the Matter of the Arbitration between Pacific Coast District Local 38 of the International Longshoremen's Association, Acting on Behalf of the Various Locals Whose Members Perform Longshore Labor and

Waterfront Employers of Seattle, Waterfront Employers of Portland, Waterfront Employers of San Francisco, and Marine Service Bureau of Los Angeles, Arbitrator's Award, Aug. 7, 1934, http://depts.washington.edu/labpics/zenPhoto/The-ILWU-and-Longshore-Workers/Documents-from-the-ILWU-Archives/Arbitration/img158_2a__Page_1.jpg. Accessed March 18, 2018.

44 *Western Worker*, Oct. 22, 1934.

45 *Willapa Harbor Pilot*, Aug. 2, 1934.

46 *Voice of Action*, July 13, 1934; Minutes of Loggers and Sawmill Workers Union 18345, May 25, 1934, International Woodworkers of America Local 3-2, Grays Harbor, Records, Aberdeen History Museum (AHM); *Western Worker*, July 23, 1934.

47 Minutes of the Meeting of ILA Local 38-92, Aug. 14, 1935, ILWU Local 1 – Raymond Records, Acc. No. 4307-001, Box 1, UW.

48 Kimeldorf, *Reds or Rackets*, 109.

49 *Western Worker*, Oct. 22, 1934.

50 *Voice of the Federation*, July 5, 1935.

51 *Seattle Post Intelligencer*, June 22, 1935.

52 Minutes of the Meeting of ILA Local 38-92, July 1, 1935, ILWU Local 1 – Raymond Records, Acc. No. 4307-001, Box 1, UW.

53 *Raymond Herald*, July 5, 1935.

54 Nelson, *Workers on the Waterfront*, 168.

55 There are few published histories of Raymond and South Bend, Washington. See L. R. Williams, *Our Pacific County* (Raymond, WA: Raymond Herald, 1930); Mrs. Nels Olsen, *The Willapa Country: History Report* (Raymond, WA: Raymond Herald & Advertiser, 1965).

56 *Voice of the Federation*, July 12, 1935.

CHAPTER 15: "ON THE FRONT TRENCH PICKET LINES"

1 *Timber Worker*, Oct. 9, 1937.

2 *Sunday News* (Seattle), July 3, 1937.

3 Kozlowski wrote in May 1939 that "as a Communist I feel that Communists need no defense." *Timber Worker*, May 27, 1939.

4 Cited in *On the Harbor: From Black Friday to Nirvana*, ed. John Hughes and Ryan Teague Beckwith (Aberdeen, WA: Daily World, 2001), 119.

5 Cecil D. Eby, *Comrades and Commissars: The Lincoln Battalion in the Spanish Civil War* (University Park: Pennsylvania State University Press, 2007), xi. At the time that Johnson, Kozlowski, and Chapin left Grays Harbor for Spain, they belonged to the FOW. By the time the soldiers returned, they belonged to the International Woodworkers of America (IWA), a Congress of Industrial Organizations (CIO) union.

6 *Timber Worker*, Oct. 9, 1937; May 27, 1939.

7 *Timber Worker*, July 9, 1937. Many Abraham Lincoln Brigade members volunteered primarily as a way to fight fascism. See Cary Nelson and Jefferson Hendricks, eds., *Madrid 1937: Letters of the Abraham Lincoln Brigade from the Spanish Civil War* (London: Routledge, 1996).

8 "Halt to Fascist Actions!" Letter from Mary Lee, chairperson of Naisjaosto, to members of the Aberdeen City Council and City Mayor, Aug. 23, 1934, Laura Law

Records, Box 12, Folder 1, SWA, Olympia, Washington; *Voice of Action*, Aug. 31, 1934.

9   *Timber Worker*, July 16, 1938.

10 *Voice of the Federation* (San Francisco), June 24, 1937.

11 *Timber Worker*, Oct. 15, 1938.

12 *Timber Worker*, July 16, 1937.

13 *Timber Worker*, May 27, 1939.

14 *Daily Worker*, Dec. 14, 29, 1926.

15 *Western Worker* (San Francisco), Jan. 1, 1937.

16 *Voice of Action*, Aug. 17, 1934; Oct. 18, 1935.

17 Robert H. Zieger, *Rebuilding the Pulp and Paper Workers' Union, 1933–1941* (Knoxville: University of Tennessee Pres, 1984), 173.

18 Julie Greene, *Pure and Simple Politics: The American Federation of Labor and Political Activism, 1881–1917* (Cambridge: Cambridge University Press, 2004), 99.

19 *Aberdeen Daily World* April 18, 1935.

20 *Voice of Action*, June 14, 1935.

21 Minutes, June 4, 1935, Sawmill and Timber Workers' Union (STWU) Local 2507, International Woodworkers of America Local 3-2, Grays Harbor, Records, AHM; Todd Goings, "Battles on the Harbor: : Inter-Labor Conflict, Anti-Communism, Women's Auxiliaries, and the Murder of Laura Law" (MA thesis, Central Washington University 2014)," 31; Lembcke and Tattam, *One Union in Wood*, 39–41.

22 Aaron Goings, "Red Harbor: Class, Violence, and Community in Grays Harbor, Washington" (PhD thesis, Simon Fraser University, 2011), 474–475; Minutes, Special Meeting, June 2, 1935, STWU 2507, International Woodworkers of America Local 3-2, Grays Harbor, Records, AHM.

23 *Aberdeen Daily World*, May 9, 1935; *Timber Worker*, May 27, 1939.

24 *Voice of Action*, June 14, 1935.

25 Lembcke and Tattam, , *One Union in Wood*, 43–44.

26 Vernon Jensen, *Lumber and Labor* (New York: J. J. Little and Ives, 1945; New York: Arno Press, 1971). 203–217.

27 David Malet, *Foreign Fighters: Transnational Identity in Civic Conflicts* (Oxford: Oxford University Press, 2013), 94–95.

28 For a history of US foreign policy during the Spanish Civil War, see Dominic Tierney, *FDR and the Spanish Civil War: Neutrality and Commitment in the Struggle That Divided America* (Durham, NC: Duke University Press, 2007).

29 Malet, *Foreign Fighters*, 96; C. E. Payne, "The Mainspring of Action," in *Fellow Workers and Friends: I.W.W. Free-Speech Fights as Told by Participants*, ed. Philip S. Foner (Westport, CT: Greenwood Press, 1981), 147; Tierney, *FDR and the Spanish Civil War*, 68.

30 *Spanish Labor Bulletin* cited in Ottilie Markholt, "Against the Current: A Social Memoir," unpublished manuscript, chap. 4, p. 14. University of Washington, Digital Archives, http://digitalcollections.lib.washington.edu/cdm/ref/collection/pnwhm/id/837. Accessed June 10, 2018.

31 The American volunteer fighting force was known widely, although incorrectly, as the Abraham Lincoln Brigade. See Eby, *Comrades and Commissars*, xi–xii.

32 Malet, *Foreign Fighters*, 98–102.

33 *Timber Worker*, Sept. 25, 1937.

34 *Sunday News* (Seattle), Jan. 10, 1937.

35 James Lerner, "I Was in Spain," *Fight Against War and Fascism* 4, no. 1 (Nov. 1936):
40–41.

36 Herman Goff to Ray, c. May–June 1937, Bob Reed Papers, Box 2, Max Farrar Folder,
Acc. No. 3512-7, UW. Herman Goff was a pseudonym used by Max Farrar.

37 *Sunday News*, March 21, 1937.

38 Cited in *Sunday News*, April 3, 1937.

39 *Timber Worker*, July 2, 1937.

40 *Grays Harbor Washingtonian*, March 25, 1938.

41 Notes from article in the *Seattle Times*, Dec. 28, 1993, Bob Reed Papers, Box 2,
Wirta Folder, Acc. No. 3512-7, UW.

42 Minutes of IWA Local 3-2, Jan. 22, 1938, International Woodworkers of America
Local 3-2, Grays Harbor, Records, AHM.

43 *Timber Worker*, July 9, Oct. 9, 1937.

44 Jeremy Egolf, typed letter by James Hassett to Dick Law, June 1, 1937, Bob Reed
Papers, Box 2, Hassett Folder, Acc. No. 3512-7, UW.

45 Herman Goff to Ray, c. May–June 1937, Bob Reed Papers, Box 2, Max Farrar Folder,
Acc. No. 3512-7, UW.

46 Jeremy Egolf, typed letter by James Hassett to Dick Law, June 1, 1937, Bob Reed
Papers, Box 2, Hassett Folder, Acc. No. 3512-7, UW.

47 *Timber Worker*, Sept. 18, 1937.

48 *Grays Harbor Washingtonian*, March 25, 1938.

49 W. C. Shifferly to Jeremy, marked as "Probably 1985," Bob Reed Papers, Box 2,
Hassett Folder, Acc. No. 3512-7, UW.

50 *Timber Worker*, July 9, 1937.

51 W. C. Shifferly to Friends, Oct. 18, 1985, Bob Reed Papers, Box 2, Hassett Folder,
Acc. No. 3512-7, UW.

52 Letter to Black and Comrades, June 27, 1937, published in *Volunteer for Liberty*,
included in the Bob Reed Papers, Box 2, Chapin, Wilfred Folder, Acc. No. 3512-7,
UW.

53 Letter to Black and Comrades, June 27, 1937, published in *Volunteer for Liberty*,
included in the Bob Reed Papers, Box 2, Chapin, Wilfred Folder, Acc. No. 3512-7,
UW.

54 Minutes of IWA Local 3-2, Dec. 17, 1938, International Woodworkers of America
Local 3-2, Grays Harbor, Records, AHM.

55 Minutes of IWA Local 3-2, Dec. 31, 1938, International Woodworkers of America
Local 3-2, Grays Harbor, Records, AHM.

56 Jeremy Egolf, typed letter by James Hassett to Dick Law, June 1, 1937, Bob Reed
Papers, Box 2, Hassett Folder, Acc. No. 3512-7, UW.

57 *Sunday News*, July 3, 1937.

58 *Timber Worker*, Oct. 9, 1937.

59 *Sunday News*, April 16, 1938.

60 Minutes of IWA Local 3-2, Dec. 31, 1938, International Woodworkers of America
Local 3-2, Grays Harbor, Records, AHM.

61 Milferd Chapin, Year: 1938; Arrival: Le Havre, France; Microfilm Serial: T715,
1897–1957; Microfilm Roll: Roll 6168; Line: 1; pp. 184–185; Ancestry.com. *New*

York, Passenger Lists, 1820–1957 [database on-line]. Provo, UT, USA: Ancestry.com Operations, Inc., 2010.

62 Sunday News, April 16, 1938.

63 Grays Harbor Washingtonian, Jan. 26, 1939.

64 Brick Moir to Jeremy, Oct. 21, 1985, Bob Reed Papers, Box 2, Chapin, Wilred Folder, Acc. No. 3512-7, Special Collections University of Washington, Seattle, Washington (UW). Wirta's first name was actually Paul. Moir misspelled Ernest Kozlowski's last name.

65 Volunteer, July 1985, included in Bob Reed Papers, Box 2, Kozlowski, Ernest Folder, Acc. No. 3512-7, UW; Grays Harbor Washingtonian, Feb. 23, 1939; Minutes IWA, Dec. 31, 1938, International Woodworkers of America Local 3-2, Grays Harbor, Records, AHM.

CONCLUSION

1 Pacific Coast longshoremen achieved a similar reduction in their work hours; as a result of the 1934 Big Strike, they won a thirty-hour workweek, consisting of five six-hour days. See Chapter 14 for further discussion of the longshoremen's activism during the 1930s.

2 For a discussion of the role played by labor bureaucrats in the decline of American labor militancy, see Paul Buhle, Taking Care of Business: Samuel Gompers, George Meany, Lane Kirkland, and the Tragedy of American Labor (New York: Monthly Review Press, 1999); Mike Davis, Prisoners of the American Dream: Politics and Economy in the History of the US Working Class (London: Verso Books, 1986).

Bibliography

ARCHIVAL MATERIALS

Aberdeen History Museum, Aberdeen, Washington (AHM)
Death Certificates of Finns in Chehalis [Grays Harbor] County, 1907–1947
International Woodworkers of America Local 3-2, Grays Harbor, Records
Marriage Records, Grays Harbor Genealogical Society
United Finnish Kaleva Brothers and Sisters Lodge 9 Collection

Aberdeen Timberland Library, Aberdeen, Washington (ATL)
City of Cosmopolis Papers
Ben K. Weatherwax, Hometown Scrapbook Collection

Butte-Silver Bow Public Archives, Butte, Montana
Butte-Silver Bow County Birth Records
Butte-Silver Bow County Marriage Records

Museum of the North Beach, Moclips, Washington
Museum of the North Beach Archives

National Archives and Records Administration, Pacific Alaska Region,
Seattle, Washington (NRA)
Records of the War Department General Staff, Military Intelligence Division

Tamiment Library, New York University, New York City
Russian Center for the Preservation and Study of Documents of Recent History
(RtsKhIDNI)

University of Washington, Seattle (UW)
Bob Reed Papers
Edwin Ames Papers
ILWU Local 1 – Raymond Records
John Caughlan Papers

Southwest Washington Archives, Olympia, Washington (SWA)
   Chehalis/Grays Harbor County Jail Record
   Grays Harbor County Coroner's Record
   Laura Law Records
   State Superior Court of Chehalis County Papers

Walter Reuther Library, Wayne State University, Detroit, Michigan (WSU)
   Industrial Workers of the World Collection

Washington State Archives, Olympia, Washington (WSA)
   Governor Elisha P. Ferry Papers
   Governor Roland Harley Papers
   Governor Marion E. Hay Papers
   Governor Ernest Lister Papers

Washington State Library, Tumwater, Washington
   Albert Johnson Scrapbooks

TRIAL PROCEEDINGS AND TESTIMONY:

State of Washington v. State of Oregon, Judd and Detweiler, 1907
State of Washington v. Hennessy, 114 Wash., 351, 195, Pac 211 (1921
State of Washington v. John Wing, Case No. 182, 1890
State of Washington v. McLennen, 116 Wash, 612, 200 Pac 319 (1921).
Francis R. Wall v. John Wing, No. 177, 1890

NEWSPAPERS

Aberdeen Daily Bulletin (Aberdeen, WA)
Aberdeen Daily World (Aberdeen, WA)
Aberdeen Herald (Aberdeen, WA)
The Agitator (Home, WA)
Albany States Rights Democrat (Albany, OR)
American Lumberman (Chicago)
Bellingham Herald (Bellingham, WA)
The Bricklayer, Mason, and Plasterer (Indianapolis)
Centralia Daily Chronicle (Centralia, WA)
Chehalis Bee Nugget (Chehalis, WA)
The Chicago Defender (Chicago)
Coast Seamen's Journal (San Francisco)
Daily Capital Journal (Salem, OR)
Daily Morning Astorian (Astoria, OR)

Daily Washingtonian (Hoquiam, WA)
Daily Worker (New York)
Day Book (Chicago)
Grays Harbor Post (Aberdeen, WA)
Grays Harbor Washingtonian (Hoquiam, WA)
Home Defender (Hoquiam, WA)
Hoquiam American (Hoquiam, WA)
Hoquiam Sawyer (Hoquiam, WA)
Independent (Yakima, WA)
Industrial Union Bulletin (Chicago)
Industrial Worker (Spokane and Seattle, WA)
Industrialisti (Duluth, MN)
The Islander (Friday Harbor, WA)
Labor Journal (Everett, WA)
Montesano Vidette (Montesano, WA)
Morning Oregonian (Portland, OR)
New Masses (New York)
The New Republic (New York)
New York Times (New York)
The Northwest Magazine (St. Paul, MN)
One Big Union Monthly (Chicago)
Oregon Mist (St. Helens, OR)
Oregonian (Portland, OR)
Raivaaja (Fitchburg, MA)
Raymond Herald (Raymond, WA)
The Seamen's Journal (San Francisco)
Seattle Post-Intelligencer (Seattle, WA)
Seattle Star (Seattle, WA)
Seattle Times (Seattle, WA)
Seattle Union Record (Seattle, WA)
Shingle Weaver (Ballard, WA)
Solidarity (Chicago)
South Bend Journal (South Bend, WA)
Southwest Washington Labor Press (Aberdeen, WA)
Spokesman-Review (Spokane, WA)
Strike Bulletin (Aberdeen, WA)
The Sunday News (Seattle)
Tacoma Ledger (Tacoma, WA)
Tacoma News-Tribune (Tacoma, WA)
Tacoma Times (Tacoma, WA)

The Timberman (Chicago)

Timber Worker (Aberdeen, WA)

Time

Toveri (Astoria, OR)

Toveritar (Astoria, OR)

Työmies (Superior, WI)

The Typographical Journal (Indianapolis)

Voice of Action (Seattle, WA)

Voice of the Federation (San Francisco)

Washington New Dealer (Seattle)

The Washington Newspaper: A Publication Dedicated to the Study and Improvement of Journalism in Washington (Seattle, WA)

Washington Standard (Olympia, WA)

Western Worker (San Francisco)

Willapa Harbor Pilot (South Bend, WA)

The Young Comrade (Chicago)

Young Pioneer (New York)

PUBLICATIONS

Aloha Lumber Company: Aloha, Wash., 1906–2006: Environment, People, Industry, Concerns. Aloha, Wash.: Aloha Lumber Corporation, 2007.

Arnold, David F. *The Fishermen's Frontier: People and Salmon in Southeast Alaska.* Seattle: University of Washington Press, 2008.

Bailey, Robert C., Dianne Bridgman, and Washington State Oral History Program. *Robert C. Bailey: An Oral History.* Olympia: Washington State Oral History Program, Office of the Secretary of State, 1996.

Basso, Helen A. "Wedding Dances." *Cowlitz Historical Quarterly* 22, no. 1–2 (Spring/ Summer 1980): 22–24.

Boxberger, Daniel. "Ethnicity and Labor in the Puget Sound Fishing Industry, 1880– 1935." *Ethnology* 33, no. 2 (1994): 179–191.

Brissenden, Paul F. *The I.W.W.: A Study of American Syndicalism.* New York: Columbia University Press, 1920.

Bruere, Robert Walter. *Following the Trail of the IWW: A First-Hand Investigation into Labor Troubles in the West, A Trip into the Copper and Lumber Camps of the Inland Empire with the Views of the Men on the Job.* New York: New York Evening Post, 1918.

Buhle, Paul. *Taking Care of Business: Samuel Gompers, George Meany, Lane Kirkland, and the Tragedy of American Labor.* New York: Monthly Review Press, 1999.

Bulletin of the US Bureau of Labor Statistics, No. 550 Cargo Handling and Longshore Labor Conditions. Washington, DC: US Bureau of Labor Statistics, 1932.

Cantwell, Robert. *The Land of Plenty.* Crosscurrents/Modern Fiction. Carbondale: Southern Illinois University Press, 1971.

———. "A Town and Its Novels." *New Republic,* February 19, 1936. 51–52.

Chaplin, Ralph. *The Centralia Conspiracy.* Chicago: Industrial Workers of the World, 1924.

———. *The Centralia Conspiracy.* In *The Centralia Case: Three Views of the Armistice Day Tragedy at Centralia Washington, November 11, 1919.* New York: Da Capa Press, 1971.

———. *Wobbly: The Rough-and-Tumble Story of an American Radical.* Chicago: University of Chicago Press, 1948.

Charette, Betty. "Finns in Aberdeen: Written for the Polson Museum, Hoquiam, Washington, 1984." Pacific Northwest Collection. Aberdeen Timberland Library Archives, Aberdeen, Washington.

Chin, Art. *Golden Tassels: A History of the Chinese in Washington, 1857–1977.* Seattle: Chin, 1977.

Cochrane, Ben H., and William Dean Coldiron. *Disillusion: A Story of the Labor Struggle in the Western Woodworking Mills.* Portland, OR: Binfords and Mort, 1939.

Collins, Joseph William. "Salmon Fishing on the Columbia." *Frank Leslie's Popular Monthly* 44, no. 4 (October 1897): 421–431.

Colman, Louis H. *Lumber.* Boston: Little and Brown, 1931.

———. "The Marker." *New Masses*, April 1928, 26.

———. "The Oiler." *New Masses*, March 1928, 20.

Columbia River Fishermen's Protective Union. *Columbia River Fisheries.* Astoria, OR: G.W. Snyder, 1890. http://digitalcollections.lib.washington.edu/cdm/compoundobject/collection/salmon/id/417.

Cone, Joseph. *A Common Fate: Endangered Salmon and the People of the Pacific Northwest.* New York: H. Holt, 1995.

Conroy, Jack. "Robert Cantwell's Land of Plenty." In *Proletarian Writers of the Thirties*, edited by David Madden, 74–84. Carbondale: Southern Illinois University Press, 1968.

Copeland, Tom. *The Centralia Tragedy of 1919: Elmer Smith and the Wobblies.* Seattle: University of Washington Press, 1993.

Dalton, C. C. *Washington Salmon Fisheries on the Columbia River.* Ilwaco, WA: Journal Job Print, 1893.

Davis, Mike. *Prisoners of the American Dream: Politics and Economy in the History of the US Working Class.* London: Verso Books, 1986.

Dawley, Alan. *Struggles for Justice: Social Responsibility and the Liberal State.* Cambridge, MA: Belknap Press of Harvard University Press, 1993.

Dennis, Peggy. *The Autobiography of an American Communist.* Westport, CT: Lawrence, Hill, 1978.

Dowell, Eldridge. *A History of Criminal Syndicalism Legislation in the United States.* Baltimore: Johns Hopkins University Press, 1939.

Dreyfus, Philip J. "The IWW and the Limits of Inter-Ethnic Organizing: Reds, Whites, and Greeks in Gray Harbor, Washington, 1912." *Labor History* 38, no. 4 (Fall 1997): 450–471.

Dubofsky, Melvyn. *We Shall Be All: A History of the Industrial Workers of the World.* New York: Quadrangle, 1973.

Eby, Cecil D. *Comrades and Commissars: The Lincoln Battalion in the Spanish Civil War.* University Park: Pennsylvania State University Press, 2007.

Engeman, Richard H. *The Oregon Companion: An Historical Gazetteer of the Useful, the Curious, and the Arcane.* Portland, OR: Timber Press, 2009.

Ficken, Robert. "The Wobbly Horrors: Pacific Northwest Lumbermen and the Industrial Workers of the World, 1917–1918." *Labor History* 24, no. 3 (Summer 1983): 325–341.

Flynn, Elizabeth Gurley. *Sabotage: The Conscious Withdrawal of the Workers' Industrial Efficiency.* Cleveland: I.W.W. Publicity Bureau, 1915.

Foner, Philip S. *The History of the Labor Movement in the United States.* Vol. 4: *The Industrial Workers of the World, 1905–1917.* New York: International Publishers, 1965; reprint, 1997.

Foner, Philip S., and David R. Roediger. *Our Own Time: A History of American Labor and the Working Day.* London: Verso, 1989.

Frank, Dana. *Purchasing Power: Consumer Organizing, Gender, and the Seattle Labor Movement, 1919–1945.* Cambridge: Cambridge University Press, 1994.

Franklin, F. G. "Anti-Syndicalism Legislation." *American Political Science Review* 14, no. 2 (May 1920): 291–298.

Freeman, Joseph. Introduction to *Proletarian Literature in the United States: An Anthology*, edited by Granville Hicks et al. New York: International Publishers, 1935,

Friday, Chris. *Organizing Asian American Labor: The Pacific Coast Canned-Salmon Industry, 1870–1942.* Philadelphia: Temple University Press, 1994.

Gambs, John S. *Decline of the IWW.* Diss., Columbia University,1932; New York: Russell & Russell, 1966.

"Gillnet Rebellion of 1896 Threatened Columbia River War." *Sou'wester* (Spring 1979): 15–17.

Goings, Aaron. "Red Harbor: Class, Violence, and Community in Grays Harbor, Washington." PhD thesis, Simon Fraser University, 2011.

Goings, Todd. "Battles on the Harbor: Inter-Labor Conflict, Anti-Communism, Women's Auxiliaries, and the Murder of Laura Law." MA thesis, Central Washington University, 2014.

Gordon, Linda. *The Second Coming of the KKK: The Ku Klux Klan of the 1920s and the American Political Tradition.* New York: W. W. Norton, 2017.

Greene, Julie. *Pure and Simple Politics: The American Federation of Labor and Political Activism, 1881–1917.* Cambridge: Cambridge University Press, 2004.

Gulick, Bill. *A Traveler's History of Washington.* Caldwell, ID: Caxton Printers, 1996.

Gunns, Albert F. *Civil Liberties in Crisis: The Pacific Northwest, 1917–1940.* New York: Garland, 1983.

Hannula, Reino. *An Album of Finnish Halls.* San Luis Obispo, CA: Finn Heritage, 1991.

Hicks, Granville, Joseph North, Michael Gold, Paul Peters, Isidor Schneider, Alan Calmer, and Joseph Freeman. *Proletarian Literature in the United States: An Anthology.* New York: International Publishers, 1935.

Higham, John. *Strangers in the Land: Patterns of American Nativism.* New Brunswick, NJ: Rutgers University Press, 1988.

Hillier, Alfred J. "Albert Johnson, Congressman," *Pacific Northwest Quarterly* 36, no. 3 (July 1945): 199.

Howd, Cloice R. *Industrial Relations in the West Coast Lumber Industry*. Bulletin of the Bureau of Labor Statistics No. 349. Washington DC: Government Printing Office, 1924.

Hughes, John C., and Ryan Teague Beckwith, eds. *On the Harbor: From Black Friday to Nirvana*. Aberdeen, WA: Daily World, 2001.

Hummasti, Paul George. "Fighting for Temperance Ideas." In *Finns in the United States: A History of Settlement, Dissent, and Integration*, edited by Auvo Kostiainen, 91–106. East Lansing: Michigan State University Press, 2014.

———. *Finnish Radicals in Astoria, Oregon, 1904–1940: A Study in Immigrant Socialism*. New York: Arno Press, 1979.

Hunt, Herbert, and Floyd C. Kaylor. *Washington, West of the Cascades; Historical and Descriptive; the Explorers, the Indians, the Pioneers, the Modern*. Seattle: S. J. Clarke, 1917.

Industrial Workers of the World. *The I.W.W. in Theory and Practice*. 5th rev. ed. Chicago: Industrial Workers of the World, 1937.

Jacobson, Matthew Frye. *Whiteness of a Different Color: European Immigrants and the Alchemy of Race*. Cambridge, MA: Harvard University Press, 1998.

Jameson, Elizabeth. *All That Glitters: Class, Conflict, and Community in Cripple Creek*. Urbana: University of Illinois Press, 1998.

Jensen, Vernon. *Lumber and Labor*. New York: J. J. Little and Ives, 1945; New York: Arno Press, 1971.

Joint Report on the Armistice Day Tragedy at Centralia, Washington, November 11, 1919. In *The Centralia Case: Three Views of the Armistice Day Tragedy at Centralia Washington, November 11, 1919*. New York: Da Capa Press, 1971.

Jones, W. A. *Salmon Fisheries of the Columbia River*, 50th Cong., 1st sess., 1888, Ex. Doc. No. 123, 46–47.

Karni, Michael G., and Douglas J. Ollila Jr., eds. *For the Common Good: Finnish Immigrants and the Radical Response to Industrial America*. Superior, WI: Työmies Society, 1977.

Kaunonen, Gary. *Challenge Accepted: A Finnish Immigrant Response to Industrial America in Michigan's Copper Country*. East Lansing: Michigan State University Press, 2010.

Kimeldorf, Howard. *Battling for American Labor: Wobblies, Craft Workers, and the Making of the Union Movement*. Berkeley: University of California Press, 1999.

———. *Reds or Rackets? The Making of Radical and Conservative Unions on the Waterfront*. Berkeley: University of California Press, 1998.

Kirby, David. "'The Workers' Cause': Rank-and-File Attitudes and Opinions in the Finnish Social Democratic Party, 1905–1918." *Past and Present* 111 (May 1986): 130–138.

Kirk, Ruth, and Carmela Alexander, *Exploring Washington's Past: A Road Guide to History*. Rev. ed. Seattle: University of Washington Press, 1995.

Knoellinger, Carl Erik. *Labor in Finland*. Cambridge, MA: Harvard University Press, 1960.

Kornbluh, Joyce L., ed. *Rebel Voices: An IWW Anthology*. Chicago: Charles Kerr, 1998.

Kostiainen, Auvo, ed. *Finns in the United States: A History of Settlement, Dissent, and Integration*. East Lansing: Michigan State University Press, 2014.

———. *The Forging of Finnish-American Communism, 1917–1924: A Study in Ethnic Radicalism*. Turku, Finland: Turun Yliopisto, 1978.

Lampman, Ben Hur. *Centralia Tragedy and Trial*. In *The Centralia Case: Three Views of the Armistice Day Tragedy at Centralia, Washington, November 11, 1919*. New York: Da Capo Press, 1971.

Laut, Agnes C. "Revolution Yawns!" *Technical World Magazine* (October 1912): 134–144.

Lavery, Jason. *The History of Finland*. Westport, CT: Greenwood Press, 2006.

Lembcke, Jerry, and William M. Tattam. *One Union in Wood: A Political History of the International Woodworkers of America*. New York: International Publishers, 1984.

Lerner, James. "I Was in Spain." *The Fight Against War and Fascism* 4, no. 1 (November 1936): 40–41.

LeWarne, Charles Pierce. "The Aberdeen, Washington, Free Speech Fight of 1911–1912." *Pacific Northwest Quarterly* 66 (January 1975): 1–15.

Lewis, Merrill. *Robert Cantwell*. Boise, ID: Boise State University, 1985.

Lindström-Best, Varpu. *Defiant Sisters: A Social History of Finnish Immigrant Women in Canada*. Toronto: Multicultural History Society of Ontario, 1988.

Loewen, James W. *Lies across America: What American Historic Sites Get Wrong*. New York: Simon and Schuster, 2007.

Magden, Ronald. *A History of Seattle Waterfront Workers, 1884–1934*. Seattle: ILWU Local 19, 1991.

———. *The Working Longshoreman*. Tacoma, WA: R-4 Typographers, 1991.

Malet, David. *Foreign Fighters: Transnational Identity in Civic Conflicts*. Oxford: Oxford University Press, 2013.

Markholt, Ottilie. "Against the Current: A Social Memoir." unpublished manuscript, chap. 4, p. 14. University of Washington, Digital Archives, http://digitalcollections. lib.washington.edu/cdm/ref/collection/pnwhm/id/837, [Accessed June 10, 2018].

———. *Maritime Solidarity: Pacific Coast Unionism, 1929–1938*. Tacoma: Pacific Coast Maritime History Committee, 1998.

Mattila, Walter, ed., *The Lewis River Finns*, 5, no. 5. Portland: Finnish American Historical Society of the West,1970.

Maunder, Elwood R., Betty E. Mitson, Barbara D. Holman, Charles Plant, Harold M. Stilson Sr., and Paul R. Smith. "Red Cedar Shingles & Shakes: The Labor Story." *Journal of Forest History* 19, no. 3 (July 1975): 112–127.

Mayer, Mayer. *Beyond the Rebel Girl: Women and the Industrial Workers of the World in the Pacific Northwest, 1905–1924*. Corvallis: Oregon State University Press, 2018.

McClelland, John Jr. *Wobbly War: The Centralia Story*. Tacoma: Washington State Historical Society, 1987.

McGuckin, Henry E. *Memoirs of a Wobbly*. Chicago: Charles H. Kerr, 1987.

Millikan, William. *A Union Against Unions: The Minneapolis Citizens' Alliance and Its Fight Against Organized Labor, 1903–1947*. St. Paul: University of Minnesota Press, 2001.

Morgan, Murray. *The Viewless Winds*. Reprint, Corvallis: Oregon State University Press, 1990.

Munk, Michael. *The Portland Red Guide*. 2nd ed. Portland, OR: Ooligan Press, 2011.

Nelson, Bruce. *Workers on the Waterfront: Seamen, Longshoremen, and Unionism in the 1930s*. Urbana: University of Illinois Press, 1990.

Nelson, Cary, and Jefferson Hendricks, eds. *Madrid 1937: Letters of the Abraham Lincoln Brigade from the Spanish Civil War*. London: Routledge, 1996.

Nelson, Eugene. *Break Their Haughty Power: Joe Murphy in the Heyday of the Wobblies*. San Francisco: ISM Press, 1993.

Norris, T. S. "Aberdeen, Washington: A New City in the Lower Chehalis Valley in the Tide Water of Grays Harbor." *Northwest Magazine* 8, no. 1 (January 1890): 14–21.

O'Conner, Harvey. *Revolution in Seattle: A Memoir*. New York: Monthly Review Press, 1964.

Olsen, Mrs. Nels. *The Willapa Country: History Report*. Raymond, WA: Raymond Herald & Advertiser, 1965.

Owen, Jerrold. "Centralia." *American Legion Weekly*, December 12, 1919.

———. "The Inevitable Clash between Americanism and Anti-Americanism." *American Legion Weekly*, December 5, 1919.

Parrish, Michael E. *Anxious Decades: America in Prosperity and Depression,1920–1940*. New York: W. W. Norton, 1992.

Passi, Michael. "Fishermen on Strike: Finnish Workers and Community Power in Astoria, Oregon, 1880–1900." In *The Finnish Experience in the Western Great Lakes Region: New Perspectives*, edited by Michael G. Karni, Matti E. Kaups, and Douglas J. Ollila, 89–103. Turku: Institute for Migration; Immigration History Research Center, University of Minnesota, 1975.

Payne, C. E. "The Mainspring of Action." In *Fellow Workers and Friends: I. W. W. Free-Speech Fights as Told by Participants*, edited by Philip S. Foner, 126–128. Westport, CT: Greenwood Press, 1981.

Pegram, Thomas R. *One Hundred Percent American: The Rebirth and Decline of the Ku Klux Klan in the 1920s*. Chicago: Ivan R. Dee, 2011.

Perez, Andrea Larson. *Astoria*. Charleston, SC: Arcadia, 2016.

"Preamble of the Industrial Workers of the World." In *Rebel Voices: An IWW Anthology*, edited by Joyce L. Kornbluh, 12–13. New and exp. ed. Chicago: Charles H. Kerr, 1998.

Proceedings of the Eighteenth Convention of the International Longshoremen's Association. July 11–16, 1910.

Proceedings of the Twenty-First Convention of the International Longshoremen's Association. July 14–19, 1913.

Quin, Mike. *The Big Strike*. Olema, CA: Olema, 1949.

Raun, Toivo U. "The Revolution of 1905 in the Baltic Provinces and Finland." *Slavic Review* 43, no. 3 (Autumn 1984): 453–467.

Reed, T. V. *Robert Cantwell and the Literary Left: A Northwest Writer Reworks American Fiction*. Seattle: University of Washington Press, 2014.

Reinikka, Merle A. *Ilwaco's Early Finns, Pacific County, Washington.* Portland, OR: Finnish American Historical Society of the West, 1992.

Remington, Arthur. *Remington's Compiled Statutes of Washington.* Vol. 1. San Francisco: Bancroft-Whitney, 1932.

Richardson, Bradley Dale. "'The Forgotten Front: Gender, Labor, and Politics in Camas, Washington, and the Northwest Paper Industry, 1913–1918," MA thesis, Portland State University, 2015.

Rideout, Walter B. *The Radical Novel in the United States, 1900–1954.* Cambridge, MA: Harvard University Press, 1956.

Rieder, Ross. "Pettus, Terry (1904–1983)," http://www.historylink.org/File/2682.

Rissanen, Aku. *Suomalaisten Sosialistiosastojen ja Työväenyhdistysten viidennen: Pöytäkirja, 1-5, 7-10 p. kesäkuuta, 1912.* Fitchburg, MA: Suomalainen Sosialisti Kustannus Yhtiö, 1912.

Rogers, Bruce. "The War of Gray's [sic] Harbor." International Socialist Review 12, no. 11 (May 1912): 749-753.

Rowan, James. *The IWW in the Lumber Industry.* Seattle: Lumber Workers Industrial Union No. 500, 1919.

Schmidt, Dorothy Neil. "Sedition and Criminal Syndicalism in the State of Washington—1917–1919." MA thesis, State College of Washington, 1940.

Siitonen, Harri. "The Ballad of Laura Luoma Law: A Forgotten Face in Finnish America Finally Resurfaces." *Finnish American Reporter,* October 1, 1994.

Smith, Adam. *An Inquiry into the Nature and Causes of the Wealth of Nations.* New York: Modern Library, 1937.

Smith, Courtland L. *Fish or Cut Bait.* Corvallis: Oregon State University, Sea Grant Program, 1977.

———. *Oregon Fish Fights.* Corvallis: Oregon State University, Sea Grant College Program, 1974.

———. *Salmon Fishers of the Columbia.* Corvallis: Oregon State University Press, 1979.

Smith, Walker. *The Everett Massacre—A History of the Class Struggle in the Lumber Industry.* Chicago: Industrial Workers of the World, 1917.

———. "The Voyage of the Verona." *International Socialist Review* (December 17, 1916): 341–346.

———. *Was It Murder? The Truth about Centralia.* Seattle: Northwest General Defense Committee, 1922.

Smits, Ina Kari, Sylvia Niemi Fisher, and Paul Kari. "The Finns in Hoquiam: Written for the Polson Museum, Hoquiam, Washington, 1984." Pacific Northwest Collection. Aberdeen Timberland Library Archives, Aberdeen, Washington.

St. John, Vincent. *The I.W.W.: Its History, Structure, and Methods.* Chicago: IWW Publishing Bureau, 1917, 1919.

State of Washington. *Second Biennial Report of the Bureau of Labor Statistics and Factory Inspection, 1899–1900.* Olympia: Gwin Hicks, State Printer, 1901.

———. *Third Biennial Report of the Bureau of Labor Statistics and Factory Inspection, 1901–1902.* Seattle: Metropolitan Press, 1903.

————. *Fifth Biennial Report of the Bureau of Labor Statistics and Factory Inspection,* 1905–1906. Olympia: C. W. Gorham Public Printer, 1906.

————. State of Washington, *Seventh Biennial Report of the Bureau of Labor Statistics and Factory Inspection, 1909–1910.* Olympia: E. L. Boardman, Public Printer, 1910,

————. *Eighth Biennial Report of the Bureau of Labor Statistics and Factory Inspection, 1911–1912.* Olympia: E. L. Boardman, Public Printer, 1912.

————. *Tenth Biennial Report of the Bureau of Labor Statistics and Factory Inspection,* 1915–1916. Olympia, WA: Frank M. Lamborn, Public Printer, 1916.

State of Washington Timber Workers' Employment Guide. Seattle: Timber Workers, 1916.

Steadman, R. W. "An Objective Appraisal of Recent Radical Writing in America." *North American Review* 247, no. 1 (1939): 142–152.

Stjärnstedt, Riitta. "Finnish Women in the North American Labour Movement." In *Finnish Diaspora II: The United States,* edited by Michael G. Karni, 260. Toronto: Multicultural History Society of Ontario, 1981.

Strong, Anna Louise. "Everett's Bloody Sunday: A Free Speech Fight That Led to a Murder Trial." *Survey* 37 (January 27, 1917): 475–476.

————. *Spain in Arms.* New York: H. Holt, 1937.

Suggs, Jon Christian. Introduction to *Marching! Marching!* by Clara Weatherwax. Detroit: Omni Graphics, 1990,

Sulkanen, Elis, ed. *Amerikan Suomalaisen Tyovaenliikkeen historia.* Fitchburg, MA: Amerikan Suomalainen Kansanvallen Liitto ja Raivaaja, 1951.

Sulkunen, Irma. "The Mobilization of Women and the Birth of Civil Society." In *The Lady with the Bow,* edited by Merja Manninen and Päivi Setälä; translated by Michael Wynne-Ellis, 49–53. Helsinki: Otava, 1990.

————. "Suffrage, Gender, and Citizenship in Finland: A Comparative Perspective." *NORDEUROPAforum* (2007): 29.

Third Annual Convention of the Maritime Federation of the Pacific Coast, June 7–July 9, 1937, Portland, Oregon, microfilm, University of Washington Library.

Thompson, Fred. *The I. W. W.—Its First Fifty Years.* Chicago: Industrial Workers of the World, 1955.

Tierney, Dominic. *FDR and the Spanish Civil War: Neutrality and Commitment in the Struggle that Divided America.* Durham, NC: Duke University Press, 2007.

Todes, Charlotte. *Labor and Lumber.* New York: International Publishers, 1931.

Trautman, William E. *Direct Action and Sabotage.* Pittsburgh, PA: Socialist News Company, 1912.

Tyler, Robert L. "The Everett Free Speech Fight," *Pacific Historical Review* (February 1954): 19–30.

————. "I.W.W. in the Pacific N.W.; Rebels of the Woods." *Oregon Historical Quarterly* 55, no. 1 (March 1954): 3–44.

————. *Rebels of the Woods: The IWW in the Pacific Northwest.* Eugene: University of Oregon Books, 1967.

United States Commission on Industrial Relations. *Industrial Relations. Final Report and Testimony,* submitted to Congress by the Commission on Industrial Relations

Created by the Act of August 23, 1912. Washington, DC: Government Printing Office, 1916.

United States Department of the Interior. National Parks Service. *National Register of Historic Places, Multiple Property Documentation Form*, July 5, 1991.

United States Department of Labor. *Hours of Work and Output*. Bulletin No. 917 of the United States Department of Labor. Washington, DC: US Government Printing Office, 1947.

United States House of Representatives. *Investigation of Communist Propaganda, Hearings before a Special Committee to Investigate Communist Activities in the United States of the House of Representatives*, 71st Congress, 2nd Session. Washington, DC: Government Printing Office, 1930.

Van Syckle, Edwin, and David A. James. *The River Pioneers: Early Days on Grays Harbor.* Seattle: Pacific Search Press, 1982.

Walmsley, A. B. "The Home Defender." *Home Defender*, May 12, 1912.

Washington State. *Extraordinary Session, 16th Legislature. Senate Journal.* Olympia, WA: Frank M. Lamborn, Public Printer, 1920.

———. Session Laws of the State of Washington. 1903. Tacoma, WA: Allen & Lamborn, 1903.

Weatherwax, Ben. "Hometown Scrapbook—No. 71—The Wobblies," Oct. 29, 1953, radio script for Station KBKW, Aberdeen, recorded in the 1950s, Pacific Northwest History Collection, Aberdeen Timberland Library, Aberdeen, Washington.

Weatherwax, Clara. *Marching! Marching!* 1935. Detroit: Omnigraphics, 1990.

Weber, Mark. "America's Changing View of Mussolini and Fascism." *Journal of Historical Review* 15, no. 3 (May–June 1995): 6–7.

Williams, L. R. *Our Pacific County.* Raymond, WA: Raymond Herald, 1930.

Willis, Steve. "Henry McCleary and the Land of the Rising Sun." *McCleary Museum Newsletter* 11, no. 3 (September 2001).

Woehlke, Walter V. "The I.W.W. and the Golden Rule: Why Everett Used Club and Gun on the Red Apostles of Direct Action." *Sunset: The Magazine of the Pacific and of All the Far West* 38, no. 2 (February 1917): 16–18, 62–65.

Zieger, Robert H. *Rebuilding the Pulp and Paper Workers' Union, 1933–1941.* Knoxville: University of Tennessee Press, 1984.

Index

Aberdeen, 3–4, 5, 6, 7, 10, 11, 12–14, 25–33, 37, 39–43, 45–68, 74, 78–79, 80, 89–90, 111–118, 121–123, 125, 130, 133–137, 142, 144–152, 155, 156, 158, 158, 167–169, 171–177, 180, 184

Aberdeen Daily World, 43, 66, 78–79

Aberdeen Free Speech Fight, 45–56; boycott and, 51–52, 55; citizens' committee violence and, 48–50, 52–54; IWW organizing, and, 45–46, 55–56; ordinances restricting speech, and, 45–47, 53

Aberdeen Herald, 29–30, 32, 45, 47, 66–67, 69, 73–74, 78, 112, 155, 158

Aberdeen Lumber and Shingle Company, 67

Aberdeen Young Communist League, 145–147

Aberdeen Young Pioneers, 145–147

Abraham Lincoln Brigade, 173, 176, 179, 180

Allen, Dudley, 48

Allison, Fred, 61, 67

Aloha Lumber Company, 120

Aloha, 120, 125

American Federation of Labor (AFL), 5, 42, 43, 52, 59–60, 80, 114, 127, 129, 171–172

American Legion, 12, 13, 101–110, 169–170, 171

American Legion Weekly, 106

Amey, Bill, 13

Andrew, Nicholas, 21

anti-radical legislation, 77, 79–80, 81–85, 87–100, 170; class legislation, 91, 96–100. *See also* Aberdeen Ordinance 1084; criminal syndicalism; Espionage Act of 1917; Sedition Amendments of 1918; Washington Criminal Anarchy Law of 1903; Washington State Criminal Syndicalism Law of 1917; Washington State Criminal Syndicalism Law of 1919; Washington State Red Flag Law; Washington State Sabotage Law of 1919

Armistice Day Tragedy, 6, 13, 101–110, 111, 154

Astoria, Oregon, 6, 12, 17, 20–24, 69, 71, 145, 159

Ault, Harry, 107

Bailey, Robert C., 69, 76

Baker Bay, 15–17, 22–23

Ballard Agreement, 129–130

Barnes, Frank, 98

Barnett, Eugene, 108

Bay City Mill, 13, 114–116

Becker, Ray, 108

Benn, Samuel, 30

Biscay, J.S., 63, 144

Black, Hugo, 127

Bland, Bert, 108

Bland, O. C., 108

Bloody Thursday, 153–154, 161, 163–165

Bordoise, Nick, 161

Bridges, Harry, 161–162

Bright, Bernard, 128

Brown, Jay G., 7, 60, 123–124

Brown, Roy, 160